D0289318

AMERICA'S
GREATEST
WALKS

AMERICA'S GREATEST WALKS

A Traveler's Guide to 100 Scenic Adventures

Gary Yanker and Carol Tarlow

With the editors of *Walking World* Magazine:
David Clow (Eastern States)
Marilyn Green (Central States)
Paula Panich (Western States)
and Catherine Gordon Ticer
   (Photo, Map and Permissions Editor)

▲▼

Addison-Wesley Publishing Company, Inc.
Reading, Massachusetts • Menlo Park, California
Don Mills, Ontario • Wokingham, England
Amsterdam • Sydney • Singapore • Tokyo
Madrid • Bogotá • Santiago • San Juan

Photo Credits and Sources

p. 6, Claire White Peterson Photo, Mystic Seaport, Mystic, CT; p. 22, photo by John T. Hopf, courtesy of Newport County Chamber of Commerce, Newport, RI; p. 45, Gettysburg Travel Council, Gettysburg, PA; p. 53, photo by Richard Frear, National Park Service; p. 56, Virginia Division of Tourism, Richmond, VA; p. 67, DeSoto Caverns Park, Childersburg, AL; p. 86, Mammoth Cave National Park, KY; p. 93, Irvin Pitts, Jr.; p. 111, State of Kansas Parks and Resources Authority, Topeka, KS; p. 115, Louisiana Office of Tourism, New Orleans, LA; p. 117, The Westin Crown Center, Kansas City, MO; p. 127, Hyatt Regency Hotel, Houston, TX; p. 145, National Park Service; p. 153, Des Moines County Conservation Board, Des Moines, IA; p. 176, National Park Service; p. 183, National Park Service; p. 186, Wyoming Travel Commission, Cheyenne, WY; p. 190, photo by C. Milliken, National Park Service; p. 195, Kurt Daley; p. 196, United States Forest Service; p. 205, National Park Service; p. 210, State of New Mexico Economic Development and Tourism Department, Santa Fe, NM; p. 246, photo by Bob Richey, Denali National Park and Preserve, AK; p. 253, Hawaii Visitors Bureau, Honolulu, HI.

Library of Congress Cataloging-in-Publication Data

Yanker, Gary.
   America's greatest walks.

   Includes index.
   1. Walking — United States — Guide-books.
2. United States — Description and travel — 1981–
Guide-books. I. Tarlow, Carol. II. Walking world
magazine. III. Title.
GV199.4.Y36 1986   917.3   85–28708
ISBN 0–201–15294–0 (pbk.)

Copyright © 1986 by Walking World

All rights reserved. No part of this publication may be reproduced, stored in a retrieval system, or transmitted, in any form or by any means, electronic, mechanical, photocopying, recording, or otherwise, without the prior written permission of the publisher. Printed in the United States of America. Published simultaneously in Canada.

Illustrations by Barbara Frake

Text design by Carson Designs Inc.
Set in 10 point Times Roman by Compset Inc., Beverly, MA.

BCDEFGHIJ–AL–8987
Second Printing, September 1987

This book is dedicated to my mother,
Lisl Yanker, who said:
"Gary, write a book with walks that I can do and enjoy."
—Gary Yanker

Contents

WALKING THE CENTRAL STATES

WALKING THE WESTERN STATES

Acknowledgments

We wish to thank all the walking enthusiasts who contributed their advice and support over the years, making this book possible.

Eastern States: Shirley R. Davis, Virginia Rice, Ruth Tedder, Theresa Dziorney, Sandi Mendelson, Nancy McCord, Peg Sinclair, Lou Rodia, Lynn O'Rourke Hayes, Jerry Petitt, Gary Bitner, Lynn Laurenti, Diana Adams, Marilyn Tanner, Bud Siemon, Colonel August Siemon, Leon Greenman, Joann Dolan, York Onnen, Sheila Buford, T. George Harris, Bill Reiss, Jerry Gorman, Betsy Livingston, Bruce Katz, Bruce Bassett, Jens Bang, Shelley Reifsnider, Bob Defer, Howard Jacobson. Ingrid and Erich Schymik, Maria von Pawelsz, Margit Dix, Craig Evans, Laura MacKenzie, Ginna Rogers Gould, Mysia Haight, Henry Laskau. Dr. Rob Roy MacGregor, Jim Kerns, Timothy Quinn, Anne Bolzoni, Ted Fields, Wendy Iseman, Kelly C. Kane, Tom and Dina Orr, Jean MacGuire, Rachel Skolkin, Lee Kass, Hank Fischer, John Mantica, Karen Kreps.

Central States: Steve Moergen, Terry Rudd, Brian Benko, Jody Weiss, Drew Mearns, Ken Freitas, John Cox, Helen Thaiman, John and Virginia Rice, Karen Tompkins-Tinch, Jim Liston, Eli Zal.

Western States: Richard Polk, Nick, Jim, Jackie, and Molly Powell, Neil Finn, Jody Lewis, Dr. Allen Selner, Bruce Cohn, Jake Steinfeld, Claire Huertel, Hattie Wright, Ron Laird, Dr. Mitch Feingold, Gail Fox, Larry Foreman, Judith and Brad Ryland, Toni Tennille, Ben Sackheim, Lori Wilt, and Janice Stoops.

Thanks also to the staff of Addison-Wesley: Robert Lavelle, Christopher Carduff, Perry McIntosh, Alison Betts, George Gibson, Mary Shapiro, Joanne Gibely, Lori Marsh, and Robert Shepard, and to Barbara Frake for the accurate and attractive maps.

Introduction

The modern walker is not someone who is merely trying to get from one place to another on foot. Instead, he or she, a savvy pedestrian, carefully chooses the location for the walk, then takes a car, bus, train, or plane to get there, saving as much time as possible for the walk itself. This is "strategic transportation," in walkers' parlance. Nor is the new walker a backpacker who chooses only wilderness trails. Backpackers are more concerned with survival in the outdoors than with a good walk. Many hikers I know walk less than 5 miles a day. They are the ones who go on weekend outings, which they spend setting up and taking down tents and packing and unpacking their hiking gear. Walkers today would rather carry light packs, do 10 to 15 miles a day, and make sure a hot shower, a glass of wine, and a well-cooked meal are waiting for them at the end of the day. Modern walkers would rather take the time to smell the flowers than set a new long-distance record. And they know they can find a good walk in either the city or the country, on pavement or on a dirt trail. The hikes and wilderness walks in this book are of the "easy hiking" variety. They require no survival skills, and all but one can be completed within one day.

A Good Walk

What makes a good walk? Perhaps the first qualification is that it be a pleasant sensory experience. *Sight:* There should be plenty of rich colors — like greens and blues, with reds and yellows interspersed — in flowers, flags, painted walls, even balloons. There should be interesting shapes and forms along the way that invite up-close study. Architecture, man-made or natural, is the best sight for a good walk: forms and shapes that are well designed are a delight to see. Walking is really the best way to observe the sights; it's the right pace and the right vehicle for getting up close. The more your eyes work with your feet, the more satisfying the good walking experience will be. *Sound:* Birds chirping, water babbling, wind rustling leaves and branches are certainly the symphonic sounds of a good walk; also, the sounds of people happily talking add to the quality of the walk. *Smell:* Spring rain, fresh-brewed coffee, smoke from a wood stove, fragrant flowers are some pleasant surprises along the walking route. *Feeling:* The cool sensation of breezes on the skin — especially the face and forearms — helps make the good walk a stimulating and energizing experience. You feel alive and relaxed. Being able to touch the things you see is a bonus on a good walk.

Other qualifications for a good walk are a good pace, continuity combined with periodic rewards, and either a spectacular view or a sense of intimacy with the environment. Let me explain these last qualifications. After sensory experience, these are qualities that are equally important to a good walk.

Continuity combined with periodic rewards. The fewer interruptions — by highways or by neglected and unclean areas — the better. Traffic noise destroys the quiet you can find on a good walk. On the other hand, a good walking route should comprise a series of intermittent, rewarding destinations to draw you on — a sight, a sound, a human encounter.

A spectacular view or a sense of intimacy with the environment. One or the other, but sometimes both (if both, you are certainly getting into Great Walk territory). The spectacular view can be either from high ground or from below. Walking in a "green tunnel," with low-lying trees and no clearing or high ground, precludes the uplifting experience of a spectacular view. A good walk requires open space, however small, along the way so you can stop to rest, observe, contemplate, and enjoy a sense of wonder, a sense of intimacy with your surroundings.

A good pace. A good walk usually lasts more than 10 minutes because that seems to be the minimum time it takes to get the body relaxed and in a walking mood. A good walk is done mostly at a stroller's pace, with opportunities to stop, to turn and look in various directions, to bend down and pick up things, even to sit for a while and gaze at a particular scene or just take a deep breath or have a friendly conversation. Once you get to know the places you like best to stop, you can pick up the pace on the rest of the walk. It's like fast-forwarding your favorite tape to the song you like best and playing it over and over again.

Contrary to the prejudice of outdoor enthusiasts, good walks can be found in cities and towns as well as in outlying areas. You need not search for the good walk only in the wilderness. Still, nature has many advantages over man-made architecture: you can find peace, solitude, and relaxation along a woodsy trail or a lonely beach, so often your desire to relax takes precedence over your desire to learn. On the city walk, unless it is in a park or other natural area, you generally learn from the people you see and meet, and from the buildings and historical sites you visit.

A good walk isn't necessarily found just in historically significant places. Many small towns were skipped over in the recording of American history. For the big-city walker (most walkers live in large metropolitan areas), a small-town walk — like the one in Perrysburg, Ohio — can be a very relaxing, even enchanting, experience. Likewise, the greatness of many of the central big city walks — like New York's Fifth Avenue, Chicago's lakefront, or New Orleans's French Quarter — may have a greater impact on a small-town walker.

The Great Walks

So, what then makes a Great Walk? Great Walks are walks that contain all of the elements of a good walk but also something extra — a kind of reward — either along the way or at the final destination, which makes the route worth traveling. If it's your first time walking a Great Walk, the reward will take your breath away. Experiencing the unexpected — a sight, some sounds, a tale told by an interesting guide — can be an "adventure." That's why the subtitle of our book is "A Traveler's Guide to 100 Scenic Adventures." We don't mean adventure in the sense of a physical challenge (the majority of Great Walks are not physical challenges) but rather in a spiritual sense.

A Great Walk, as distinguished from a good walk, is really a matter of a consensus of opinion. In other words, which good walks are considered tops among walking enthusiasts? A walk need not be perfect to be considered great. It can contain a flaw or two, which gives it even more character. For example, we can ignore the dusty streets of Taos (muddy in spring, icy in winter) in order to experience an artists' town of the Old West. That there is only one historical monument in Perrysburg, Ohio, does not detract from the unique experience of a true, preserved, small town. Not having Colorado's highest peak in the background takes nothing away from the beautiful maroon colors of the Rocky Mountains. How great a walk is depends on the cumulative effect of its many elements, as finally evaluated by walkers themselves.

How We Put This Book Together

From literally thousands of good walks, including more than 300 nominated by walking enthusiasts, my co-editor, Carol Tarlow, and I selected the 100 we considered to be the greatest. We were assisted by three regional editors: David Clow (Eastern States), Marilyn Green (Central States), and Paula Panich (Western States). We also had the help and advice of many other enthusiastic walkers, as mentioned in the Acknowledgments.

Probably one-third of the Great Walks in the book are already known to experienced walkers. They often appear in regional walking books, buried among descriptions of other trails. So deciding on the Great Walks was at first just a matter of taking a poll. But other Great Walks — like Pinnacle Gulch Trail in Bodega Bay — were uncovered, too. These "secret" walks, as well as some other little-known ones, were nominated by walking enthusiasts from all over America. And a few walkers from other countries also took the time to nominate walks for us. These nominators are not walking "experts," such as hike leaders, but rather walking enthusiasts who, like the majority of our readers, approach walking with a fresh eye. That's why we have so many Great Walks that most people never heard of. And, in cases of the better-known walks, our walking enthusiasts bring to them a new perspective that is probably a better one than that of the jaded eye of the experienced walker. After all, are we not redefining the old art of walking for a new generation of walkers?

The Walker's Road Map

We organized the Great Walks from the point of view of the motorist, since walking and motoring are America's favorite ways to sightsee. Most traditional hiking guides give only sketchy directions on how to get to trails; and walkers are often uncertain about leaving well-traveled roads in search of hidden trailheads they may never find. Maps for the 10 major subregions show where the Great Walks are located in relation to major cities. The map accompanying each walk — or the detailed description — will guide you along your way.

If you think there is a Great Walk in your state that we have overlooked, turn to the nomination form at the back of the book and submit your choice. It will be considered for our next edition. Be sure to support your choice of walk with good arguments.

Types of Great Walks

The Great Walks in this book fall into one of four major categories: City Walks (including Suburban and Town Walks), Country Walks, Wilderness Walks, and Beach Walks. The book contains at least one Great Walk from each of the 50 states as well as the District of Columbia and even the Virgin Islands. Half the walks are in cities, suburbs, and towns. The next largest group (about one-third) are Wilderness Walks. The remaining walks are fairly evenly divided between Country and Beach Walks.

From the motorist's and city walker's viewpoint, these walks fall neatly into geographical regions formed by concentric circles extending out from the cities at their center. If you are traveling to a Great Walk, most likely you will start from a city and work your way out to its suburbs, then farther out to the countryside, and still farther to the beach or wilderness area. Each additional distance involves greater traveling and preparation time.

For the motorist traveling from state to state, the cities, connected by the interstates, amount to intermediate destinations along the motoring route. If you are a frequent traveler like me, you will probably be using a city as your port of entry to any geographical region. Each Great Walk cites the city it's near. The regional maps also indicate the major cities near the chosen walks.

Greatest Walks Overall (Gary Yanker Picks Them)

I could not resist the temptation to provide you with "the greatest of the greatest" walks and walking areas. These are based on interviews with walkers throughout the U.S., consultations with our editors, and my own personal experience traveling throughout America over the last 10 years in search of the best walks.

Greatest Walking States Overall: California and New York (a tie)

Greatest Country Walking State: Connecticut

Greatest Wilderness Walking State: Wyoming

Greatest Mountain Walking State: Colorado

Greatest Canyon and Desert Walking State: Arizona

Greatest Beach Walking State: New Jersey

Greatest Big City Walking State: California

Greatest Small Town and Suburban Walking State: Ohio and Missouri, a tie

Greatest Walking City: New York and San Francisco (a tie)

Greatest Town Walk: Savannah, Georgia

Greatest Country Walk: Steep Rock and Vermont trails (a tie)

Greatest Beach Walk (sandy beach): Assateague Island, Maryland/Virginia

Greatest Beach Walk (shoreline): Pacific Palisades, Santa Monica, California

Greatest Wilderness Walk: Cascade Canyon, Grand Teton National Park, Wyoming

Greatest Historical Walk: Boston's Freedom Trail and Gettysburg (a tie)

Preparing for Your Walking Adventure

Equipping Yourself

Comfortable shoes are the tour walker's basic equipment. I never travel without them, because no matter where I am there's always an opportunity for a good walk. Clothing depends on the type of walk you are taking. In general, you will be more comfortable if you wear several layers. They can be put on or taken off as comfort dictates. For example, the hike up Squaw Peak near Phoenix almost always makes you sweat; it will also give you a nice suntan. Short pants and a T-shirt are the best outfit for it, or for any other walk in the Great Southwest. Carry warmer clothing along in a day-pack for cooler evenings when the sun goes down. Even on short walks in the Southern Region, carry a water bottle or canteen. Next to walking shoes, the day-pack is perhaps the best piece of walking equipment you can bring along. It leaves your arms free and allows you to carry cameras, additional clothing, a snack, and other personal effects to make your walk even more enjoyable.

For walks longer than 2 miles, I usually bring along some water and a few pieces of fruit if I suspect that none can be found along the way. Summer and Sunbelt Walks are more enjoyable with a hat or sunglasses, and sunscreen is a must for those of you with sensitive skin. It's wise to take along a sweater or a jacket on afternoon and evening walks, even if it's too hot to wear at the beginning of the trip. If the walk is longer than 4 miles, it is by definition an "exercise walk." That means bring along a change of socks and a water bottle, wear sweats, and be sure you have comfortable walking shoes. If you plan to go walking every day, I suggest that you change off with two pairs of shoes, giving one a chance to air and dry out. This is a good idea anyway, even if you don't do a lot of walking. Your feet sweat inside your shoes, and the accumulated moisture needs a chance to escape.

While it may seem obvious, walkers who travel in wet weather need to be reminded to wear leather shoes or rain-protective apparel. I find that, even on an exercise walk, one should stay as comfortable as possible and most of all have dry feet. Many Great Walks can be taken in inclement weather if you have raingear that repels rain and snow. And many Great Walks are at their best during late fall and early winter when the trees are bare. The Cuyahoga Valley Walk in Ohio provides greater views of the valley when you are able to see through the trees, as do many walks in the East, where thick foliage blocks the view during the summer months, creating a kind of "green tunnel."

Many of the Great Beach Walks are beautiful in the rain. But without proper raingear you will be uncomfortable, because your wet body will tend to cool down fast. Stay dry while you are walking. You will enjoy the sights much more that way.

Don't attempt a Mountain Walk when it's wet. Wet ground makes traction difficult, and walkers often trip and fall. Also, be careful when you take a City Walk in the rain. Slick pavement can be hazardous.

Getting in Shape

I have often said that the walking tour itself is its own exercise training. If you are really out of shape, exercise infrequently, and do little or no walking, tackle only those walks that are 2 miles long — or under — to start. If you get tired, stop and rest. If any pain persists, stop walking and seek medical attention. Otherwise, build up your mileage gradually in ⅛- to ¼-mile increments.

Most of the walks in this book can be completed within a day. The fitter you become, the more miles you can do. For example, if you are in poor condition, choose tours in the ⅛- to 2-mile range; then walk them slowly with frequent reststops. (You will want to do this anyway — to take in the sights.) If you are in fair shape, you can walk 2 to 4 miles without stopping and therefore should be able to handle comfortably the walks in this book that are in the 1- to 4-mile range.

Less than one-fourth of the Great Walks are 6 miles or longer. If you can walk 4 to 6 miles without aches or pains, you are ready to try a 6- to 10-mile walk. Allow one hour for each 2- to 3-mile distance for Wilderness Walks, including a 5- to 10-minute reststop, as well as various other stops to sightsee along the way. You need to be in good shape before taking on a 6- to 10-mile walking tour; or at least be ready for some muscle soreness (calves, buttocks, inner thighs) the next day. Also, if you were not careful to wear shoes with cushioning and arch support, you'll have some foot pain and blisters or tender spots. Take care to prepare yourself better for the longer walks. Don't try walks over 10 miles unless you are in excellent shape. Gradually build up your stamina: reach each mileage level, mastering it to the point of comfort, before proceeding to the next.

Future Editions

With your help, we hope to provide further regional editions — as well as international guides — of the best and greatest walks. Please use the nomination form on the last page for your Great Walks candidates. In addition to hiking trails under 15 miles — or one day's walk — we are interested in guided walking tours, unguided city strolls near the center or near large hotels, nature and wilderness areas near major cities, and any trails near major airports for air travelers who want to get out and stretch during layovers. Other categories include the best park walks in cities, the nearest climb walks (including high-rise buildings you can walk up), and the best indoor walks (including air-conditioned shopping malls, atriums, and museums, as well as underground passageways).

Let your imagination do some work, too. There are probably golf courses that qualify as Great Walks. And we are interested in those little-known walks tucked away on the coast or in the backwoods somewhere. It is our goal to create a "park-and-walk" footwork network, making walking more accessible and an integral part of our modern life, much as it is in Europe where footpaths connect many of the cities.

Gary Yanker

AMERICA'S
GREATEST
WALKS

Walking the Eastern States

FROM STROLLS through America's oldest cities to hikes up the most remote mountaintops; from quiet walks along miles of seashore to rambles in autumn forests ablaze with color, the Eastern United States offers a huge variety of wonders.

It was the retreat of the glaciers from the Northeast region more than 10,000 years ago that allowed the great forests of New England to develop. In the fall these trees provide one of nature's most beautiful works of art — a spectacular painting, the sugar maple (the State Tree of Vermont) at its center, in hues ranging from bright yellow to crimson red. Dogwood, oak, and birch add their own splashes of color; and mountain laurel, rhododendron, and azalea are among the shrubs that contribute to this glorious canvas. Autumn is the crowning season of America's Northeast, but equally wonderful is winter, when the region lies peacefully beneath a carpet of glistening snow. Bundled up warmly, the winter walker is rewarded, not only by nature's startling white beauty, but also by the warmth and good companionship that come later in front of a blazing fire.

The landscape changes dramatically as you go south. Then the great deciduous forests of the Northeast are replaced by live oaks, swamp cypress, Spanish moss, and palm trees. Here the seasons are less extreme, and the profusion of color from the myriad of flowers and trees lasts almost year round.

Birds (loons and ibis, great blue heron and egrets, to name just a few) and some of the best seafood found anywhere (Maine lobster, Florida stone crab, Maryland blue crab, and a host of Atlantic oysters) are rewards walkers can expect to find along the Atlantic Coast, in addition to the region's miles of beaches of soft sand and assorted delicately formed seashells.

Walkers from other parts of the country can enjoy some of the very things easterners tend to take for granted — the history and romance of the region. A walk from the Massachusetts State House atop Beacon Hill east toward Boston Harbor, for example, takes the walker through three centuries of historic sites. Today, thousands of people pass them on their way to work, or pass under them as they crowd into subways to beat the snarling beast called "Boston Traffic." Even the villagers in the most picturesque Atlantic coastal towns find it necessary, even easy, to live

1

with their history shoved a little to the side. Easterners inhabit the shells and husks of the past and build the present around them. Sometimes the beauty so readily apparent to visitors is unappreciated by them, and it is not until they show their visitors around — to watch the Cardinal of Boston bless the fishing fleet in Gloucester Harbor, to touch the Liberty Bell, or to read the words of Lincoln's Second Inaugural Address on his Memorial — that its magnificence touches them. Yes, they agree then, the East . . . it really is pretty nice after all.

The country was born here; many have died here; still more have come here and stayed, and their children still call this place home. Beneath the soil and the paved roads that you walk on in New York, Boston, and Charlottesville lie the footsteps of countless nameless soldiers of the Revolutionary War. In Gettysburg and Savannah, echoes of millions of bullets fired during a single day of the Civil War are heard in the statues and graveyards honoring the dead. The East is a visual digest of the world and of American history, best read on foot, page by page. The walks in this book are just a beginning. We hope they will lead you on to your own discoveries, discoveries as wonderful as this one, described to us by a friend, who takes walks as often as he can.

"One late autumn night I was walking alone on a New England beach. There was nothing there but the sound of the surf and the wind under a slate-colored sky. At the very edge of the tide I saw tiny darts of light in the water. The sea was tossing phosphorescent jellyfish onto the sand. Flashes of green light, like lightning bolts you could hold in your palm, shot through each of them. I wanted to show someone, but no one else was there. The ocean and the sky were the same color that night, so they looked seamlessly dark, overwhelming and mighty. And it felt as though that tremendous power was speaking to me in these little messages of light. What it said I'm still not sure, but I'll remember it forever."

Part 1

NEW ENGLAND

Connecticut, Maine, Massachusetts, New Hampshire, Rhode Island, Vermont

1. Mystic
2. Steep Rock Mountain
3. Acadia National Park
4. Boston
5. Concord
6. Franconia Notch
7. Newport
8. The Long Trail

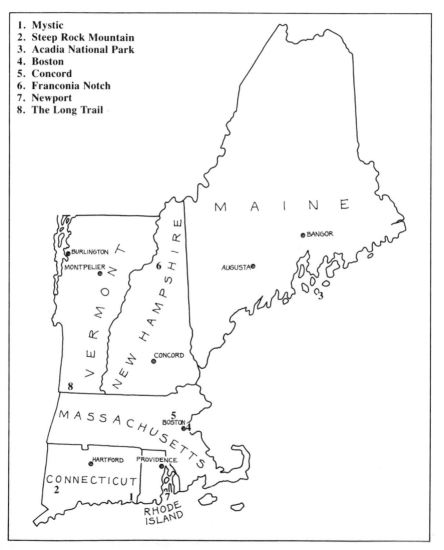

Connecticut

MYSTIC

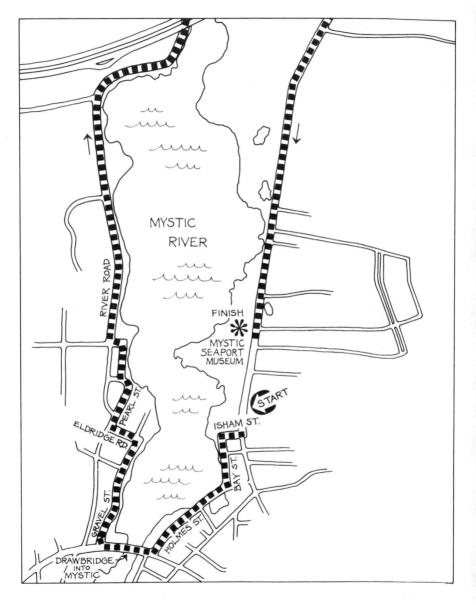

Directions: Mystic is in the southeastern corner of Connecticut, on the Atlantic Coast, within a few miles of I–95. Get off I–95 at Exit 90 onto Greenmanville Avenue (Route 27) and head south. Park in the South Lot of Mystic Seaport (the third traffic light from the exit).

Best Season: Mystic is beautiful year round, but this is one place you might want to see at Christmastime. Being a New England seacoast town, it takes on a special character in winter. But don't go Christmas Day; the Seaport is closed then.

Length: This 5½ mile walk takes about four hours. You'll want to spend time in Mystic Seaport Museum, though, so allow yourself a full day.

Degree of Difficulty: Easy.

Mystic River Walk

Nothing else so beautifully marries form and function as a sailing vessel, and Mystic reflects some of the same sturdy elegance. Much of its seagoing past remains in the downtown area, and in Mystic Seaport Museum it's still very much alive.

Lisa Brownell nominated this 5½ mile loop walk. It winds along both sides of the Mystic River and ends at the Seaport Museum.

From your car, walk south (left as you leave the parking lot) on Route 27 and take your first right (Isham Street). When you reach the water's edge, turn left on Bay and follow the river along Holmes Street. Take a right on Route 1 (Main Street) and walk over the drawbridge into downtown Mystic.

The first right over the bridge is Gravel Street, once the home of sea captains and sailors. Many of the homes you pass on the left are historic, built during the early 19th century. Number 13 Gravel is reputedly a "spite house," built deliberately to block a neighbor's view of the water. Number 29, like other homes on the street, has been occupied by not one, but two sea captains — one a submariner.

Bear left on Eldridge Road and walk one block to Pearl Street. Walk to your right along Pearl to River Road where you have a great view of the ships and buildings at Mystic Seaport Museum. Follow River Road past the wildlife sanctuary, where you'll see some of the ducks and swans that live on the river; then bear right at the intersection with Route 27, past the Mystic General Store. The signs will take you back toward the lot where you parked your car and to Mystic Seaport Museum. Along the way you'll pass close by Olde Mistick Village and the Mystic Marinelife Aquarium. If you have time, stop for a visit. The aquarium, especially, is excellent.

Mystic Seaport Museum is a tour by itself. It is a nonprofit, educational maritime museum emphasizing the great era of Atlantic maritime commerce. It includes more than 60 historic buildings, four major vessels,

a planetarium, a library, and a tremendous collection of maritime artifacts. One-day adult admission is $9. It's worth every cent.

The museum is the site of George Greenman & Co., builders of some of the fastest sailing ships. Fittingly, the last of the great whaling ships is berthed here: the *Charles W. Morgan,* built in 1841. It, and others, such as the training ship *Joseph Conrad* and the fishing schooner *L. A. Dunton,* are open for boarding. The largest collection of small craft in the United States is also on display.

Lisa Brownell recommends that, if your visit is short, you begin a tour of the Museum at the Stillman Building near the North Gate entrance. There the display on "New England and the Sea" will acquaint you with the oceangoing heyday of the place. The exhibit of scrimshaw and ship models is superb.

The Museum is laid out like a small town, with streets and separate buildings of various styles. There are stores, a school, a chapel, a cooperage, a tavern, and a bank, along with ships and a working preservation shipyard. The Children's Museum will help your kids understand how their 19th-century seagoing counterparts lived — they can even play with 19th-century toys. The Planetarium offers daily presentations on celestial navigation and other subjects relevant to the seadog and pleasurable to the landlubber. The Museum is a wonderful collection of new and old buildings, many brought here from other sites in New England, some on their original sites.

For a special experience (May–October), take a cruise on the 1908 steamboat *Sabino*.

The Mystic Seaport Museum offers a variety of special programs and events — lectures, music, demonstrations, and so on. To plan your trip, call (203) 572-0711.

STEEP ROCK MOUNTAIN

Directions: From Route 202, take Route 47 to Washington Depot, located in northwestern Connecticut. Turn at Parks Drug Store, keeping the river on your left. When the road bears to the right, keep straight. You are now entering Steep Rock Preservation. Park the car just before the bridge, where you will see a path with a fence rail across it. That is the old railroad bed that begins the walk.

Best Season: Fall; spring and summer are also good. Difficult in winter.

Length: About an hour of walking time round trip. Count on another half hour or hour (at least) to picnic at the top, or just to sit down and take in the view.

Degree of Difficulty: Easy.

Places to Visit: Washington and Washington Depot, two of Litchfield County's loveliest towns, typify New England charm. Special points of interest include the American Indian Archaeological Institute in Washington, which houses early American Indian artifacts, a life-size Indian Long House, a museum and a museum shop, and the Gunn Memorial Historical Museum, also in Washington. In Washington Depot, the Hickory Stick Bookshop is a wonderful place to browse; and, before you begin your walk, plan to stop at the Ice Cream Depot. It's located on your right, about a quarter of a mile down the road from where you turn at Parks Drug Store to get to Steep Rock. People come from all over to get the Depot's famous homemade ice cream and ice-cream cones.

Steep Rock Mountain Walk

The beautiful Shepaug River runs through Steep Rock Preservation, over 2,000 acres of untouched woodland. It is open to the public for picnicking and hiking. Outdoor horse shows are held in the horse corral during the summer; and many a "Huck Finn" has jumped into Mitchell's hole

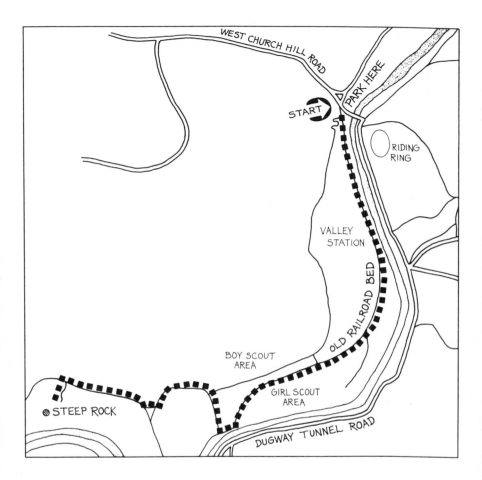

— the deepest part of the river and a favorite spot for swimmers. In the early spring, canoeists dot the river. At this time the annual "Pooh Stick Race" is held, beginning at the bridge and ending at the bend.

There are many wonderful walks throughout Steep Rock: around the "clam shell," for example; through the old railroad tunnel; in the Hidden Valley; wading along the river's edge. The winning walk was sent in by Nancy Ware, an 18-year resident of the area. It begins along the dirt path, parallel to the river. Shortly after this path turns to cinder, you cross a small gully. Right after that, the path bears to the right and you begin your climb up the mountain. The terrain never gets very steep, and you can wend and wind your way up at your own pace, enjoying the fresh pine scent or stopping now and then to examine a wild flower or fern or to listen for the sound of the Shepaug River below.

After about two miles the sky begins to appear through the pine boughs. Before long you're at the top, overlooking the "clam shell" and the Shepaug River, which wraps itself around the land below. The lookout along a rock ledge is protected by a fence. A small memorial plaque reads: "In memory of Robert Frost, who died October 31, 1957, age 11." Because of the fence, there is no danger now, but the memory of young Robert Frost, who fell from the mountaintop when there was no fence, makes the view just that much more awesome.

The top of Steep Rock Mountain is for contemplation. It is a quiet place that invites quiet thoughts. "I don't recommend the walk in winter," says Ms. Ware, "but any other time is just about perfect. The New England foliage from the top of Steep Rock is breathtaking, so I especially like the walk in the fall, and never miss a trip up the mountain in October."

Maine

ACADIA NATIONAL PARK
Penobscot and Sargent Mountains

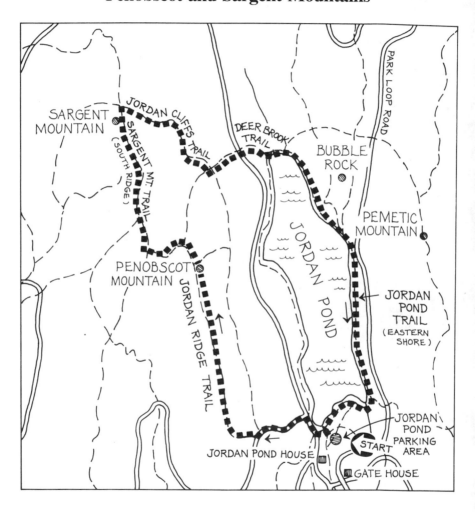

Directions: Acadia is on Mount Desert Island, surrounded by French-man Bay, Blue Hill Bay, and the Atlantic Ocean, about two-thirds up the coast of one of God's favorite states — Maine. The only way on to the island is via Route 3, to Bar Harbor, which you can pick up from U.S. 1. Continue on Route 3 to the Visitor's Center, three miles north of Bar

Harbor. Stop there for a trail map. "The Penobscot–Sargent Mountain area contains one of the most intricate webs of backcountry trails in Acadia," says Park naturalist Lois Winter. "A trail map is essential." At the Visitor's Center ask for directions to the Jordan Pond parking area (not to be confused with the Jordan Pond House parking area) where this walk begins.

Best Season: Fall. Park naturalist Robert Rothe, who suggested this walk, calls fall in Acadia "idyllic — nature in its glory."

Length: Acadia offers trails in remarkable profusion, from little half-mile loops to 7 miles round trip. Time is disproportionate to distance; some of these walks are real climbing hikes. For example, the Penobscot and Sargent mountains walk is a 5-mile loop, certainly a "good hike." You should probably allow at least four hours, so that you'll have plenty of time to enjoy the panoramas, as well as the up-close scenery such as picturesque little Sargent Pond, nestled between the two mountains.

Degree of Difficulty: According to Robert Rothe, the walk up Penobscot and Sargent mountains can be "a great test of stamina, depending on your level of fitness." The paths in Acadia vary from very easy to strenuous. If you prefer something easier, ask for suggestions at the Visitor's Center.

The Penobscot and Sargent Mountain Hike

The name "Acadia" was first given to the North Carolina coast by the Italian navigator Verrazano. The green shoreline made him think of descriptions of the Arcadian landscape of Ancient Greece. European cartographers, never having seen the New World, allowed the name to drift north to the Maritimes. The early French colonists called this part of North America "L'Acadie"; hence the name of one of the most popular parks in the National Park System.

What makes Acadia so popular? In addition to its remarkable scenic variety and 120 miles of trails, the Park staff offer a number of guided nature walks. There are, for example, three-hour birding hikes; walks that teach the glaciation and geological history of the island, still deeply scarred and rutted by the Ice Age; walks to see beaver; and walks that explore the shoreline life forms at low tide. Acadia is a mountain and forest and seacoast park all in one, and several guided activities are available every day to help you appreciate it all. And every night too, for that matter: the "Night Prowl" explores the forest after dark, and "Stars over Acadia" takes in the clear night sky. Some of these walks require a reservation. Call (207) 288-3338 for information.

Robert Rothe recommends the hike up Sargent and Penobscot mountains. It's five miles of great hiking and gets you to the second-highest point in the Park (1,373 feet), overlooking the mountains to the east and Somes Sound to the west. "It's less developed than Cadillac Mountain (the highest point at 1,530 feet, and accessible by car) — and Cadillac is a little anticlimactic," says Rothe, "considering that you climb a pretty strenuous trail only to find cars parked at the summit. And, you won't be disappointed with the views; they are spectacular."

From the Jordan Pond parking area, walk down the gravel road, which serves as a boat launching access for Jordan Pond. When you reach the shore of the pond, turn left on the trail and follow it to the southwest tip of the pond. There you'll join a carriage path which crosses over Jordan Stream. There are more than 51 miles of these old carriage paths throughout the Park. They pass over cut granite bridges and were designed especially to afford visitors the best opportunity to enjoy the natural scenery of the Park. They are another reason Acadia is special.

Turn right and walk several hundred yards to an intersection with another carriage path. Turn left and follow this carriage path for about half a mile. You'll pass over a stone carriage road bridge and by the Jordan Cliffs Trailhead sign. About 100 feet beyond the sign is another trailhead sign: Penobscot Mountain. Start up the trail (called the Jordan Ridge Trail) and walk up to the summit. The view here is stunning; you won't want to leave. From the summit of Penobscot Mountain, follow trail signs to Sargent Pond, a peaceful little place where you can pause for contemplation or just to relax for a moment before starting up Sargent Mountain, where you'll find more impressive vistas.

When you're ready to take the second part of the loop back to the parking area, follow the Jordan Cliffs Trail east, southeast off the summit to Deer Brook Trail. Turn left and follow the Deer Brook Trail east. Cross over the carriage path at Deer Brook Bridge and continue on to the north end of Jordan Pond. Follow the trail along the eastern shore of Jordan Pond, back to the Jordan Pond parking area.

Massachusetts

BOSTON
The Freedom Trail

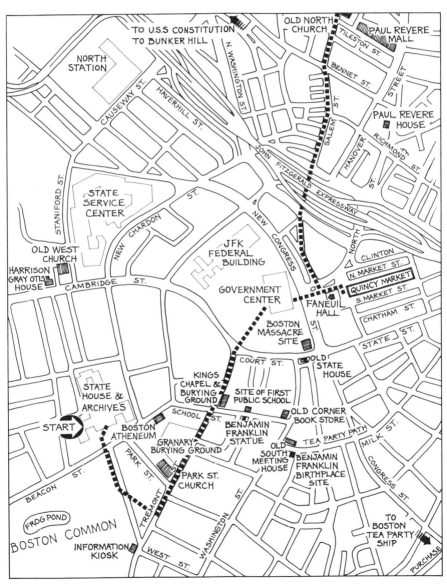

Directions: Routes 1, 93, 95, 3, and the Massachusetts Turnpike will take you to Boston. Driving in Boston is a tribal rite, laden with ceremony and danger. If you must participate, follow the signs for downtown. There are a number of costly parking garages available. Stay near Beacon Hill if possible, and ask directions often.

Best Season: Spring and fall. The beauty of winter in Boston is breathtaking, but very cold. On weekdays the city is crowded with business people; tourists pack it on weekends.

Length: Although the Freedom Trail is only about 5 miles round trip, allow at least a day for Boston. There are lots of planned stops along the Trail and many others you'll want to make on the spur of the moment.

Degree of Difficulty: Easy.

Boston's Revolutionary Walk

The Freedom Trail is marked by a line of brick, inlaid in the sidewalk, or a line of brick-red painted footsteps. Begin at the New State House (1795). Its gold leaf-covered dome is a highly visible landmark. Cross the Boston Common, where you might find an outdoor art exhibit, or street music, to Tremont Street. The corner of Park and Tremont is a favorite haunt of America's best street artist, Bob "Sidewalk Sam" Guillemin. He may be laying out a Rubens in chalk as you pass. Beyond the Park Street Church on Tremont is the Old Granary Burying Ground (1660), resting place of Paul Revere, John Hancock, the artist John Smibert, and the victims of the Boston Massacre. Benjamin Franklin's parents lie under the central obelisk. King's Chapel (1749–1754) and its even older burying ground (1630) lie just up the street. Visit the Chapel; it's a masterpiece. Tremont will take you into Government Center, a daunting desert of brick, overlooked by Boston's new City Hall.

Faneuil Hall and the Quincy Market oasis are on the other side of Congress Street. Faneuil Hall (notice the impressive golden grasshopper weathervane) was built in 1742 by Peter Faneuil as a meeting hall and marketplace. It remains a vital civic center today; and Quincy Market has emerged from heavy restoration to become a touristy, slick, but nonetheless pleasant gathering place. Its assortment of shops and restaurants is delightful, and its open stalls are filled with everything from fish to flowers. You may want to spend some time here, browsing through the shops and sampling the clam chowder or fried clams for an authentic taste of New England.

From Quincy Market, continue along the Freedom Trail, under the Crosstown Expressway into the North End, the Italian enclave of the city. The Trail will guide you to the Old North Church. An equestrian statue of Paul Revere stands in the Prado, a sunny little plaza where people from the neighborhood like to play chess and *bocce*. In the church tower, on the night of April 18, 1775, two lanterns hung to tell Revere that the British were arriving by sea. The next day, in Concord, the Colonials faced the Redcoats with muskets ablaze.

Follow the Trail to Copps Hill Burying Ground where you can see across the Harbor to Charlestown, Bunker Hill, and the frigate, *Constitution*. If it's a nice day and you have time, take a side trip to Charlestown to see the diorama of the Battle of Bunker Hill inside the Monument and to go aboard the *Constitution* ("Old Ironsides").

There's more to the Trail. Just follow the signs and you'll see modern and ancient Boston rubbing shoulders in the unique way that gives this city its special charm.

CONCORD
A Quiet Walk

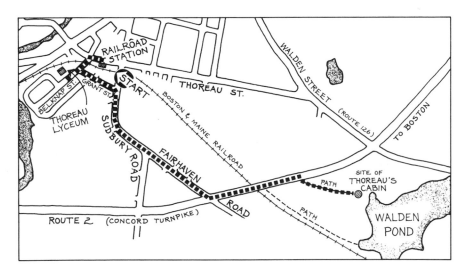

Directions: Concord is about 20 miles west of Boston. Take Route 2 west and follow the signs for Concord Center. At Monument Square, turn left onto Main, and fork left at the Concord Library. Proceed past it to the light and take a left. A restored train station will be on the right. You can park there.

Best Season: All year round is good, and early morning is best. The walk is extraordinarily pretty in the fall, when the leaves are turning; and in the winter, when the woods are muffled under the snow and you have the route to yourself.

Length: This walk is about 5 miles. Allow two to three hours at a good pace, but leave time to saunter, if you can.

Degree of Difficulty: Easy.

Finding Walden Pond

"I was seated by the shore of a small pond, about a mile and a half south of the village of Concord and somewhat higher than it, in the midst of an extensive wood between that town and Lincoln, and about two miles south of our only field known to fame, Concord Battle Ground; but I was so low in the woods that the opposite shore, half a mile off, like the rest, covered with wood, was my most distant horizon."

The town of Concord will quickly reveal the more popular tourist attractions like the Battle Ground. This lesser-known tour, however, is for the walker who seeks Walden Pond, the "small pond" where Thoreau spent two years living deliberately.

Walk west from the railroad station, keeping the tracks on your left. The first left turn is Belknap Street, and one block down it is the Thoreau Lyceum. The closest thing to a museum of Thoreau, it contains several exhibits, including the desk on which Thoreau is thought to have written his masterpiece, *Walden*. There is a good bookshop there, and a full-scale replica of the sturdy little house Thoreau built by the pond in 1845. The Lyceum, open Monday–Saturday, 10–5 and Sunday, 2–5, charges a nominal admission fee.

The folks at the Lyceum will help you find the pond. Go back to Grant Street and follow it until you reach Sudbury Road. Turn right there and continue on Fairhaven. Cross Route 2 and follow it left, uphill. After passing a railroad bridge, you'll be able to find your way into the woods on your right. The pond is there.

The path around the pond has been extensively restored. Today Walden lives a dual life: it is both a literary shrine and an active recreation resource. Recent landscaping has made the two compatible. The path will guide you to the site of Thoreau's house, on the north side. The dimensions of the house are marked by granite shafts. Over the chimney foundation a marker reads, "Go thou my incense upwards from this hearth."

Elsewhere in Concord you will find the house on Main Street where Thoreau died, and Sleepy Hollow Cemetery where he shares "Authors' Ridge" with Emerson, the Alcotts, and Hawthorne. But it is at Walden, secluded from the traffic, ground fog drifting over the water, the sun coming up, where the academic crust falls away from Thoreau's memory, and you have him fresh: "I learned this, at least, by my experiment; that if one advances confidently in the direction of his dreams, and endeavors

16

to live the life which he has imagined, he will meet with a success unexpected in common hours. . . . In proportion as he simplifies his life, the laws of the universe will appear less complex, and solitude will not be solitude, nor poverty poverty, nor weakness weakness. If you have built your castles in the air, your work need not be lost; that is where they should be. Now put the foundations under them."

New Hampshire

FRANCONIA NOTCH

Directions: Franconia Notch State Park, in the middle of New Hampshire amid the White Mountains, is split by Route 3, accessible via I–93. Follow Route 3 to the parking area at Lafayette Campground, where this walk begins.

Best Season: Summer is best for its comfortable weather; fall is best for scenery. In fact, Franconia Notch is one of the best fall foliage districts in the country.

Length: The walk described here loops from the Old Bridle Path to the Falling Water Trail and is about 8 miles round trip. Allow a full day for the walk itself; you will need another full day to discover the many wonders of Franconia Notch.

Degree of Difficulty: Moderately difficult. The trail is steep in places, rising to a top height of 5,249 feet. Dress warmly and wear good shoes.

Franconia Notch and the Summits of Lafayette and Lincoln Mountains

Franconia Notch is a natural amusement park. Concentrated within its relatively small area are many wonderful walks, some dramatic rock formations, covered bridges, fishing, and picnicking.

The Notch is a seven-mile-long valley between the Franconia and Kinsman ranges of the White Mountains. Its most famous feature is a 40-foot outcropping on the side of Cannon Mountain. The Old Man of the Mountains is a stunning sight: a nearly perfect profile of a stern-faced, square-jawed New Hampshire native. The profile is invisible from most of the area, but along Route 3, near Profile Lake, it stands out so clearly that no imagination is required to see the forehead, sharp nose, mouth, and chin. Discovered by white men in 1805, the Old Man of the Mountains is now the state symbol of New Hampshire, possibly because it looks like, and is about as loquacious as, a purebred Yankee.

A number of trails snake through the Park, offering remarkable contrasts. For example, you could spend a full day walking the rigorous route from Profile Lake up the Green Leaf Trail to Mount Lafayette, past the Appalachian Mountain Club hut. From Lafayette you can stay above treeline on the Franconia Ridge Trail, all the way across the Ridge to Mount Lincoln and Mount Liberty. This rugged, day-long walk is for experienced hikers. Less strenuous is the short hike from Echo Lake, in the north part of the Park, to Bald Mountain via Artist's Bluff.

The walk we are suggesting is a fairly strenuous one. It begins at Old Bridle Path trailhead directly across the highway from Lafayette Campground. The trail rises two miles to Greenleaf Hut at treeline, then ascends another mile above treeline to the summit of Mt. Lafayette (5,249 feet). At the summit is the junction of the Franconia Ridge Trail which is part of the Appalachian Trail System that stretches from Maine to Georgia. The ridge trail leads south to the summit of Mt. Lincoln (5,108 feet). Pause here to enjoy the magnificent setting before beginning your descent on the Falling Waters Trail which leads back to Lafayette Campground.

About four miles south of the Lafayette Campground, off of Route 3, is one of the most popular sites in the Park — the Flume. Take time to visit this 700-foot-long crack in the earth and the swift mountain stream that runs through it. There is a small boardwalk down the middle, and it's a cool, green, awesome place to walk. The Basin, just south of Lafayette Campground, is a natural dish cut into the granite by centuries of flowing water. There's a footbridge over it for viewing. Boise Rock, also along Route 3, south of the Old Man of the Mountains, is a glacial boulder with a colorful history: an 18th-century traveler, caught in a blizzard, spent two days in the shelter of the rock. He killed his horse, cut it open, crawled inside, and survived until rescuers came to carve the frozen beast away. Finally, not to be missed, is the Cannon Mountain Aerial Tramway, which runs to the summit of Cannon Mountain. It's as close as you can get to a bird's-eye view of this beautiful park.

Rhode Island

NEWPORT
The Cliff Walk

Directions: Newport is on an island surrounded on the north and east by the Sakonnet River, on the west by Narragansett Bay, and on the south by Rhode Island Sound and the Atlantic Ocean. From Boston, take Route 128 to 24 south and follow the signs to Newport via the Sakonnet River Bridge to 114 south. From New York, take I–95 north to 138 east, and follow the blue road signs for Newport Bridge, which takes you into town. If possible, take the latter route; Newport Bridge is a toll bridge, but it's one of the prettiest suspension bridges in the East.

Best Season: A summer day is wonderful for taking the Cliff Walk. The ocean breeze makes it very comfortable, even in the hottest part of the season. Winter might be too cold and icy, and many of the Newport mansions are closed. A couple taking the Cliff Walk on a blustery day in fall would probably have it all to themselves.

Length: The Cliff Walk is about 3½ miles long, and takes between 90 minutes and two hours to go one way. If you don't want to retrace your steps, arrange for someone to meet you at the other end, Bailey's Beach.

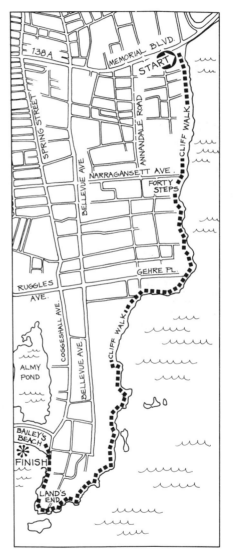

Degree of Difficulty: Moderate. There are some rough places along the way, and on windy days especially parts of the trail can be a bit dangerous. Be careful.

The Cliff Walk

Newport's Cliff Walk is concrete proof that the best things in life are free. Wealthy owners of some of the mansions you pass along this route tried to keep this wonderful part of the world all to themselves, but the courts ruled that fishermen needed free access to the sea; walkers too benefit from this ruling.

Begin the walk on Memorial Boulevard at Newport Beach. This is a great place to swim and body surf, so you might want to spend the morning here, eat lunch, and take the Cliff Walk in the afternoon.

The walk winds along Rhode Island's shoreline, past some of the most wildly opulent mansions ever built in America. Called "cottages" by their builders (the only understatement about them), these palaces are on your right as you follow the walk; the water is on your left; none of the homes is accessible from the ocean side. These homes are open to the public from April until late fall. For additional information about the mansions, write to the Convention and Visitor's Bureau, Inc., P.O. Box 237, Newport, RI 02840.

The first part of the Cliff Walk descends a stairway, known as the Forty Steps, which takes you down to the water's edge. The first building you come to is Ochre Court, built in 1890 by the architect Richard Morris Hunt. Now it is the Administration Building for Salve Regina College. Hunt was about as prominent in his day as an architect could be. He was the first American to attend the Ecole des Beaux-Arts. A founder and president of the American Institute of Architects, he was a preferred tastemaker for American high society. His commissions included buildings at Yale and Princeton, as well as the U.S. Capitol Building. Hunt designed the New York residences of John Jacob Astor, William K. Vanderbilt, and others who knew the value of a dollar, thereby placing a shell of continental grandeur and taste around fortunes that were thoroughly American. Naturally Hunt was the man to design their modest Newport retreats, and any Renaissance, Gothic, Genoese, or other bit of architectural confectionery that could be bought, Hunt could deliver, and did.

The millionaire builders lived by the law of competition, and it extended to their architectural creations. The Breakers, the next house on the route, was built by Hunt in 1895 for Cornelius Vanderbilt. For sheer size, mass, and opulence, the Breakers is staggering.

Around the bend is Rosecliff, built in 1902 by Stanford White (Hunt died in 1895) for Mrs. Herman Oelrichs. Rosecliff is modeled after the Grand Trianon of Versailles. The heart-shaped stairway is justly famous. Some scenes from *The Great Gatsby* were filmed here. Remember Robert

Redford glancing back at the colossal terra-cotta castle and asking Sam Waterston, "My house looks well, doesn't it?" What a silly question!

Next is the Beechwood Museum, Mrs. Astor's summer home. Live theatrical performances and a multi-image program help you feel more at home.

The Marble House is another Hunt *tour de force*, built for William K. Vanderbilt. It's one of the most luxurious of all Newport houses. The kitchen of the Marble House will give you an idea of the scale on which these people lived and entertained. It looks like the kitchen of an elegant turn-of-the-century ocean liner. You'll have to pass underneath the Marble House's Chinese Tea House here to continue the Cliff Walk.

Belcourt Castle is next, but it's invisible as the Cliff Walk winds around Land's End and goes on to Bailey's Beach. Pause here to take in the beauty of the place and perhaps to ponder on a Biblical verse from 1 Timothy 6:10. "For the love of money is the root of all evil, which some have coveted after, they have erred from the faith, and pierced themselves through with many sorrows." Whatever the lives of Newport's multimillionaires may have been — tragic or otherwise — they could not have been ordinary.

Vermont

THE LONG TRAIL

Directions: The Long Trail extends the length of the state from Canada to Massachusetts, merged for about a third of the way with the Appalachian Trail. Blackinton, Massachusetts, the southern terminus, is so small it doesn't even appear on some maps. The closest town is Williamstown, in Massachusetts' northeast corner, on Massachusetts State Highway 2. To get an excellent guidebook with trail maps, write to the Green Mountain Club, Box 889, 43 State Street, Montpelier, VT 05602.

Best Season: "The end of June through mid-October," says Harry T. Peet, Jr., Executive Director of the Green Mountain Club. "Earlier than that, things tend to be a little wet at the higher elevations, and the June weather is pretty unsettled up here. After that it calms down. Early October can be cold, but the fall foliage is magnificent."

Length: Somewhere between two hours and two months. The trail and its subsidiary footpaths total about 440 miles. People who walk it tell us it is impossible to select one special section. It's all wonderful, they say. The consensus is that people have to walk it for themselves to find their favorite part.

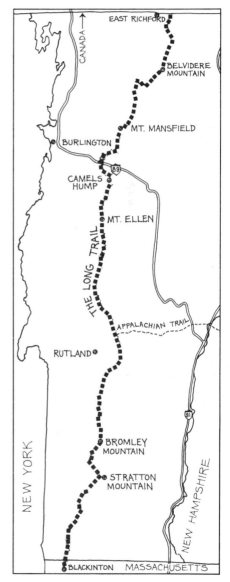

Degree of Difficulty: From easy to strenuous and rugged, depending on where you walk. Study the trail on paper before you set out to study it on foot. The weather in northern New England, in any season, changes in an instant. The Green Mountain Club will provide you with invaluable information on what precautions you should take.

The Long Trail

While we couldn't possibly put together a collection of America's greatest walks without including the Long Trail, all of the people who nominated this walk remarked that there's no one best part. So we invite you, the reader, to explore the many beauties of the granddaddy of all the great American long-distance hiking trails. Conceived in 1910, it gradually cut through the forests and mountain highlands of Vermont until its continuous walking paths linked Massachusetts and Canada. Now the main trail winds 265 miles long, and its offshoots add about 175 miles more to the system. The point of it all is the pleasure of beautiful hiking; the trail was developed to provide the best views and to take the walker around the prettiest lakes and gorges. "Certainly that was the idea," said Harry Peet. "The Green Mountain Club has never been favorably disposed toward speed records."

In other words, take your time. You'll see about 10,000 years' worth on this trip. Vermont shows the deep scars of millenia of glacial movement. In her northeastern hardwood and coniferous forests very little has changed in hundreds of years.

How best to enjoy the Long Trail? In short or long hikes, it offers details as intimate as the trillium, bloodroot, and jack-in-the-pulpit that line the path and the 200 species of birds that dart around it, and views as wide and powerful as the great worn tops of Stratton Mountain and Camel's Hump. Harry Peet said, "I think part of what the Long Trail has to offer is that on any given trip you can head out on a small part of it and find variety. The northern part of the state offers higher elevations and more ruggedness; the southern part has more scenic lakes and ponds. For solitude we suggest the upper parts; for beauty and social hiking, stay to the south."

If you don't live in Vermont, you might consider joining the Green Mountain Club as an At-Large member. The Club membership is divided into At-Large and Section members. Each section runs its own activities: day hikes, snowshoe hikes, cross-country skiing, and so forth, and they welcome the public along. Some hikes require expenses; most are free. For more information, get in touch with the central office at the address listed above under "Directions."

Part 2

THE MID-ATLANTIC REGION

Delaware, District of Columbia, Maryland, New Jersey, New York, Pennsylvania, Virginia, West Virginia

1. Winterthur
2. Annapolis
3. Baltimore
4. Cape May County
5. Midtown Manhattan
6. The Financial District
7. Niagara Falls
8. Gettysburg
9. Philadelphia
10. Independence National Historic Park
11. Presque Isle State Park
12. Assateague Island
13. Charlottesville and Monticello
14. Georgetown
15. Washington, D.C.
16. Harpers Ferry

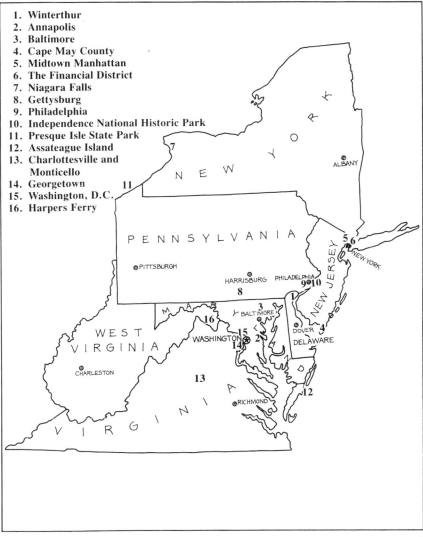

Delaware

WINTERTHUR

Directions: The Henry Francis du Pont Winterthur Museum and Gardens are six miles from Wilmington, Delaware, in the Brandywine Valley, on Route 52, halfway between New York City and Washington, D.C. Take exit 7 off I–95 in Wilmington and follow the Brandywine Valley Trail signs.

Best Season: Winterthur's 963-acre grounds are magnificent even under snow, but in spring the colors are almost audible. Literally hundreds of thousands of flowers are in bloom: daffodils, azaleas, primroses, and the unique hybrid rhododendrons that so delighted Henry Francis du Pont. The Christmas season sees 21 rooms in the Museum decked in period decoration according to early American holiday tradition. In short, there's no "best" time to visit — all of Winterthur's times are best.

Length: About three centuries. Winterthur is another of those walks whose time is disproportionate to its length. You will probably want to spend a full day here, exploring the beauty of the place. There is a restaurant and an outdoor café. All tours of the Museum are with guides, but there are self-guided walking tours of the Gardens. For further information, call (302) 654-1548.

Degree of Difficulty: Easy.

Winterthur Gardens and Museum

A walk through Winterthur is a splendid walk through a most unusual museum. It houses what is probably the country's finest collection of American decorative arts, containing nearly 200 room settings and over 70,000 objects (furniture, textiles, paintings, prints, pewter, silver, ceramics, glass, needlework, and brass) made or used in America between 1640 and 1840. The rooms themselves are exhibits, with beams, windows, fireplaces, and floors installed into the building fabric.

Thus, Winterthur is not a glass-case type of museum. The room settings are like stage sets awaiting characters. Even the most magnificent and renowned objects are displayed with a sense of warmth and intimacy: the set of silver tankards made by Paul Revere in the du Pont Dining Room, for example, might elsewhere be watched over by an armed guard; here it sits on a sideboard against a wall. So, at Winterthur you not only see objects from the past, you also get a feeling for the people who used them.

Some highlights of the Museum tour include the Chinese parlor, decorated with wallpaper painted in China about 1770. From floor to ceiling, it shows scenes of daily life in an Oriental village in rich tones of gold, hazel, and azure. The Montmorenci Stair Hall, perhaps the most famous room at the Museum, has a giant free-hanging spiral staircase sweeping down in a graceful curve. In contrast to the luxury of most other rooms is the Shaker Dwelling Room, with its spartan straight-backed chairs and unadorned white walls.

Even without the exquisite Museum, Winterthur would be worth a visit. Its spectacular gardens contain more than 200 acres of English-style naturalist plantings, designed subtly to imitate the informality of natural settings. Henry Francis du Pont was an amateur gardener in the finest sense: a *lover,* captivated by beautiful, unusual plants and tireless in acquiring them. Winterthur is actually several gardens: the Azalea Woods, which blossom in May with white, mauve, salmon, red, and pink; the Magnolia Bend, where huge trees are covered with white, pink, and pink-purple in mid-April; the Winter-hazel Walk, pale-yellow and lavender in early April; the Sycamore Area, blossoming from spring to fall. The tallest tree in Delaware is in the Chandler Woods, just beyond the visitor parking area. In total, there are 13 garden areas.

Winterthur's admission price of $7 includes the Two Centuries Tour of the Museum, a tram tour of the gardens, as well as the self-guided garden tour. Other tours are extra.

Maryland

ANNAPOLIS

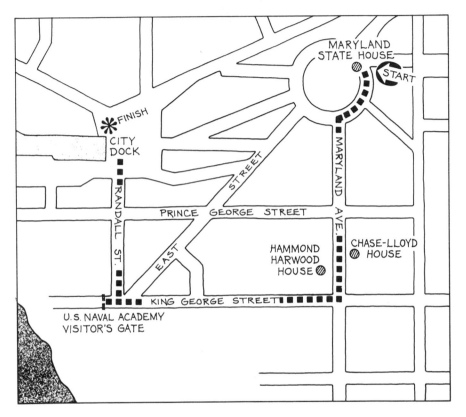

Directions: Take Route 50 to the Rowe Boulevard exit and follow signs to the Capitol Building.

Best Season: All year. Annapolis can be especially pretty in the summer, if you enjoy the sea. Boating season is from spring to fall.

Length: 4–5 miles, up to 2½ hours.

Degree of Difficulty: Easy.

Exploring Historical Annapolis on Foot

The capital of Maryland, Annapolis successfully mixes ancient elements with modern commercial needs, and it does this without being

Disney-like or touristy. The Annapolis skyline is a particular joy, lacking the commercial towers that would rob the town of its old flavor.

Annapolis was planned in 1695 by Governor Francis Nicholson, a Renaissance man of sorts, who was responsible for the two circles around which the city plan is based. Linda Vanderhoff, who nominated Annapolis for best city walk, likens it to a "royal crown," explaining that "Its unique city plan of circles is the jewellike attraction for which it is internationally famous. . . . To walk through the tree-lined, brick-paved streets is to experience an intimate relationship with the past." Today's Annapolis is a warren of small streets with some fascinating stops.

Begin at the State House (1772). It is the oldest capitol in America still in continuous legislative use. It stands in State Circle and is Annapolis's most visible building. Proceed down Maryland Avenue to the Chase-Lloyd House, an 18th-century Georgian mansion where "Star-Spangled Banner" writer Francis Scott Key was married. Across the street is the Hammond-Harwood House, which is open to the public as a museum. It is one of the finest Georgian mansions in America.

A right on King George's Street will take you toward the sea and the U.S. Naval Academy. The Naval Academy Chapel has some remarkable stained-glass windows and massive bronze doors designed by a 19-year-old woman.

The next stop is City Dock. If you love ships, City Dock will keep you occupied for an entire afternoon. Plan to spend some time there, exploring the Chesapeake Bay boats and sleek yachts.

Annapolitans enjoy talking about their town. It has just 30,000 or so people — small for a state capital — so stop along your walk to ask questions of the friendly shopowners. Everyone has a favorite historic site, and you can enjoy most of them within a few hours in this compact, picturesque town.

BALTIMORE

Directions: Baltimore lies on the western side of the Chesapeake Bay, between Washington, D.C., and Philadelphia, along the Boswash Corridor. Take I–95 from the south, I–83 from the north, or I–70 from the west. Follow the signs to the Inner Harbor.

Best Season: Spring, summer, and fall.

Length: Since this walk offers a thousand distractions, it's going to take an afternoon or longer, although it's only a mile or so long.

Degree of Difficulty: Easy.

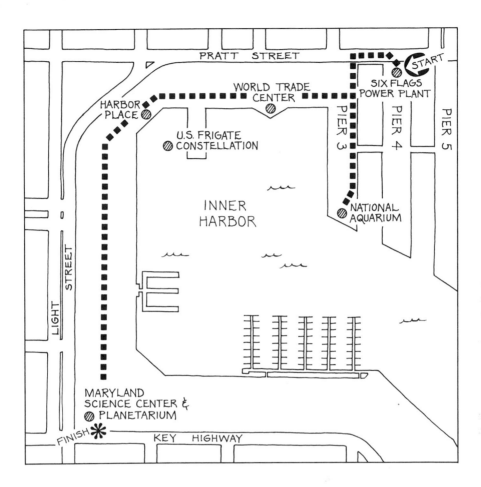

Baltimore — a "Reborn" City

Not so long ago, Baltimore was the sort of place you could find under any mossy rock. Thanks to some enlightened leadership, some public soul-searching, and some federal and private development money, Baltimore has been reborn as one of the East's most hospitable, most delightful cities.

Its chief attraction is the Inner Harbor, a public shopping/recreation area that comprises a Rouse Company festival market, the National Aquarium, a World Trade Center, an 18th-century warship, and an indoor amusement park, not to mention a lot of good places to eat, sit, walk, and watch people. Bring money to cover the admission fees to places such as the Aquarium and the new power plant.

Perhaps you've seen enough of the hanging-fern-and-white-wine variety of marketplace, and are tired of the oh-so-trendy imitations of Vic-

31

torian design that seem to spread like a rash across the face of every city in the country. So why another? The answer is money. The Inner Harbor isn't Baltimore's only success story, but it's the one that attracts most of the rejuvenated tourist traffic to a city that has to fight for every dollar it gets. Eighteen million people visit Harborplace, the Rouse Company's festival market, every year. One-fifth of them come from out of state. That traffic pumps millions of dollars into Baltimore's economy, helps revitalize neighborhoods, creates jobs, and increases the city's tax base.

Yes, festival markets are trendy, and yes, a buck is a lot for an ice-cream cone. But if there's no other pleasure for you here, take this to heart: people on foot are an extremely powerful force in reshaping cities for the better, and no city shows it as well as Baltimore.

This walk begins at Six Flags Power Plant, on the old Pier Four at the east end of the harbor. This was a municipal power plant just a few years ago. Now it's a temple of Victorian polychrome craziness, like Main Street in Disney World turned outside-in.

Next, visit the National Aquarium on Pier Three. It's the distinctive pyramidal concrete-and-glass building with the multicolored mural facing onto the harbor. Under that pointed glass canopy is a lush miniature Amazon Rain Forest with flying as well as swimming inhabitants.

The U.S. frigate *Constellation* is next. Built in 1797, it was the first commissioned ship in the United States Navy. Costumed guides aboard will explain her in detail.

The pentagonal skyscraper overlooking the harbor is the World Trade Center. Twenty-seven stories tall, designed by I. M. Pei, it features an observatory and exhibits on the top floor.

The *Constellation* overlooks the two Harborplace buildings. Ben Thompson, who designed the renovation of Faneuil Hall Marketplace in Boston, created the two pavilions. They're jammed with restaurants and shops.

At the far end of the harbor walk, along the south side, you'll come to the Maryland Science Center. It's a fine way to cap this trip, but remember, the Inner Harbor walk is only an introduction to Baltimore. The restored downtown and neighborhoods present many other walking opportunities. Baltimore has sacrificed none of its ethnic genuineness by inviting the world to visit, so walk the neighborhoods around downtown to see the Washington Monument at Monument and Saint Paul streets, or Babe Ruth's birthplace at 216 Emory Street, or the H. L. Mencken Home at 1524 Hollins Street. You'll enjoy youself in this city. It knows what it's doing.

New Jersey

CAPE MAY COUNTY

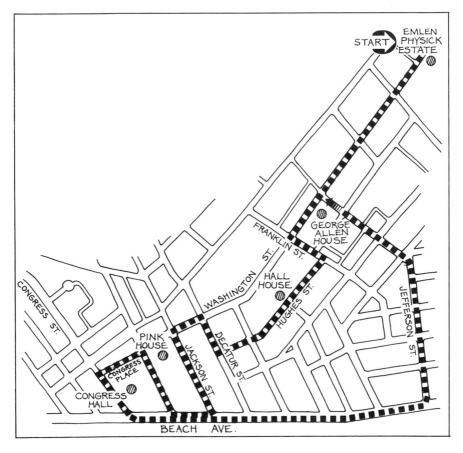

Directions: Cape May County is the southernmost county in New Jersey. Its principal cities run along the Atlantic Coast. Either the Garden State Parkway or the less-traveled Route 9 will take you there. Ocean Drive connects all the towns along the Coast. The walk described here takes place in Cape May City.

Best Season: Cape May is beautiful between spring and fall. During the Christmas season, a Candlelight House Tour is given by the nonprofit Mid-Atlantic Center for the Arts, which, during the year, offers several other tours of the Victorian houses in Cape May City and sponsors a "Victorian Week" in early fall. For information, call (609) 884-5404.

Length: About 2 to 2½ miles. Allow at least an hour and a half.

Degree of Difficulty: Easy.

Exploring the Cape May Seashore

Ocean City, Strathmere, Sea Isle City, Avalon, Stone Harbor, Wildwood, Cape May City: their names alone make these shore towns enchanting. Each has its own personality and appeal. Stone Harbor, for example, is the only heronry in the United States, a must for bird-watchers. Wildwood boasts an internationally famous boardwalk, lined with games, arcades, restaurants, and rides. Cold Spring Village is a reconstructed South Jersey farming village, a living outdoor museum with fifteen 18th- and 19th-century buildings.

Presidents Pierce, Buchanan, Lincoln, and Grant preferred Cape May City. It has the same clean, white beaches that all the other towns have as well as a lovely boardwalk overlooking the surf, which shelves gradually enough to be safe even for children. But Cape May City's chief treasure is her collection of Victorian houses. The whole city is a National Historic Landmark.

A fire in 1878 destroyed 30 acres of homes, nearly half the town, then as now a fashionable retreat for the wealthy. The best carpenters and craftsmen were recruited to rebuild Cape May City, and the result was the elaborate and ornate pastel-colored cottages with huge porches and thick, intricate carving called gingerbread.

The Mid-Atlantic Center for the Arts sponsors a number of guided walking tours of the Historic District. A "Cottages at Twilight" tour opens five fine homes for the evening; "Mansions by Gaslight" covers four particularly opulent buildings; and an evening walk called the "Stained Glass Tour" (a feature of "Victoria Week" in October) shows homes with colored windows lit from behind. Gas lights on the street cast a mellow, old-time glow along the way. The effect is spectacular.

The walk we have chosen begins at the Mid-Atlantic Center and passes by a good sampling of Cape May's famous homes. The Center is located at the Emlen Physick Estate at 1048 Washington Street. Physick, a member of a prominent Philadelphia medical family, commissioned Frank Furness, a local architect remembered for his exuberant Pennsylvania Academy of Fine Arts, to design the big stick-style house with its exaggerated detail. The 16-room house, now a museum of Victorian furniture and artifacts, is a masterpiece of the period's domestic architecture. As you walk down Washington Street, you'll pass the George Allen House, an Italian villa at #720. Take a left to Franklin and a right on Hughes, the oldest residential street in the city. Make sure to see the Hall House at 645 Hughes, notable for its multi-colored exterior.

Walk right on Decatur and left on Washington to Jackson. Now you'll pass the Gibson House, with its elaborate roof shingles and cornices. Go left on Perry to Beach Drive. The famous "pink house," built in 1879, and the "Seven Sisters" houses, built in 1892, are on your left.

Toward the Point, Congress Hall, where several presidents vacationed, is a highlight of the tour. From there you can walk along Beach Drive to get to Jefferson Street, which leads back to Washington and the Physick estate.

New York

NEW YORK CITY
Central Park and Midtown Manhattan

Directions: Begin this walk at City Hall, at the foot of the Brooklyn Bridge. We suggest you take public transportation to get there; this is a long walk and best taken just one way.

Best Season: Spring through fall. A summer weekend, if not too hot, can be perfect.

Length: The full route is almost 4 miles, one way. With all the things to do and see along the way, give it a full day. Or skip most of Fifth Avenue and head straight for the corner of Fifth and East 59th Street, to spend an afternoon crossing the Park.

Degree of Difficulty: Easy. The only hazard is you may spend too much money. It's probably wise to leave your credit cards at home for this walk. Bring about $20 in ones, though; that's good for trying every dish in the world's most diverse food and entertainment smorgasbord.

Walking the "Wonderful Town"

Will and Ariel Durant fit *The Story of Civilization* into 20 heavy volumes: a monumental achievement. H. G. Wells stuffed *The Outline of History* into just two. But nobody ever aspired to squeeze more into a smaller space than E. B. White did when he wrote a short

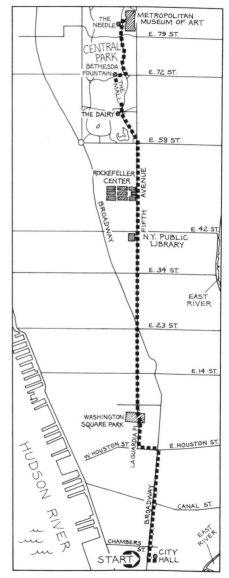

essay — just 30 pages or so — and called it "Here Is New York."

Until now. There are hundreds of wonderful walks in New York City. We've chosen just two, with no illusion that they alone represent "New York." But they will give you an idea of the city's diversity and will inspire you to discover other areas on your own.

From City Hall at the statue of Nathan Hale, walk straight up Broadway to East Houston Street. (The locals know it's HOW–ston, not HEW–ston.) Go left on Houston to get to LaGuardia Place, and follow that up into Washington Square.

Here's where you spend your first one dollar bill. The street musicians in the Square are good, sometimes excellent, as is the floor show of sidewalk speechmakers, NYU students, sunbathers, and beautiful people. New Yorkers know all there is to know about peaceful coexistence. The arch commemorating the centennial of Washington's inauguration is the entrance to Fifth Avenue.

The Avenue: Try resisting Godiva chocolates, Mark Cross leathers, Steuben Glass, Elizabeth Arden, F. A. O. Schwartz, Alfred Dunhill of London, Bergdorf Goodman, Van Cleef and Arpels, Saks Fifth Avenue, Gucci, Cartier, Barnes and Noble, Scribner's, Gucci (that's right, two Guccis), Fortunoff, and Trump Tower. You'll also pass the Bank of New York, the Seaman's Bank for Savings, Manufacturer's Hanover Trust, the Bank of Ireland, Banco do Brasil, Banker's Trust, Israel Discount Bank, and the National Bank of North America (one of which you may now be tempted to rob, if you took our advice and left your credit cards at home). You'll also pass Northwest Orient, Olympic Airways, Lufthansa, and Alitalia, offering you a choice of destination (should you now be a fugitive from the law). Then again, remember those singles in your pocket. You may find nothing quite so luxurious as a glass of fresh-squeezed orange juice; on Fifth Avenue in summer they sell it on every corner. (In winter you can substitute roasted chestnuts.)

Fifth Avenue will carry you past the Main Branch of the New York Public Library between 40th and 42nd. It's free, and it's worth a visit, because there is always some wonderful exhibition in progress. Continue along the Avenue and you'll come to Rockefeller Center between 50th and 51st streets and St. Patrick's Cathedral across the street. The RCA Building at Rockefeller Center is better known as "30 Rock," where NBC-TV has studios for the *Today Show* and *Saturday Night Live,* among others. NBC studio tours are available Monday through Saturday. Pay particular attention to the "Channel Gardens." Radio City Music Hall is part of the complex, too.

Continue up Fifth Avenue, past the Plaza Hotel at 59th Street, to Central Park. It was during the late 18th century that a movement for a park in New York began. Not until the mid-19th century, however, was it really underway. At that time the green landscape that is now Central Park was a garbage dump, overrun by dogs and goats, dotted with tumbledown squatters' shacks. This particular piece of land was given over to recreation only because it was less valuable for commercial purposes than the waterfront. With a physical and political wilderness stretching before him, Frederick Law Olmsted and co-designer Calvert Vaux set out in 1858 to cut a diamond with an axe and a shovel. *Voila!* Central Park.

The East 59th Street entrance will guide you to the Dairy. In 1870 it housed a goat and a cow to provide milk for children. Today it's the Park Reception Center. Maps and exhibits are available free. The Zoo is nearby.

The Mall in Central Park is a favorite gathering place for street musicians. If you're partial to dixieland jazz, you'll find some truly superb talents here who like nothing better than to spend Sunday afternoons playing for passersby. Continue on to Bethesda Fountain.

Around the lake to the right, you'll be guided to Cleopatra's Needle. Its original home was 12th-century B.C. Egypt, which was considerably kinder to it than 20th-century New York. If you've made it to the Needle, you've made it to the Metropolitan Museum of Art. The Temple of Dendur is one of three million artifacts and artworks on display. Plan to spend as much time as you can here. A lifetime probably isn't enough.

The same is true of New York City itself.

NEW YORK CITY
The Financial District

Directions: From midtown Manhattan, drive or take public transportation to the World Trade Center. (There is ample parking there, if you do decide to take a car.)

Best Season: Year round, but for the real flavor of Wall Street, be sure to go on a weekday.

Length: About 3 miles, but there are lots of diversions. Allow at least three hours. If you stop at the South Street Seaport, plan on a full day.

Degree of Difficulty: Easy. Like most big cities, however, New York has a way of making its own hazards. Don't invite trouble.

A Walk around Wall Street
One of the best ways to enter New York is on foot over its grandest entrance: the Brooklyn Bridge. If you've started this walk on the Manhattan side, at the World Trade Center, walk across the bridge, turn around and start a slow saunter back. New Yorkers celebrated the centennial of the Brooklyn Bridge in 1983 with a smashing display of fire-

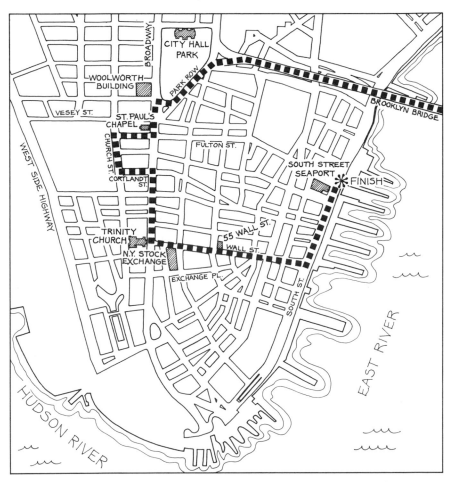

works, and rightly so. It's an extraordinary walking experience. At midpoint, facing Manhattan, Governor's Island and the Statue of Liberty are on your left, along with lower Manhattan and the gleaming World Trade Center, which towers over everything else; to the right, midtown sprawls out with the sharp points of the Empire State and Chrysler buildings pulling threads off the clouds. The Manhattan Bridge, to your right, is a pretty counterpart to the Brooklyn. As you approach the foot of the bridge, the tower of the Woolworth Building is on the left; that of the Municipal Building is on the right. Together they stand like a pair of Gothic sentries, welcoming you in.

Lower Manhattan's small, irregular streets are a remnant of 17th-century New Amsterdam. Broadway, for example, was a principal thoroughfare from around the 1630s. Wall Street is so named because it ran the length of the cross-island palisade erected in 1663 to protect against

English attack. Other streets were created pretty much as needed, without any particular plan. That's why lower Manhattan is such a rabbit warren, compared to the regular grid of the rest of the island.

At the foot of the Brooklyn Bridge is City Hall. Built in 1802–1811 on what has always been the town common, it's remarkably modest considering the size of New York. The giant Municipal Building behind it handles most of the city's office needs.

Across City Hall Park at 233 Broadway is the Woolworth Building, which was built in 1913 to serve as the headquarters of the dime-store empire. It's been topped by taller buildings, but never yet outdone for elegance. Be sure to see the lobby.

The stone church just to the south on Broadway is St. Paul's Chapel, the only church left in Manhattan that was built before the Revolutionary War. After taking the oath of office on April 30, 1789, the first president of the United States came to St. Paul's to pray. Behind St. Paul's there's a wonderful Alexander Calder stabile, at the corner of Church and Vesey.

You won't need specific directions to find your way to the next stop. Just look up. The twin towers of the World Trade Center are looming over you. Enter Tobin Plaza from the east. If you like, there's a stunning view from the Observation Deck and the rooftop promenade of #2 World Trade Center. The plaza below doesn't offer much, but there's an interesting contrast between the two slick, modern towers and the Woolworth Building, which pokes its funky head up over one of the Center's low buildings. Remember the climber who machined his way up the side of one tower a few years ago? The grooves into which he threaded his climbing device have been closed up — for a full five stories off the ground. We hope you didn't bring your equipment along for nothing! And speaking of impossible dreams, reserve ahead (*way* ahead) to dine in the sky at Windows on the World.

Follow Broadway past the imposing black bulk of the Marine Midland Bank (it has that big red cube in front) to Trinity Church at Broadway and Wall. The church is special, and the graveyard is a must for history buffs. Alexander Hamilton, first Secretary of the Treasury, was buried here in 1804, after taking a mortal wound in a duel with Aaron Burr, then vice-president. Hamilton's son died the same way, at the same dueling ground, using the same pistol, three years before. Hamilton's grave is close to a commemorative marker to Robert Fulton, who lies on the other side of the church.

Trinity Church faces down Wall Street. On a weekday, this heart of the financial world is a rippling ocean of gray flannel and golden dreams. At 55 Wall Street is an intimidating monument to George Washington. On this spot he took the first oath of office. The New York Stock Exchange is between Wall Street and Exchange Place. It's free, and open 10–4 on weekdays.

When you come to the end of Wall Street, take a left on South and go to the South Street Seaport. If you're prejudiced against festival marketplaces, you'll really hate this one. It has nothing to recommend itself except good food, cold drinks, nice shops, big ships, and a dazzling view of the Brooklyn Bridge. Better skip it. From here, you can walk back to the World Trade Center for your car, or take public transportation anywhere else.

NIAGARA FALLS

Directions: Niagara Falls is in the western part of New York State, just north of Buffalo. Follow I-90 to exit 50; take I–290 to I–190 north and go to the Robert Moses Parkway north. Take this to the end and park in the state parking lot at Prospect Park (at the Falls).

Best Season: Niagara Falls is a tourist town 365 days a year; it supports festivals and attractions year round. For information and a visitor guide, call the Niagara Falls Convention and Visitor Bureau at (716) 278-8010.

Length: This walk is about 1½ miles, but you won't want to zip through it. Take your time and enjoy some of the best views in America.

Degree of Difficulty: Easy, but keep an eye out for the Viewmobile trains that sometimes use the same roads you will be walking on.

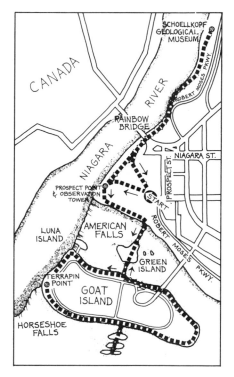

Goat Island Trail

Niagara Falls is a great walking experience. Ask Rosemary E. Thompson, who told us "The trail around Goat Island enables me to view the upper Niagara River before the water trails past the Three Sisters Islands, forming foaming wild rapids. For years coronary and bypass surgery patients have made this their prescribed daily exercise walk. It's a natural high, and the roar of the water is a tranquilizer after a day of work."

Or ask Henry Brodowski, who wrote to us: "It's the most scenic, relaxing walking and viewing area in the world."

Or take the testimony of the Reverends Andrew Reed and Thomas Mattheson, who in 1834 proposed: "Niagara does not belong to Canada or America. Such spots should be deemed the property of civilized mankind, and nothing should be allowed to weaken their efficacy on the tastes, the morals, and the enjoyment of mankind."

Looking at Niagara Falls now, it's hard to believe that in 1884 it was a collection of scummy industries, using the water flow for power, and scummier tourist traps that sold views of the falls for cash. Today it's clean of its former exploiters, and free forever to enhance our "tastes, our morals, and our enjoyment."

The walk around Goat Island was designed by the Niagara Reservation Centennial Commission and the Greater Niagara Frontier Council of the Boy Scouts of America. It covers the American side of the falls, but provides a good view of the Canadian side. Where the best views are is somewhat of a controversy. Many people feel they are from the Canadian side, overlooking Horseshoe Falls. If possible, try to see both sides and judge for yourself.

Begin this walk at the Visitor Center at Prospect Point, then cross the lawn to the New York State Observation Tower. This is the starting point for boat tours to the falls on board the *Maid of the Mist*. There's an elevator at the tower to take you to the top, for a panoramic view of the whole falls, or to the bottom, for an up-close view of the American Falls.

Continue now along the path to Prospect Point, overlooking the American Falls, which are 175 feet high and 1,100 feet wide. Only 10 percent of the water not diverted for electric or industrial use goes over the American Falls, but it's still a mighty torrent. Turning east, upstream, you'll pass the American rapids. Take a right over the pedestrian bridge to Green Island, in the middle of the rapids, the former site of a paper mill. From there go on to Goat Island, named after the animals that used to graze there. A loop footpath will take you around the island to Luna Island and Bridal Veil Falls. There is a statue of Nikola Tesla, the inventor of alternating current, here where he first tested his idea.

Terrapin Point, farther along, gives a great view of the Canadian side of the falls. This is where barrel-jumpers like to start their bumpy journeys. Winding around Goat Island will bring you to Three Sisters Islands, in the middle of the river, and up to Parting of the Waters, where the river is split into Canadian and American branches. Finishing the loop around Goat Island and heading back toward Prospect Point brings you to the footbridge you first crossed. Continue by it, retracing your steps to the New York State Observation Tower.

Head along the path under the tower, following the river downstream to the Schoellkopf Geological Museum (pass under the Rainbow Bridge).

Walking along the river, you'll see some of the remains of the old industrial plants that used the falls. Power generated by the huge water motion helped build prosperous factories along the Niagara's banks.

Stop at the Schoellkopf Geological Museum. Here you can see a multi-image presentation detailing the geological history of the falls, plus exhibits and interpretive programs. Schoellkopf also offers nature walks. Ask for information at the museum. There is a fine view of the falls from their overlook.

Return to Prospect Park the same way you came.

Pennsylvania

GETTYSBURG

Directions: Gettysburg is in south-central Pennsylvania, close to the Maryland border. From the east, take I–76 west to U.S. 15 and then State Highway 116. From the South, I–83 to U.S. 30 will lead you right into the heart of town.

Best Season: Anytime in spring, summer, or fall. The Gettysburg Travel Council can tell you when special events, such as the Blue Grass Festival and the Civil War Collectors Show, are scheduled. Call (717) 334-6274 for information.

Length: Total distance is only about 4 miles, but between car touring and walking, Gettysburg will take a full day.

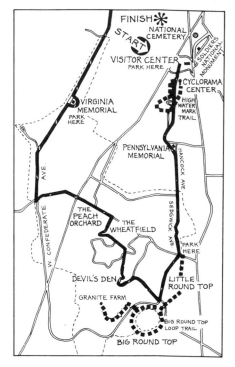

Degree of Difficulty: Easy, but Gettysburg is still woods and fields, so beware of animals, snakes, and ticks.

Preserving Memories in Gettysburg

"The world will little note, nor long remember what we say here, but it can never forget what they did here. It is for us, the living, rather to be dedicated here to the unfinished work which they who fought here have thus far so nobly advanced."

Lincoln was wrong in one sense — the world has greatly noted and long remembered what he said that day in November, 1863, at the dedication of the National Cemetery at Gettysburg; he was right in another sense — it has not forgotten the tens of thousands of Union and Confederate soldiers who fought here. A walk through Gettysburg is a tour of the ways Americans preserve their memories.

To see the Cemetery, stop first at the National Park Service Visitor Center, just outside Gettysburg on Washington Street. The Park Service guide will help you plan your tour, and there are maps available. The Center also features an Electric Map exhibit showing the field and the events of the battle, plus a staggering collection of weapons and artifacts of the fight. Be sure to pick up the free Park Service map. It describes two excellent walking tours.

A few yards from the Visitor Center is the "Cyclorama." This is a giant circular painting described in detail by a Park Service guide, depicting a critical moment during the third day of the battle. The Cyclorama exhibit costs $1 and helps orient you when you step back outside. The battlefield is extensive, with many important natural features and landmarks, some of which you could easily miss. Use the Cyclorama as a starting point. Also, there is the first draft of the Gettysburg Address, one page written in pencil on the night before the dedication of the National Cemetery. Lincoln used these notes that day.

You'll want to combine driving and walking in order to see as much of the field as possible. In fact, it might help to take the Park Service auto tour in order to familiarize yourself with the stops. Then, park back at the Visitor Center and begin your walk.

From the Cyclorama, start at the High Water Mark Trail. This covers the temporal and geographic point of climax, where the Army of the Potomac successfully fought back the ill-fated Confederate advance known as "Pickett's Charge." As with so many sites on the battlefield, the High Water Mark still has artillery pointed toward their targets during the fight.

Some stone walls and trees remain, too. It's remarkably easy to visualize the fight because the landscape is so well preserved. All that seems conspicuously out of place are the monuments scattered in profusion around the battlefield, marking the spots where both sides fought and fell.

The High Water Mark Trail, about one mile long, circles back to the Cyclorama. From there, return to your car and drive down Hancock Avenue (south) toward the most noticeable of Gettysburg's monuments, the Pennsylvania Memorial. Now you are on Cemetery Ridge, along which the Union forces formed defenses toward the end of the first day's fighting. The plaques of names on the Pennsylvania Memorial will help you understand the sheer numbers of men who clashed here.

Park at Little Round Top. It's a short walk to the point where General Gouverneur Warren looked down on a concealed Confederate position to the west. He ordered a cannon shot into the woods. Sunlight glinting off long lines of bayonets confirmed his suspicion. Only his order to reinforce the position prevented its falling into Confederate hands, giving them a vantage point from which to shell the entire Union line.

The monuments on Little Round Top are worth reading carefully. It's still the best place from which to see the southern part of the battlefield, where the heaviest fighting took place.

Follow the markers to Big Round Top. The Loop Trail here is about a mile long and clearly marked. This very green, quiet walk is pleasant relief from the sun. Still more markers will guide you to Granite Farm (open only in summer), which lay in the hands of both armies at different times during the fight. The house served as a field surgery. A guide there will explain the fighting and answer questions about how farming was conducted here.

Return from Granite Farm to your car and drive south and west to Devil's Den, a rock formation that gave cover to southern sharpshooters. From there follow the auto tour past the Wheatfield and the Peach Orchard and up West Confederate Avenue to the Virginia Memorial where you can park your car.

The Virginia Memorial marks General Robert E. Lee's position during Pickett's Charge. You can see the grove of trees on the opposite side of the field that was the focus of the thrust, and the Union artillery that sawed holes through the ranks of charging rebels.

The end of your tour should be the National Cemetery, even if you stopped there before your walk. Drive back to the Visitor Center, park, and enter the Cemetery from there. Now that you have seen the battlefield, you will appreciate what happened here at Gettysburg. Many Union soldiers are buried here. Many could not be identified. In the shadow of the Soldiers' National Monument, marking the spot where Lincoln delivered the Gettysburg Address, lies grave after grave marked "Unknown." Their memory is preserved and, as Lincoln said, "The world . . . can never forget what they did here."

PHILADELPHIA
Forbidden Drive

Directions: Fairmount Park, Philadelphia. From I–95, enter Philadelphia's Historic District. Take Market Street west, around City Hall, then follow the Benjamin Franklin Parkway to Kelly Drive, to Lincoln Drive. Take Lincoln north, turn around, and park at the east end of the trail entrance, on the southbound side of Lincoln Drive.

Best Season: A spring morning. Early starters can lunch at Valley Green and be back by mid-afternoon.

Length: 5½ miles one way; round trip about five hours, allowing for stops and walks down some of the side trails.

Degree of Difficulty: Moderately easy. Rolling, unpaved, well-lit path. (More difficult side paths lead into the surrounding hills.)

Walking along the Forbidden Drive

Forbidden Drive is five and a half miles of magnificent walking inside Fairmount Park, the largest city park in the world. You'll feel so secluded among the birdsongs and soft noises of Wissahickon Creek that you'll find it hard to believe the walk is entirely within the limits of America's fifth-largest city.

Forbidden Drive is "forbidden" only to motor traffic. Riders on horseback and horse-drawn carriages are welcome, and hardy cyclists and joggers often use the

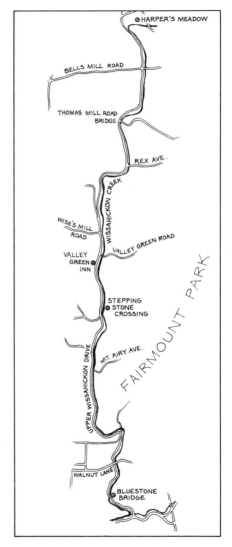

trail. Mainly, though, it belongs to walkers. And what a great escape it is, winding beside and above the creek, under and around giant rock cliff-sides and old trees. If you can do it on a weekday, chances are you'll have it almost all to yourself.

Forbidden Drive is mainly free from "sights," except those that nature intended. There are some noteworthy man-made embellishments: the towering arches of the Henry Avenue Bridge are compatible in scale and massiveness with the cliffs along the way; the old Thomas Mill Road Bridge, spanning the Wissahickon Creek, is a surprise, especially for people who have never seen a covered span, let alone one in a big city. Valley Green, an 18th-century inn, renowned by Colonists for its pancakes and catfish ("Wissahickon" is a corruption of the old Indian word for "catfish creek"), is now a welcome stop on this long pleasant walk, offering lunch or dinner on a broad front porch or in a cozy inside dining room. The ducks like to gather there for food, too.

What makes Forbidden Drive one of America's 100 greatest walks? It offers green and unspoiled solitude inside a city of over 3.5 million. "It's inspirational," says Rod Clabo, who nominated the Forbidden Drive, "loved by those who go there to unwind, relax, or gain a moment of solitude." He treasures it; so will you.

PHILADELPHIA
Independence National Historic Park

Directions: Downtown Philadelphia; accessible from I–95. Follow the signs to "Historic District," and park near the Visitor Center at Third and Chestnut streets.

Best Season: Early or late summer; but since there are frequent indoor stops, and shorter lines, if any, in the winter, tours at that time can be fine too. The old buildings are particularly beautiful beneath a blanket of snow on a January night.

Length: This will vary, depending on how much you want to see and how much time you have. The entire Historic District lies inside one square mile, but it can take a full weekend to appreciate it thoroughly.

Degree of Difficulty: Easy.

Walking in and around Independence Park
Begin at the Visitor Center at Third and Chestnut where you can get acquainted with the Park before starting out on your walk. The Center is

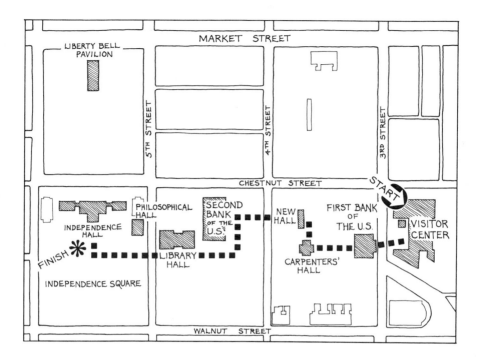

open daily from 9–5, as are all the historic buildings. (There are more historically significant buildings within Independence National Historic Park than in any other square mile in the United States.) You can pick up free maps at the Center, and guides are available to answer questions. There are also short films on the area and some very good exhibits. There is no admission charge to any of the buildings on the tour — after all, they belong to you. Advance information can be obtained by calling (215) 627-1776, a 24-hour information line.

When you leave the Center, walk across 3rd Street to the First Bank of the United States (1795–1797). The bank was the first home of the U.S. Treasury Department. The exterior has been carefully preserved; inside are changing exhibits.

A few steps west of the First Bank is Carpenters' Hall (1770–1774), one of the jewels of the Park. The First Continental Congress met here in 1774; the assembly helped forge the Colonies of Britain into the nation of America. New Hall (1790, rebuilt 1960), in the forecourt of Carpenters' Hall, is the museum of the history of the U.S. Marine Corps.

Continue walking across 4th Street to the Second Bank of the United States (1818–1824). Built in strict Greek Revival style to recall the Parthenon, it is now the National Portrait Gallery.

On the south side of the Second Bank, a pleasant cobblestone path leads past Library Hall, which houses the collection of the American Philosophical Society. The society's headquarters are across 5th Street in Independence Square.

You'll want to spend some time at Independence Hall, originally called the State House, because that's what it was for the Pennsylvania Provincial Assembly. The low section was built in 1732–1736; the tower was added after 1750. Between 1790 and 1800 it was the capitol of the United States, but its most significant assemblies were in 1776, when the delegates of the Second Continental Congress adopted the Declaration of Independence, and in 1787, when the Constitution was drafted and approved there. Independence Hall has been meticulously restored to its 18th-century character. Still in the Hall is the chair in which President Washington sat during the Constitutional Convention. On the table before it is the silver inkstand used to sign both the Declaration and the Constitution.

And don't miss the Liberty Bell, which is now housed in a new glass pavilion north of Independence Hall, across Chestnut Street. The only virtue of this regrettable box is that it makes the Bell easy to see.

These are the principal sites of the Park, but there are many more. Some of the very best are just a few blocks away. Christ Church, for example, is where Washington and Franklin worshipped. Elfreth's Alley is America's oldest continually occupied street. While the core of the Park looks somewhat over-manicured, the sites on the perimeters blend into the cityscape of 20th-century Philadelphia.

PRESQUE ISLE STATE PARK

Directions: Presque Isle State Park is located next to Erie, Pennsylvania. Take I–95 or I–79 to State Highway 832. Follow 832 north about five miles to Presque Isle.

Best Season: Summer is the tourist season, and millions visit for beautiful Great Lakes swimming, bird-watching, picnicking, and fishing. Winter is for hardier souls, but it offers some rare sights, including 25-foot ice dunes formed by the wind tearing over Lake Erie.

Length: Between 2 and 16 miles; thirty minutes to six hours.

Degree of Difficulty: Easy, but watch out for running deer.

Presque Isle Walks

Presque Isle is a unique sickle-shaped peninsula that curves seven miles out into Lake Erie. On its 3,000-plus acres are miles of beautiful

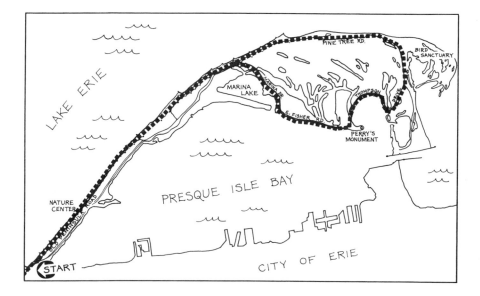

beaches, seven miles of hiking trails, swamps and ponds, and a bird sanctuary. Robert J. Baumann nominated Presque Isle as a place for great walks in several categories. "This is a family-type park," he says, "and age is no barrier because you can choose how far you go." And he adds, "The sunset most of the time is really spectacular."

Presque Isle was also nominated by W. Robert Chandler, who points out the variety of walks that can be enjoyed on the peninsula: "America's greatest walk is without a doubt enjoyed at Presque Isle State Park. City, country, beach, wilderness, unguided and guided tours — it qualifies for all of them."

Park your car near the Park entrance gate and begin your hike on Old Peninsula Road. This part of the Isle is only a few hundred feet wide. Soon after you begin, you'll pass the Nature Center. Stop to see how this strange geological formation came to be, and how many different types of birds and animals call it home.

Your walk will take you along the outer, northern perimeter of the Peninsula, facing Lake Erie until you pass some Park offices and swimming areas. As the peninsula widens, you can leave the beach area and head into some of the trails. They're all marked — Presque Isle is not wilderness, but the crowds won't keep you from enjoying the trails that run through the ecological reservation and the bird sanctuary. Ponds of varying size and age dot the Isle at its broadest point, and they're carefully preserved for wildlife.

On the northeastern tip of Presque Isle, off Pine Tree Road, is the bird sanctuary; and, if you don't think of yourself as a bird-watcher, you will undoubtedly become one at Presque Isle. Located right on the migratory path between the southern U.S. and Canada, Presque Isle is a stop-over for over 300 species. May is an extremely active month; after the tiring flight over Lake Erie, thousands of birds descend on Presque Isle to mend for the next leg of their trip. Over a hundred species nest here.

A trail winds through the sanctuary in an elongated circle to take you back along the south side of the Isle, facing Presque Isle Bay and the city of Erie. A monument to Commodore Perry is along the way. He used the Isle as a naval base for engaging the British during the War of 1812. The walk will take you past more modern ships docked at Marina Lake, and then back along the route by which you entered.

Virginia

ASSATEAGUE ISLAND NATIONAL SEASHORE

Directions: Assateague is the easternmost point of both Maryland and Virginia (the border crosses the island), located at the end of a 10-mile stretch of winding road passing through desolate marshlands. To get to the Virginia end, take U.S. 15 to State Highway 175, which crosses Chincoteague Island, home of the delicious Chincoteague Oysters. (But not the ponies, which reside on Assateague.) When you arrive on Assateague, it is a good idea to stop at the National Wildlife Refuge Information Center and at the National Park Service Visitor Center. Both places will help you get acquainted with the island. Or, before you go, write to the National Park Service, Assateague Island National Seashore, Route 2, Box 294, Berlin, MD 21811. They'll send maps and information on the variety of programs offered on the island. Assateague is a carefully preserved natural landscape; visitors must obey the rules.

Best Season: Spring, of course, is gorgeous, with pink azaleas in full bloom along the paths, and dogwood adding bursts of white. Summer and fall are also beautiful times to visit the island, which is open from 4:00 a.m. to 10:00 p.m. from spring to fall, and from sunrise to sunset at other times of the year. It's a popular place, so the earlier you go, the more you'll have it to yourself.

Length: Assateague has over 20 miles of unspoiled beach and wildlife trails. It's a weekend's worth, at least.

Degree of Difficulty: Moderate. You need to be in pretty good shape to take advantage of the beach and trails. Be careful of the sun; it can be deceiving.

Assateague Island Walks

Get up at 4:00 a.m. to go to the beach? Well, this isn't just any beach. It's a bird-watcher's paradise, filled with ducks, snow geese, ibises, herons, and egrets; 262 different species of birds visit the island throughout the year. A barrier island, formed by sand from Atlantic storms, Assateague is also home to a variety of marsh and forest wildlife and flora. Herds of white-tailed deer roam the island, and there are otters, muskrats, opossums, and even some oriental elk, called sikas. And, finally, Assateague has two herds of wild ponies, believed to be the descendants of Spanish horses that swam ashore from a wrecked galleon. They roam the island freely under the care of the Chincoteague Volunteer Fire Company and the National Park Service.

One of the best ways to get to know Assateague is on a guided "Interpretive Program." These are walks, guided by park naturalists, through beach or marsh or forest, demonstrating crabbing or clamming or a variety of other ways to appreciate the island. For example, the "Island History and Ecology Walk" examines the island's past and some rarely seen barrier island life forms. The "Life of the Beach and Surf Walk" reveals just what you're sharing your day at the beach with. The staff is dedicated and enthusiastic. If you go for a weekend, this is the way to spend the first day. Some walks require a reservation, especially during the busy summer season. Call (301) 641-1441 or (301) 641-3030 for details.

There are auto roads on the island, but they're small and unobtrusive. Most of the place is reserved for movement by the ways nature intended: wings and feet. You're going to feel right at home.

CHARLOTTESVILLE AND MONTICELLO

Directions: U.S. highways 29 and 250 and I-64 converge at Charlottesville, home of the University of Virginia. Monticello is south of Charlottesville on State Highway 20.

Best Season: Early fall, for the beauty of the Virginia foliage, and winter, for the solitude on the grounds of the University.

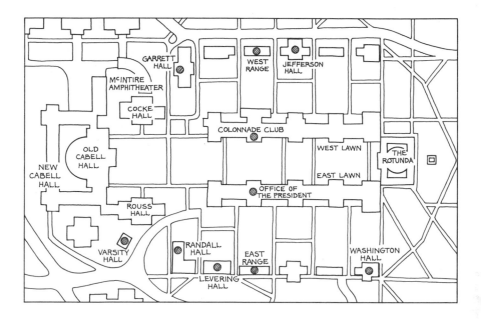

Length: The University of Virginia and Monticello are located within five miles of each other. Each tour is no more than a mile, but allow lots of time for each. Admirers of Thomas Jefferson will want to spend a full day in the area.

Degree of Difficulty: Easy.

The University of Virginia: Jefferson's "Academical Village"

By his own request, Thomas Jefferson's gravestone at Monticello makes no mention of his having been president of the United States. "Here was buried Thomas Jefferson," it says, "Author of the Declaration of American Independence, of the Statute of Virginia for Religious Freedom, and Father of the University of Virginia." It seems he wanted to be remembered less for his duties and more for his beliefs.

The University of Virginia remains a fresh testimony to the unique breadth of his mind. He began working on it at the age of 75, surveying the land himself and drawing up a design for an "academical village" that would showcase the variety of classical design he loved.

The Lawn is his masterpiece. Jefferson's work is in a giant U-shape. At the head is the Rotunda, the library, based on the design of the Pantheon in Rome. The self-guided walking tour of the University begins here. The arms of the "U" are formed by Colonnades, punctuated five to a side by 10 pavilions, in 10 variations of classical order. Behind each is a garden. Two of the Pavilions are, respectively, the UVA Faculty Club

and the president's office. The rest are faculty residences. The Colonnades form covered walkways running from building to building. The technical virtuosity of the architecture is never oppressive or stuffy; in fact, there is something plain and humble about the whole plan. This must be a reflection of Jefferson himself. The outstanding characteristic of the design is just how sensible it all is. The only lamentable building on the Lawn is the modern addition, Cabell Hall, designed by Stanford White, which closes the vista Jefferson intended.

Be sure to walk behind the gardens. The sinuous Serpentine Wall runs there, just one brick thick. Edgar Allan Poe's room and Woodrow Wilson's are in the "Hotels" on the outer perimeter of the gardens.

Monticello

The University was a late occupation of Jefferson's life. His own home, Monticello, was a lifelong pleasure. He worked on it between stints as a member of the Continental Congress, governor of Virginia, minister to France, secretary of state, vice-president, and president, for 40 years.

Monticello is a distillation of Jefferson's extensive travels, his passion for invention, and his love of nature. It speaks again and again of his insatiable curiosity. The paintings and rich furnishings might belong to any well-heeled gentleman of the time, but the mechanical conveniences

Jefferson himself created — the dumbwaiter hidden in the fireplace, built to carry wine up from the cellar; the four-way music stand for string quartets; the swivel chair; the Great Clock in the Entrance Hall, run by Revolutionary War cannonballs used as weights — show an innovative mind having a rare sort of fun.

Monticello is a museum, strictly speaking, but it's alive and vibrant with the personality of its creator. That makes it a home.

Washington, D.C.

GEORGETOWN

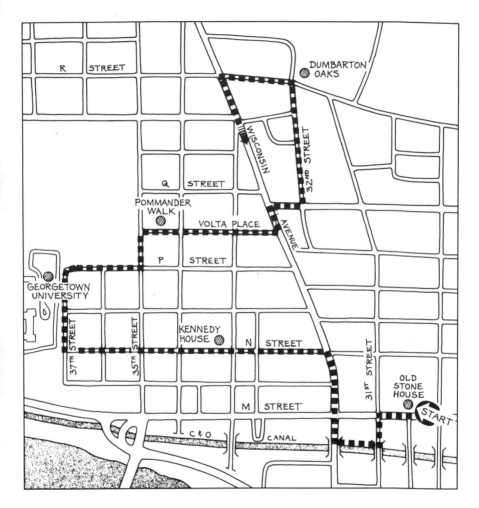

Directions: Georgetown lies along the Potomac to the northwest of the White House. Pennsylvania Avenue will take you to M Street, and M Street to Wisconsin Avenue, the central spine of Georgetown.

Best Season: Roses, fuschia, and day lilies bloom in July at Dumbarton Oaks, but any day between April and September looks good in Georgetown. It's a great place to spend an evening out, too.

Length: About 2 miles, but it will take four or five hours to see the sights: Georgetown is a dazzling collection of buildings, shops, and people.

Degree of Difficulty: Easy.

Walking Georgetown

Laid out in 1751, Georgetown is older than Washington, and its smaller scale and warmer feel contrast nicely with the cool, giant government buildings to the southeast. Kristine Stevens of Pathfinder Tour Consultants has designed a four-mile, self-guided tour of Georgetown that includes 23 sites. For further information about this Georgetown tour, contact Thomas G. Murphy of the Washington, D.C., Convention and Visitors Association, (202) 789-7007, who nominated Georgetown as one of America's greatest walking cities.

For a shorter, two-mile walk, begin at the Old Stone House, 3051 M Street NW, which dates from 1766. It's the oldest in the neighborhood. From there, 31st Street will take you to the Chesapeake and Ohio Canal (1823), a reminder of Georgetown's industrial past. The C & O once serviced over 150 miles. There are pretty restored houses and shops along its path now.

Wisconsin Avenue will lead you north to N Street. Senator John F. Kennedy bought 3307 N Street (built in 1812) shortly before he, his wife, and their infant daughter moved to Pennsylvania Avenue. Smith Row, a block of simple, handsome Federal houses, is on your way.

Follow N Street to Georgetown University, dominated by the Rhinecastle of the Healy Building (1879). George Washington's nephews went to school here, and Washington himself addressed the student body from the steps of Old North.

P Street up to 35th will take you north to Volta Place. Pomander Walk, between 34th and 33rd, off Volta Place, is a pedestrian haven of tiny restored houses facing onto a narrow alley. Follow Volta to Wisconsin Avenue, take a right onto O and another left onto 32nd, and head for Dumbarton Oaks at 1703 32nd Street NW.

If you love gardens, grand houses, pre-Columbian art, Byzantine art, diplomatic history, or all of the above, don't miss Dumbarton Oaks. Ambassador and Mrs. Robert Woods Bliss shaped the estate with eclectic, excellent taste. The house is open 2–5, Tuesday–Sunday. The gardens are open 2–6, with an admission charge of $1. The gallery of Byzantine and Hellenistic art is one of the best in the country. The pre-Columbian collection is housed in a new wing by Philip Johnson. The 16 acres of trees, terraces, pools, and flowers at Dumbarton Oaks are as grand as almost any other garden on earth.

Back on Wisconsin Avenue, the fortress-like Soviet Embassy at 2600 is a striking contrast to the clean, soaring Washington National Cathedral at Wisconsin and Massachusetts avenues. Further along Massachusetts

Avenue are the embassies of Japan, Britain, Brazil, Venezuela, Zambia, and Paraguay, as well as other significant buildings. Massachusetts will take you back into central Washington via Dupont Circle.

THE MALL

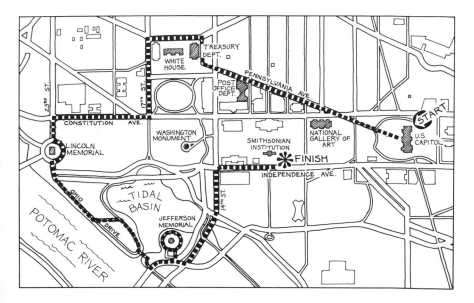

Directions: I–95 and Route 1 will take you into Washington from the north and south; 123, 7, and 59 from the west. The Capital Beltway that encircles Washington gives the driver lots of options to enter the city. New Hampshire, Pennsylvania, and Connecticut avenues, among other roads, lead off the Beltway into the heart of Washington.

Best Season: Washington looks best in spring, particularly when the cherry blossoms are in bloom. And a late-night tour of the floodlit monuments any time of the year can be thrilling (but don't do it by yourself).

Length: Washington's most significant sites are collected in the areas of the Mall, but by no means is all of Washington here. The tour described is about 3 miles.

Degree of Difficulty: Easy.

Walking the Capital Mall

It is, of course, entirely predictable that Washington, D.C., should appear in such a book as this. Tonia Brown, who nominated the nation's capital, has walked in 48 of the 50 states; Washington, D.C., is one of her most memorable walks. No other city in America touches us quite so much or offers quite such a concentration of grandeur, hubris, and elegance.

Ironically, the design of Washington, capital of the world's most successful democracy, followed the example of Paris and Versailles, seats of monarchy. The planner was an eccentric Frenchman, Pierre Charles L'Enfant. His gravesite, just above that of President Kennedy in Arlington National Cemetery, shows his original design.

Our walk begins at the Capitol. L'Enfant placed it on what was the highest rise overlooking the Potomac. President Washington laid the cornerstone of the Capitol in 1793, and the building evolved continually until after the Civil War. Not many people know that the dome is made of cast iron.

A walk down Pennsylvania Avenue will take you on the same route followed by presidents on Inauguration Day. The Old Post Office on the way is worth a visit; beautifully restored, it is now home to a number of restaurants and shops. Not so impressive is the plaza farther up the avenue, laid out as a map of the old plan for the city. The Department of the Treasury completes the vista; behind it is the White House.

The Washington Monument was supposed to have been located at the crossing of the axes from the Capitol and the White House, but the land was too marshy at that point to support the massive shaft. It's open until midnight during the summer, for a dazzling nighttime view from the top.

Walk from there toward the Lincoln Memorial. On your right, past the little lagoon, is Washington's most chilling monument, the new Vietnam Veterans Memorial. Nothing you have heard, good or bad, about this singular remembrance can really prepare you for the grief, terror, pride, and love embodied in its black stone.

The Lincoln Memorial is next. Daniel Chester French's massive seated Lincoln is deeply stirring. E. J. Applewhite, in *Washington Itself,* says the great marble face "expresses not power, but gentleness, compassion, and loneliness."

The Jefferson Memorial lies on the other side of the Tidal Basin to the southeast. Like the Lincoln, it was not anticipated by L'Enfant's design, which had the great green sweeps before the Capitol and the White House running unobstructed into the Potomac. After visiting the Jefferson Memorial, you may want to rent a paddleboat at 15th Street and Maine Avenue SW for a ride in the river's Tidal Basin.

Heading north again on 14th Street will take you back onto the Mall and into the midst of the ten buildings comprised by the Smithsonian Institution. Their attractions are almost limitless, but the favorites seem to be the new East Wing of the National Gallery (not part of the Smithsonian), and the National Air and Space Museum. There is an open sculpture garden before the Hirshorn Museum.

Needless to say, there's much more to Washington than we can describe here. The Washington, D.C., Convention and Visitors Association can help you get to know the capital. Their number is (202) 789-7000.

West Virginia

HARPERS FERRY

Directions: Harpers Ferry sits where the Shenandoah River meets the Potomac, in northeast West Virginia on the West Virginia/ Maryland border. It can be reached on foot via the Chesapeake and Ohio Canal from Washington, D.C., or by car via the main route into town, U.S. 340. Park your car in the parking area near the Visitor Center on Shenandoah Street.

Best Season: Summer and fall weekends are recommended.

Length: The walk described here is relatively short, but you could easily spend four or five hours in Harpers Ferry. Also, other hikes, such as the Grant Conway Trail, across the river in Maryland, are part of the larger National Historic Park. The Appalachian Trail runs through the town, and the Appalachian Trail Conference Headquarters is there, too. So Harpers Ferry can be a stop on a much longer walk.

Degree of Difficulty: Easy.

A Walk through History at Harpers Ferry

Harpers Ferry is significant for its own history and for the national history it anticipated with almost eerie coincidence. Most of us know that in 1859 the abolitionist fanatic John Brown led a quixotic raid on the federal arsenal at Harpers Ferry, intending to arm a slave uprising in the South. The details are less well known: the U.S. Marines who captured him were commanded by Col. Robert E. Lee and Lt. J. E. B. Stuart. Lee was in charge of Brown's execution, protested by Ralph Waldo Emerson and Henry David Thoreau. One of the militiamen who participated in

Brown's hanging was John Wilkes Booth. Brown's last message to the world, handed to his jailor on the day of his death, said, "I, John Brown, am now quite certain that the crimes of this guilty land will never be purged away but with blood." Sixteen months later came the shelling of Fort Sumter, the outbreak of the Civil War. The memory of John Brown inspired the Union troops with a battle song: "John Brown's body lies a-mouldering in the grave, but his soul goes marching on. . . ."

Begin the walk at the Park Visitor Center, the restored Stagecoach Inn, on Shenandoah Street, the main street of Harpers Ferry. From here, the Park Service conducts hourly guided tours during the summer months; otherwise, it's a good place to get maps and orientation information.

The cluster of buildings on Shenandoah between the Visitor Center and Potomac Street is the historic center of Harpers Ferry. Next to the Visitor Center is a blacksmith shop, and across the street are a Union guardhouse and a mid–19th-century dry goods store. Down the block are the Civil War Museum, the John Brown Museum, and "John Brown's Fort," the Armory firehouse where Brown took refuge during his raid. Restored businesses, a tavern, a post office, and a candy store are around the corner. The whole place is charming. Narrow streets and beautiful stone and brick buildings dot the steep hillside.

Once you've explored central Harpers Ferry, walk back past the Visitor Center and away from the center of town along Shenandoah Street. You'll pass an old Armory workman's home on your right. Just beyond that, on the right, is Jefferson Rock. From here Thomas Jefferson, in 1783, proclaimed the view "stupendous . . . worth a voyage across the Atlantic."

Continue up Shenandoah to the footbridge on your left. Cross the canal and turn right over the bridge. You are now on Virginius Island, once an industrial center spotted with water-powered factories. Continue along the trail to the site of Hall's Rifle Works. Established in 1819, the Rifle Works produced breech-loading flintlock rifles using interchangeable parts (a principle that later led to mass-produced goods). Follow the trail, which soon passes under the B & O Railroad tracks, then runs parallel to the Shenandoah River, passes by some old mill ruins, and ends up in the parking lot across from the Visitor Center.

Part 3

THE SOUTHEAST CORNER

Alabama, Florida, Georgia, Kentucky, Mississippi, North Carolina,
South Carolina, Tennessee, Virgin Islands

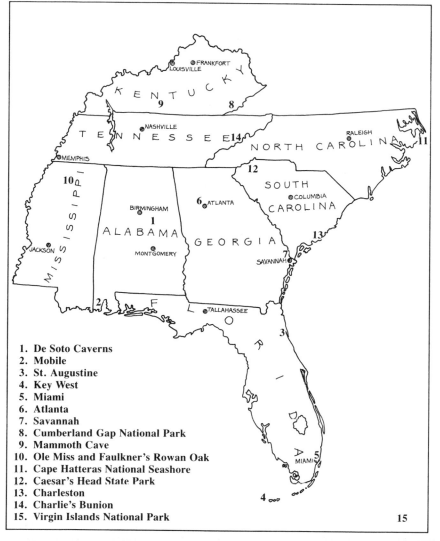

1. **De Soto Caverns**
2. **Mobile**
3. **St. Augustine**
4. **Key West**
5. **Miami**
6. **Atlanta**
7. **Savannah**
8. **Cumberland Gap National Park**
9. **Mammoth Cave**
10. **Ole Miss and Faulkner's Rowan Oak**
11. **Cape Hatteras National Seashore**
12. **Caesar's Head State Park**
13. **Charleston**
14. **Charlie's Bunion**
15. **Virgin Islands National Park**

Alabama

CHILDERSBURG
De Soto Caverns

Directions: De Soto Caverns are in Childersburg, Alabama, on Highway 76, about 35 miles southeast of Birmingham; visitors simply pull into the parking lot and go to the Gift Shop to arrange their walks.

Best Season: The caverns are open 7 days a week from March 1 through September 30; they are open year-round on weekends.

Length: The guided tour makes 20 stops during its ⅓ mile and takes about an hour. It is also possible to arrange to spend a night inside the caverns, or to take a tour by candlelight, a mysterious and exciting way to view the sparkling draperies of onyx. Call (205) 378-7252 for further information.

Degree of Difficulty: Easy to moderate. There are stairs throughout and well-surfaced trails. Temperature is constant at 58 degrees, so sweaters are a good idea when walking inside.

A Cave Walk through History

The cathedral-like onyx chambers of De Soto Caverns are the legendary birthplace of the Creek Indians, the center of the spirit world from which their ancestors emerged to form the great Indian nation that encompassed all of Alabama and Georgia at the height of its power. George Stiggins, the only Creek Indian to write a story of his people, described the caverns as peopled by fairies, assistants to the "Master of Breath" who gave and took life. The caverns were being used for tribal ceremonies when Hernando De Soto explored them in 1540. Today concerts are given in the awe-inspiring Kymulga Room, where the acoustics are especially wonderful. Guided walks, like the one described here, give visitors an opportunity to explore the fascinating history of the place.

As you walk back into the caves, you'll see a burial ground 2,000 years old, used by the descendants of Asians who, having crossed the Bering Strait, slowly moved down the length of the country into Mexico. Experts believe that one of them — whose skeleton they found in these caves — was a giant over seven feet tall.

Later, these same caves provided shelter for early pioneers, and during the Civil War they were an important source of bat guano and saltpeter used by Confederate soldiers to make gunpowder. The walking tour takes you to the leaching trench and vat used in the saltpeter operation. The need for gunpowder in the South was so great that young men were urged

66

to work the mines rather than fight. The caverns played a major and lucrative role in the war as the price of saltpeter rose to 59 cents per pound, and the boiling and purifying process to convert saltpeter into gunpowder was carried on right in the cave.

During Prohibition the caverns found another use: moonshine entrepreneurs turned them into a dancing and gambling den. A still remains in the cave, shown on the tour as a remnant of the days of the "Bloody Bucket," the name given to this unusual speakeasy because of the shootings and fighting that took place there.

In addition to the historic sights along this cave walk, there are spectacular, sometimes comic, formations to stroll through, under, and around — the Frozen Waterfall, for example; Sandman's Castle; the 30-foot-high, free-hanging Onyx Draperies; Fat Man's Squeeze; and Bugs Bunny's Den with its huge carrot-shaped formations. Old Man North Wind looks like a piece of carefully executed sculpture, cheeks puffed out; and the Wishing Pond and Waterfall are enchanting. These strangely beautiful formations are composed of cave onyx, a variety of travertine; they began to form 60 million years ago.

The climax of the walk is the Creation Sound and Light Show, about halfway through the tour. Roy Hughes, who nominated the walk, describes the Great Onyx Cathedral as "over 12 stories high and larger than a football field. It has huge, beautiful formations and an amphitheater inside, where they do a sound and light show on the Book of Genesis, using the formation of a cave through the ages to help tell the Creation Story."

The walk ends where it began, at the Gift Shop. Here you can buy bits of cave onyx and Indian souvenirs. Lunch and snacks are available at the De Soto Hillside Cantina, and the picnic area has a covered pavilion for wet weather.

MOBILE
Historic District

Directions: Mobile is in the southwest corner of Alabama on the Gulf of Mexico. From I–10, take the Water Street exit. Turn left at the first light (Government Street) and left again at the next light (Royal Street). Go to Mobile's official welcome center, Fort Condé, near City Hall at 111 South Royal Street. Brochures and a map of the walking tour are available here.

Best Season: March through June, and September through November; in other words, try to avoid summer. A walk in the early evening after the gaslights are lit is particularly delightful.

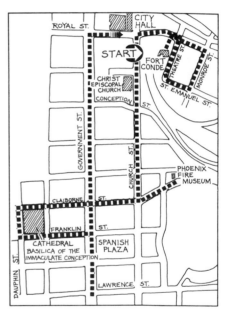

Length: Over 2 miles, about three and a half hours.

Degree of Difficulty: Easy.

Church Street East Historic Tour

"Mobile" is what the 17th-century French Colonists called the lands of the local Indians, the Maubilians, which meant "canoe peddler." Mobile has at various points in her history belonged to the French, the British, the Spanish, the Confederacy, and the United States. It was the capital of French Louisiana. Today visitors to Mobile can wander for hours through blocks of charming streets lined with beautiful old historic buildings and stately oak trees.

"The Church Street tour is particularly rich in history," says Russell Nolen, who nominated this walk. Church Street East is the largest of Mobile's historic districts, featuring over 50 noteworthy buildings. The walk begins at Fort Condé Village, where a military installation built by the French, Spanish, and English has guarded Mobile since the early 1700s. Fort Condé Village, which features brick-paved streets and charming small shops and homes, is still in the process of being restored.

There are several historic buildings in the Village, an area of about two square blocks circumscribed by the Water Street/Route 10 loop interchange. To tour the Village clockwise from Fort Condé, turn right into Royal Street and make rights on Monroe, St. Emanuel, and Theatre streets. The Condé-Charlotte House at 104 Theatre Street is a museum operated by the Colonial Dames of America. Open 10–4 Tuesday through Saturday, it contains, among other things, remnants from the wall of Mobile's first jail. At the corner of St. Emanuel and Monroe is an antebellum cottage. You might want to spend the rest of your life on its delightful veranda.

To leave the Village, turn left on Royal from Theatre Street. At the corner of Royal and Church, note the Italianate-style City Hall. Built in 1857, it is the oldest city hall still in use in America. Then turn left onto Church and you'll soon see Christ Episcopal Church on your right. Designed in Greek Doric style, the church contains two Tiffany stained-glass windows. Continue down Church and take a left onto Claiborne. At 203 Claiborne, the Phoenix Fire Museum, you'll discover highlights of the history of firefighting in Mobile. This museum was once the sight of the Phoenix Fire Company.

Cross Church again and continue on Claiborne, noting the elegant Greek Revival townhouse at 350 Church and the example of antebellum servants' quarters at 108 Claiborne. Yes, that's right, servants' quarters.

Continue on Claiborne, crossing Government Street (we come back to it) and Conti Street, and pause to view the Cathedral-Basilica of the Immaculate Conception. It's an amalgam built in increments, beginning in 1835. The stained-glass windows are magnificent. Left on Dauphin Street takes you to an 1852 residence with an original wrought-iron balcony. Southern houses make an art of external features; balconies and porches conjure up images of graceful relaxation.

Turn left on Franklin to Spanish Plaza, which commemorates the Spanish period of Mobile's history (1780–1813). The City Museum, located across Franklin Street, is a fine place to get in out of the sun for awhile and to look into Mobile's past.

To conclude the walk, saunter along Government Street and note the interesting buildings along the way. On the corner of Lawrence and Government, for example, is an old Italianate townhouse. It was built by a prominent Mobile merchant in 1876.

From Government Street, return to Fort Condé — or turn left at Conception and proceed to De Tonti Square, a nine-block historic district bounded by Claiborne, Conception, St. Anthony, and Adams streets. Named for Henri De Tonti, an Italian who became an explorer for the French, De Tonti Square has a tranquil charm all its own. Of particular interest is Richards–D.A.R. House, at 256 North Joachim. It's a house museum with iron lace depicting the four seasons.

There's also a unique museum moored near Fort Condé: the $200 million, 700-foot-long U.S.S. *Alabama*. If you have time, go on board. It's a walking tour in itself. Allow half a day to tour the battleship and adjoining grounds. Also on display are World War II aircraft and the submarine, U.S.S. *Drum*.

Florida

HISTORIC ST. AUGUSTINE

Directions: St. Augustine is located in northeast Florida, south of Jacksonville. Take I–95 to Route 16 and continue to Route 5. Follow signs to the Visitor Information Center and park on the east side of St. George Street, just inside the city gates.

Best Season: Spring or fall.

Length: Three to five hours. You'll probably want to spend a full day exploring St. Augustine and browsing through the city's many craft and specialty shops.

Degree of Difficulty: Easy.

Walking Tour of San Agustin Antiguo, Old St. Augustine

Founded as a Spanish military outpost in 1565, St. Augustine is the oldest city in the United States, rich in colorful history and a reminder of Spanish power in the New World. The old city, San Agustin Antiguo, has been restored, and guides dressed in period costume recreate both Spanish and British Colonial lifestyles.

The self-guided walk begins on St. George Street, the heart of the restored city. Here narrow second-story balconies hang out over the street, creating a wonderful old-world atmosphere. Cars are not allowed in the restored area of St. George Street, so walkers can wander leisurely without worry. However, April Athey, Travel Media Liaison for the Florida Department of Commerce's Division of Tourism, who submitted the walk, cautions those on foot. "Watch out," she warns, "for horse-drawn carriages that clatter about on the cobblestones!"

Stop first at the Casa de Ribera for tickets to the six restored buildings on the walk. Located at 22 St. George Street, the Casa de Ribera has been restored on its original Spanish foundations and represents the home of a wealthy old Spanish family. The Casa de Gallegos, across the street, provides a glimpse of 18th-century domestic life. It was the home of a Spanish soldier and his family, and has a detached kitchen, as well as a formal garden with numerous flowering plants and fruit trees. Farther on along St. George Street you'll come to the Casa de Arrivas, a silversmith's shop, which still has its 1740 ground-floor walls. Stop here for awhile to watch a master silversmith at work, using only 18th-century tools.

On the left you'll see a beautiful Greek Orthodox Shrine, and as you continue up the street you'll pass by two archaeological sites: De Hita Gonzales and De Mesa Sanchez. Next to the De Mesa Sanchez site, you can see a demonstration of 18th-century cabinetmaking at the Pellicer House. Across the street, at the Sanchez de Ortigosa House, there is an exhibit of 18th-century textile making.

Continue your walk up St. George, past Cuna Street, stopping to peek in the craft shops there before going on to Treasury Street. Here, on the corner of Treasury and St. George, is the Dr. Peck House, built in 1690 for the Spanish Treasurer.

Don't hesitate to leave St. George Street to explore some of the side streets along the way. The Cathedral of Saint Augustine, for example, is to the left, down Cathedral Street, and the Lightner Museum is two blocks to the right, down King Street. Built by railroad magnate Henry Flagler as a hotel in 1888, today the museum is filled with crystal, art glass, porcelain, and Victorian furniture.

Turn left off St. George on Artillery Lane where the Oldest Store Museum provides an opportunity to shop in an authentic 18th-century store, and then continue on to Aviles Street. Here you'll find small shops and an art gallery in what was once a Spanish military hospital.

Walk back to Artillery and turn right, then left on Charlotte Street. If time permits, stop at the wax museum on Menendez Avenue and at the marketplace at the end of the Plaza de la Constitución. The walk continues down Charlotte Street, turns left on Cuna, and ends up where it started, at the beginning of St. George.

For further information about this unique walking tour, call the Historic St. Augustine Preservation Board at (904) 824-3355, or write them at P.O. Box 1987, St. Augustine, FL 32085.

KEY WEST
Pelican Path and Hemingway House

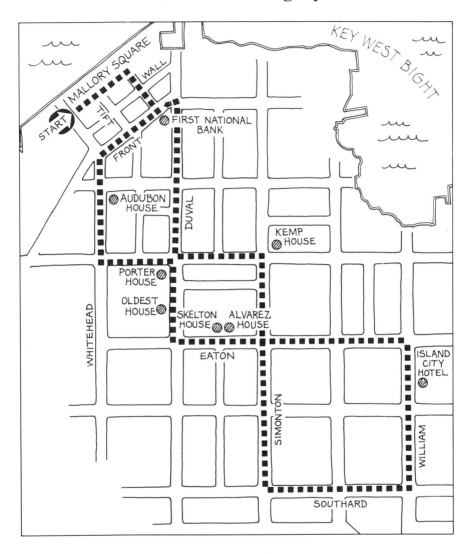

Directions: Key West lies at the southernmost tip of Florida, southwest of Miami. The only way in or out by road is along U.S. 1, which runs from island to island through the Keys. If you see fish in the car, you've gone too far. Park at Mallory Square.

Best Season: Winter and spring.

Length: The Pelican Path is about 1½ miles long. If you go through all the buildings at once, it will take less than two hours, taking time to notice all the unique architecture. Leave extra time for a detour to the Hemingway House.

Degree of Difficulty: Easy.

Pelican Path and the Hemingway House
     Key West is one of the loveliest and most distinctive cities in the country. Its mixed racial and cultural history has produced a tropical town with Caribbean overtones in its flora and architecture and a European sophistication in its culture. Carole Heinlein, who nominated the walk, enjoys one of Key West's other attractions as well: the flowering trees that cover the island. "Especially the poinciana blossoms with huge fiery red flowers that begin to blossom in April and May," she explains. "Orchid trees with white or lavender flowers bloom most of the year and are especially beautiful in winter. The bougainvillea trees flower in purple, orange, and white, and the hibiscus and frangipanni are all over. It's just fantastic here when the trees are in flower."
     The Pelican Path was developed by Key West's Old Island Restoration Foundation (O.I.R.F.) to guide visitors through the old section of the island. It's marked by black and yellow pelican signs, displayed along the streets. With one deviation (the Hemingway House), the walk described here follows the Pelican Path.
     Begin at the headquarters of the O.I.R.F., where volunteer members will give you a brochure that describes the various buildings along the walk. It includes a map showing the route of the walk. From here, follow the pelican signs to Front Street and turn right. Front Street was the early commercial center of Key West, where ships from all over the world brought in goods.
     Continue along Front Street, turn left on Whitehead Street, and stop at the Audubon House on your left. This was one of the first Key West houses to be restored. John James Audubon visited here while painting the "Birds of America." Today it is a museum of his works, featuring many rare books and paintings. It is managed in cooperation with the Florida Audubon Society.
     From Whitehead Street, turn left on Caroline Street. Here there are a number of interesting homes, among them the J. Y. Porter House, where Dr. J. Y. Porter II was born and died. Dr. Porter's research into yellow fever led to present-day U.S. quarantine laws.
     Turn right on Duval Street where you can visit The Oldest House. Not surprisingly, it is the oldest house on the tour, built in 1829. From Duval, turn left on Eaton and notice the Skelton and Alverez houses, two fine examples of the charm of Key West. Continue on Eaton to William

Street and turn right. There are several beautiful buildings on William Street, including the Island City Hotel, which, once condemned by the city, has been lovingly restored.

Walk right at Southard Street and continue to Simonton. You will pass the houses of many wealthy Key West merchants along the way. Turn right on Simonton. (Simonton was named for businessman John W. Simonton, who paid $2,000 for Key West. He bought it from its Spanish owner, Juan Pablo Salas, in 1821.)

At the corner of Caroline and Simonton streets is the Richard Kemp House, which beautifully reflects the clean lines of sailing ships. Many of the Old Key West homes were built by the same craftsmen who built the vessels that worked the tropical trade routes.

A left on Caroline Street takes you past five more interesting Key West houses that demonstrate a wide variety of architectural styles, from the brick Bott House to the Milton Curry House, styled after a Newport cottage.

Back at Duval Street, turn right and continue back to Front Street. At the corner of Front and Duval, stop in at the Florida First National Bank to see part of Tiffany's solid gold table service.

This brings you to the end of the Pelican Path, but there is another highlight to your visit to Key West: the Ernest Hemingway house at 907 Whitehead Street. Hemingway owned this mansion between 1931 and 1961. He wrote *A Farewell to Arms, Death in the Afternoon,* and *For Whom the Bell Tolls,* among other works, in the study built in the old carriage house. Guides are available to take you on a room-by-room tour. The present owner, Mrs. Bernice Dickson, bought the house just four months after Hemingway's death. With it came the family furnishings, so it strongly reflects the personality of its famous owner. Furniture and chandeliers bought on world travels still fill it. The swimming pool is particularly interesting — ask the guide to tell you about the penny pressed into the cement.

There is a small admission fee to see the house, a shrine for Hemingway admirers from around the world. It also serves as home to dozens of cats, descendants of the 50 or so that lived there as Hemingway family pets.

MIAMI
Art Deco Tour

Directions: The walking tour begins at the headquarters of the Miami Design Preservation League at 1236 Ocean Drive, in Miami Beach.

Best Season: Just about any time of the year is good for this walk, but it has to be a Saturday, and there is a $5 fee. The walk begins at 10:30 a.m. The itinerary includes buildings that are under restoration; so if you can arrange to be there during a really spectacular project, you'll get a glimpse of the old and the new at once. Call ahead for information: (305) 672-2014; departure location may change.

Length: Allow about an hour and a half for this walk, which follows no fixed route but changes to allow visitors to see new restorations or to enter buildings of new interest. It's about 2 miles long.

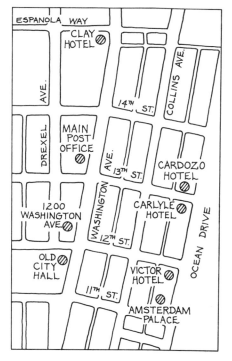

Degree of Difficulty: Easy.

Art Deco in Miami Beach — A New Look for the 1930s

The Thirties went to Miami Beach to retire, but they're forever young in the Art Deco District, a square mile of historically certified apartments and hotels extending from 6th to 23rd streets and from Ocean Drive to Flamingo Park. More than 800 buildings on 125 city blocks make up the District, the only National Historic District consisting of buildings constructed in the 20th century.

Richard Hoberman, Dade County's Assistant Director for Historic Preservation, frequently guides the tour. He explains that "Art Deco was very popular in Europe in the Twenties, and became the style for building in America during the 1930s and '40s. At that time Miami Beach was in a real building boom, the most active in the country. The pent-up demand of the Depression was released as the economy improved, and the light-hearted, colorful deco style was perfect for the area as Miami Beach emerged as a resort for wealthy Americans seeking a less expensive place than Europe to vacation. What was built here is called 'Tropical Deco,' colorful, festive buildings characterized by rich materials, neon, flags and finials, etched glass, and smooth, streamlined shapes."

Hoberman's favorite building is the Amsterdam Palace, an apartment house built to resemble the 1510 family home of Christopher Columbus in Santo Domingo. Other major stops include the hotels Victor, Carlyle, and Cardozo, all sleek, sexy, and newly restored; the post office; a stop at the beach; and a foray into the adjacent Washington Avenue neighborhood. This is a unique opportunity to see a neighborhood still undergoing an economic revival and to get a glimpse into both the past and the future of design.

Georgia

ATLANTA

Chattahoochee River National Recreation Area

Directions: To get to the Loop trailhead from downtown Atlanta, take 75 north and then 285 east. Exit on Powers Ferry Road/Northside Drive (exit 15, the first exit you see). Turn right to go inside the "Perimeter" (as the looped 285 is known locally) for one mile. Turn right on Indian Trail and follow the gravel road for about a quarter of a mile to the parking lot and the sign: "Chattahoochee River National Recreation Area." To get to the trailhead for the Cochran Fitness Jogging Trail, turn left off of exit 15, cross back over 285, and turn left at Interstate North Parkway. Drive about one half mile and cross the river and park on the right-hand side. You'll see another sign: "Chattahoochee River National Recreation Area, Cochran Shoals Unit."

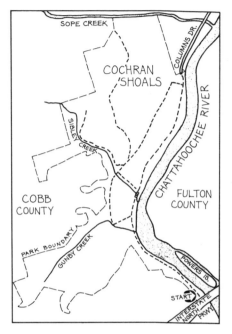

Best Season: Year round, but be prepared for rain any time. Since the weather can be changeable, it is best to dress in layers. Hiking boots or tennis shoes are advisable, depending on the season.

Length: A ranger-led walk in the area will take three hours; they are given two weekends per month from September through May. (The rangers are too busy to lead walks in summer, when they have to supervise the influx of rafters to this popular area.) Call (404) 394-7912 or 394-8335 to arrange for a guided tour. The Loop Trail is not measured; you should allow about three hours. The Cochran Fitness Jogging Trail is a 3-mile loop along the river.

Degree of Difficulty: Moderate. The Loop Trail is slightly steep in some areas, but park interpreter Cathy Jones says there's no problem if walkers take care to maneuver slowly. Watch out for snakes; but, as in most wilderness areas, the reptiles won't trouble you if you leave them alone. Black snakes are out in springtime; copperheads are also around, but rarely observed.

Loop Trail and Cochran Fitness Jogging Trail

Just 30 minutes from Atlanta, these two trails in the Chattahoochee River National Recreation Area are so close together you can take your pick or enjoy both. The name "Chattahoochee" derives from an Indian word that means "river of the painted rock." The Loop Trail is verdant and peaceful. You'll see changing color in autumn and multihued rocks among fragrant pines, redbuds (pale rosy pink flowers in spring), white dogwoods, buckeyes, rhododendrons, and the quintessential trees of the south, magnolias. Wildflowers bloom along the flood plain, especially the lilylike trillium, and beavers and ducks splash along in the river as you walk by. There is an old cabin ruin and a rock shelter, once used by the local Indians, along the meandering trail.

If you want to jog or bicycle along "The Hootch," as the river is affectionately known, the Cochran Fitness Jogging Trail might be just what you're looking for. It is very popular among people who live in Atlanta, says nominator Susan Sales. There are exercise stations along the path, some open fields, picnic tables, and beaver dams on the little creeks that feed the Chattahoochee.

HISTORIC SAVANNAH

Directions: Savannah is located on the Georgia coast. Take I–95 to I–16, which brings you into Savannah's Historic District. Look for Broad Street and park near the Savannah Visitors Center at 301 West Broad Street.

Best Season: Spring, when the flowers are in bloom, but fall and winter are good, too.

Length: Savannah's Historic District is 2.2 square miles. Allow five or six hours for a leisurely "stop-when-you-like" walk.

Degree of Difficulty: Easy.

Savannah, the "Walking City"

Savannah, the Colonial capital of Georgia, offers an almost endless variety of walking opportunities. A number of walking tours have been laid out and are described in brochures. A "waterfront tour," for example, begins in the oldest part of the city and follows cobblestone streets along the riverfront. A walk "around the squares" provides an up-close view of the "Savannah grid," originally designed by James Oglethorpe in the 18th century and still one of the most brilliant examples of the best in city planning. Oglethorpe, who founded Savannah in 1733 as a haven for English debtors, was a military man. His little stockade, carved out of the Georgia wilderness on the banks above the Savannah River, was a variant on military camp design as old as the Romans. From Oglethorpe's original four green squares, or "mini-parks," the city grew by repetition to more than 25. By the time of the Civil War, when Sherman began his devastating march to the sea, each green square was fronted by homes and churches befitting the prosperous cotton port.

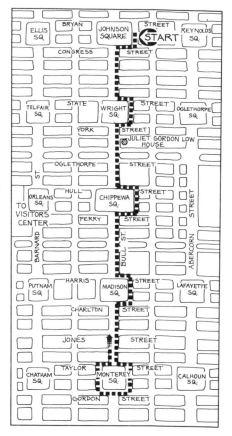

Fortunately Sherman treated Savannah kindly, and its legacy survives in magnificently restored mansions and historic buildings. The trips between these sites make Savannah special. As a walking city, it is the jewel of the United States. Massive trees, covered with Spanish moss, overhang shady walks and benches. Automobile traffic in the heart of the city is forced by the squares to flow at a sane and quiet pace, so the pedestrian crossing the street from square to square holds command.

To get an up-close view of Oglethorpe's squares, begin at Johnson Square on Bull Street, between Bryan and Congress. This beautiful square, resplendent with two fountains, was the first of Savannah's green mini-parks and home to the city's first inn and general store.

Continue along Bull Street to Wright Square, between York and State streets, where you'll find a large boulder honoring Indian Chief Tomo-Chi-Chi, who was friendly to the Colonists and gave them his blessing to settle in the area. Two blocks south of Wright Square, on the corner of Bull and Oglethorpe, is the home of Juliette Gordon Low, who founded the Girl Scouts in 1912. Your next stop along Bull Street is Chippewa

Square, between Perry and Hall. Named for the 1814 Canadian "Chippewa Battle," this square hosts a bronze statue of Oglethorpe, created by Daniel Chester French.

Madison Square is next, between Harris and Charlton streets. Here a statue of Sargent William Jasper commemorates one of the soldiers who died in the Siege of Savannah in 1779. Continue along Bull Street and stop between Taylor and Gordon streets at Monterey Square, named for the 1846 Mexican Battle of Monterey. Here another statue honors a Polish nobleman, Casimir Pulaski, who also lost his life in the 1779 Siege of Savannah.

Monterey Square is the last of the squares along Bull Street. Circle it and retrace your steps two blocks up Bull Street, then take a stroll east or west down the tree-shaded brick sidewalks of Jones Street. Several of the elegant townhouses here have been converted to inns and restaurants. The Eliza Thompson House at 5 West Jones Street is a luxurious example of old world comfort, offering guests complimentary champagne, continental breakfast, and romantic rooms with canopied beds and other antique furniture. For a memorable, down-to-earth, home-cooked meal, stop at Mrs. Wilkes' Boarding House at 107 West Jones Street. Open for breakfast and lunch only, this place offers some of the best southern cooking found anywhere.

If you prefer a guided tour of Savannah, the nonprofit Historic Savannah Foundation offers a two-hour, two-mile walking tour with a trained guide. The tour departs daily at 9:30 a.m. from the Hyatt Regency Hotel at 2 West Bay Street. For reservations call (913) 233-3597. Martha Rudd, who nominated Savannah as the best city walk, says, "The only hazard is that the walk is so fascinating and beautiful you won't want it to end." She encourages people everywhere to come see for themselves that "Savannah is truly a pedestrian paradise. You can walk for hours and never be bored."

Before beginning your walking tour or tours of Savannah, it's a good idea to stop at the Visitors Center at 301 West Broad Street. There you'll find all sorts of information about the city and the various ways to see it. Trained guides will give you suggestions and maps of the town. The Center also features two multimedia programs on Savannah's history. Jenny Stacy of the Visitors Bureau, who also submitted Savannah as the best city walk, suggests picking up the Savannah Visitors Guide Map, a comprehensive and informative guide to the Historical District.

Plan to see Savannah your own way, at your own pace, but be sure to include a stroll north toward the river. You'll amble down Factor's Walk, a remnant of the 19th-century cotton trade, and along the restored Riverfront Plaza. As you come back through town, pay particular attention to restored homes such as the Davenport House (1815–1820) and the Owens-Thomas House (1816–1819), which capture the essence of antebellum elegance. Both charge admission. They're worth it. A free attraction is the Colonial Park Cemetery, resting place of Declaration of Independence signer Button Gwinnett.

Savannah's more-than-250-year history has matured the city, which now boasts 5,000 giant oaks, a host of magnificent, stately homes, and a worldwide reputation for hospitality.

Kentucky

CUMBERLAND GAP NATIONAL PARK

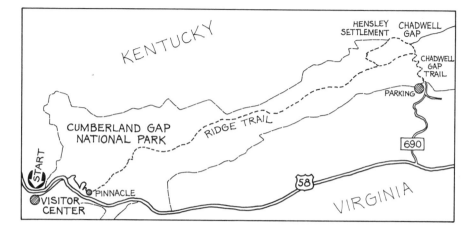

Directions: Cumberland Gap National Park is at the meeting point of the Kentucky, Virginia, and Tennessee borders. From Lexington, north of the park, take I–75 to 25E to Middlesboro, Kentucky, where the Visitor Center is located. From Knoxville, in the south, take I–75 north to 25W to Lafollette, Tennessee. Then, take Route 63 to Harrogate, Tennessee. From there, take 25E to Middlesboro, Kentucky.

Best Season: Mid-October, when the fall colors peak. Middlesboro holds its annual Cumberland Mountain Fall Festival then, with crafts demonstrations and interpretations of the traditional mountain folk cultures. Lodging is available in Middlesboro.

Length: The walk includes 2.1 miles on the Chadwell Gap Trail and .9 miles on the Ridge Trail, making it 3 miles one way from the trailhead to Hensley Settlement. The park has several long and short trails, totaling nearly 50 miles. Some make fine day hikes; others, particularly Ridge Trail, require an overnight stay at designated backcountry campsites. Even the short trails are rugged and require more time than flat-terrain walking. Two miles that add two thousand or so feet to your elevation above sea level add up to a morning's work.

Degree of Difficulty: Moderate. Be sure to call the park for seasonal warnings — (606) 248-2817 — and permits, especially if you plan to camp.

The Chadwell Gap Trail

The Cumberland Gap is a natural gateway in the long palisade formed by the Appalachian Mountains. It has been a buffalo trail and a link in the Warrior's Path that provided the Cherokee and Shawnee access to Kentucky hunting grounds. Beginning in 1750, it was the door to the West for white Colonists.

Cumberland Gap National Historic Park lies along the elongated peak of Cumberland Mountain. Magnificent trails form a fish-skeleton, with the Ridge Trail leading along the high ground and lesser trails branching off toward the valley on either side.

The Visitor Center is the place to begin. Pinnacle Road leads from there up to the Pinnacle Overlook, 2,400 feet above sea level and directly above the Gap itself. From here there are magnificent panoramas, stretching for miles and miles.

Wesley Leishman, Chief of Interpretation for the park, who recommends the Chadwell Gap Trail, suggests you follow Route 58 from the Visitor Center to the small Virginia town of Caylor, where you can pick up the Chadwell Gap trailhead. The trail will lead you back into Kentucky, then back to Virginia, and finally back into Kentucky again (the border runs along the ridge of the mountain). The highpoint of this walk is the Hensley Settlement, a colony established in the early 1900s by the Hensley and Gibbons families. Leishman describes it as "an outstanding cultural restoration. It's a group of farmsteads with 70 acres under cultivation and 34 historic structures, houses, farms, fences, and other outbuildings. It's like taking a walk back in time. For example, there's a one-room schoolhouse with the old-style potbellied stove." Here you can experience what life was like for the early settlers in Kentucky.

The historian Frederick Jackson Turner, in effect announcing a new era of American civilization in his 1893 paper, "The Significance of the Frontier in American History," said, "Stand at the Cumberland Gap and watch the procession of civilization, marching single file — the buffalo, following the trail to the salt springs, the Indian, the fur trader and hunter, the cattle raiser, the pioneer farmer — and the frontier has passed by." The 1890 census revealed the end of the great westward colonization — American settlement at last reached from sea to shining sea. Today the Cumberland Gap is no longer a door from place to place, but it remains for the walker a special moment, from time to time.

MAMMOTH CAVE

Directions: Mammoth Cave National Park is in south-central Kentucky. To get there from the north, take I–65, 31W, or 31E; from the east, the Bluegrass Parkway, the Cumberland Parkway, or U.S. 68; from the west, U.S. 231, Green River Parkway, and the Western Kentucky Parkway; and from the south, U.S. 68 and 31W. All lead to State Route 70 and 255, which lead to the park. Stop at the Visitor Center to pick up tickets for your cave walk and to get a schedule for the various walking tours.

Best Season: Mammoth Cave is a very popular attraction year round, and especially in summer. If you'd like to avoid the crowds, spring or fall are best because children are in school and traffic is lighter. In July or August, you'll be in a crowd, whether you like it or not.

Length: This varies considerably. Plan to spend a day here so that you can combine the cave walks with walks along the various aboveground trails.

Degree of Difficulty: Some of the cave walks are very strenuous, up and down steep hills and steps and through narrow underground passages. The cave is cool (in the 50s) and humid. Even if you go in July, wear sturdy shoes and warm clothes. The park above ground is populated by snakes, ticks, and other wildlife. Dress accordingly.

Mammoth Cave

Mammoth Cave is the largest known cave in the world. If you can imagine such an underground network, it stretches and winds for 360 miles, and that's only what has been explored to date. Some of these miles inside the earth are open to the public via tours that vary in length and route. The shortest, a half mile, is reserved for handicapped visitors; the longest, a half day hike through a rugged four miles of underground passageways, includes steep inclines and more than 700 steps.

Lewis Cutliff, who enthusiastically recommends the walks in Mammoth Cave, explains how the cave came to be: "The cave was formed by water during the Mississippian Era, when water covered much of North America. Limestone deposits formed and then eroded as the sea disappeared. Over the eons, 300 million years or so, the draining water cut little channels in the stone, and as the water receded and the channels grew, the passages we know today were formed."

These passages lead through giant cathedral-like rooms and stalactite-filled corridors, up steep hills and over deep pits. The brilliant colors of the limestone formations are dazzling and the formations are fantastic. The "Frozen Niagara," for example, that culminates the half-day tour and is the main feature of a tour of its own, is a water-formed limestone for-

mation resembling a waterfall. The "Snowball Dining Room," also on the half-day tour, really is a place to eat — lunch is served from a counter in a subterranean room that can accommodate 250 people.

Of particular interest is the "Lantern Tour," given seasonally, which crosses three miles and four thousand years, past prehistoric artifacts and diggings left from an 1812 saltpeter mining operation that dug minerals to be made into gunpowder. Lanterns are the only illumination, so the cave is revealed to you as it was seen by explorers a century ago.

In addition to the cave walks, there are 52,000 acres in Mammoth Cave National Park that provide wonderful opportunities for the walker. On your way to the Visitor Center, you'll get a glimpse of the countryside around Mammoth Cave as you pass through a forest filled with shagbark hickory, beech, maple, ash, and sycamore trees, as well as dogwood and mountain laurel. There are 34 miles of backcountry trails, including short trails such as Big Springs (just one mile) and White Oak (2½ miles), and long trails such as Good Springs, which is a loop trail of 10 miles. Access to the backcountry trailheads is across the Green River; there are two cave ferries to get you and your car to the other side: the Honchins and the Mammoth. On the south side of the Green River there are several short, aboveground, self-guided walks. One of the most interesting is the Cave Island Nature Trail along which the walker can see clues of the underground cave's existence. This one-mile walk begins near the Historic Entrance and ends at the Visitor Center.

Mississippi

OLE MISS AND FAULKNER'S ROWAN OAK

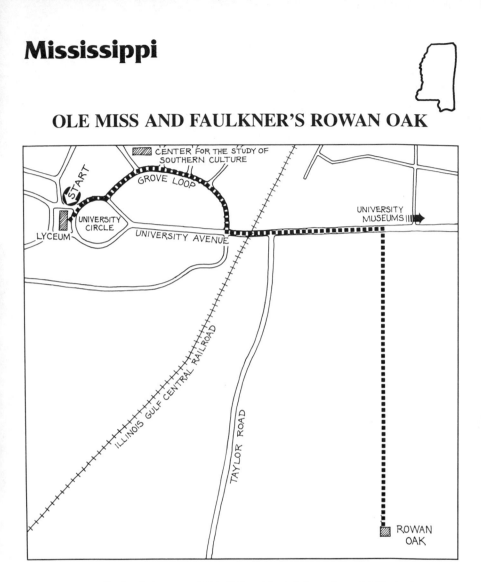

Directions: Oxford, home of Ole Miss (the University of Mississippi), is in the northern part of the state, almost due south of Memphis, Tennessee. Take I–55 to Route 6.

Best Season: Late September or early October.

Length: About 2 miles in total, and two hours.

Degree of Difficulty: Easy.

Ole Miss and Rowan Oak

Begin this walk with a leisurely tour of the University of Mississippi's lovely campus. Ole Miss is perhaps best known as a perennial football powerhouse, but whether you're a football fan or not, you'll enjoy a walk around these beautiful grounds.

A good place to start is at the Lyceum, the Administration Building, on University Circle. Built in 1841, it's an excellent example of antebellum Greek Revival grandeur, complete with columned portico. As you exit the Lyceum, walk to your left, picking up Grove Loop to the Center for the Study of Southern Culture, housed in an antebellum observatory. Admission here is free, and you may want to stop for a look at artifacts and audiovisual exhibits of southern life.

Continue past the Grove, turn left on University, and walk the few blocks to the University Museums. These are also free, and contain wonderful collections of art, archaeology, history, and science. (The Millington-Barnard Collection of antique scientific instruments is fascinating.)

Walk behind the complex of museums to the parking lot and look for the path leading into the woods. Follow this path for about 15 to 20 minutes to Rowan Oak, home of William Faulkner for 32 years. Faulkner had a long and unusual relationship with Ole Miss. In fact, walking around the University and its environs in Oxford is almost like a trip to Yoknapatawpha County itself. Faulkner's father was business manager of the school for some years, and Faulkner attended school there for two. Later he was postmaster of the University post office and night fireman of its power station. The thread that tied his literary and odd-job lives together was his home, Rowan Oak.

The house was a tumbledown mansion when Faulkner bought it in 1930. Nor was Faulkner himself a great success at that time, but both house and writer underwent renewals during the years he lived there. He plumbed and wired the house himself and laid new floors to replace the ones ruined by the small livestock that once tenanted the first floor. Many of his major works were written at Rowan Oak, beginning with *Light in August,* but it was not until late in his career that Faulkner was financially well-off, so he continued to make repairs, large and small, to the house with his own hands. He added rooms, including his office, and planted trees and flowers to brighten the grounds. He often asked publishers for an advance so he could continue to improve the place.

Today the University of Mississippi maintains Rowan Oak much as it was when Faulkner died in 1962. His favorite green chair still sits in the library, where he liked to write in longhand on hand-lined paper. The portable typewriter he used for notes is still in the office. The most unusual notes are written right on the wall: an outline for *A Fable* remains where Faulkner worked it out on the plaster.

North Carolina

CAPE HATTERAS NATIONAL SEASHORE
Pea Island Wildlife Refuge

Directions: Enter Cape Hatteras National Seashore from the north via U.S. 17 and 158, or from the west via U.S. 64 and 264. The National Park Service Group Headquarters is at Fort Raleigh National Historic Site on Roanoke Island. The Whalebone Junction Information Center is on Brodie Island at the beginning of Route 12. From Brodie Island continue south along the coastal road to Pea Island Refuge Headquarters.

Best Season: Spring and summer are best for observing nesting birds (although parts of Pea Island may be closed in spring to protect the birds during this time). October through November is the best time to see the huge variety of migratory birds, and the winter months are best if you want to see waterbirds, such as snow and Canada geese.

Length: The Pea Island Nature Walk is 4 miles round trip.

Degree of Difficulty: Easy to moderate. Swim only on guarded beaches. Cape Hatteras Seashore undergoes constant changes from shifting sand and water, and the currents can be dangerous. The Park Service map will help you find good swimming. Protect yourself against sunburn and insects. Drive and park only in designated areas — it's easy to get stuck in the sand.

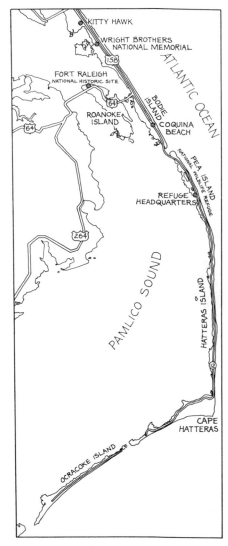

Cape Hatteras Seashore and Pea Island Nature Walk

Cape Hatteras National Seashore is a long string of barrier islands forming the east coast of North Carolina, separated from the mainland by Pamlico Sound. The Seashore has something for everyone: long sandy beaches for walking and beachcombing; marshes for birding; woodlands for hiking. History buffs will want to look for the remains of the many ships wrecked by natural and man-made causes. The *Laura A. Barnes,* for one, is visible near Coquina Beach, and many more lie off the Outer Banks, victims of German submarines that prowled the coastal waters during World War II. Blackbeard used the shallows around the Ocracoke Island Inlet as a hiding place.

On your way to Pea Island Wildlife Refuge there are two significant and very different historical sites at the north end of the seashore. First (if you arrive from the north on U.S. 12) is the Wright Brothers National Memorial, a tribute to the enterprising, bicycle-making brothers, Orville and Wilbur Wright, who used the Kill Devil Hills (south of Kitty Hawk on today's Route 12) as testing grounds for their bizarre experiments with kites and powered aircraft. On December 17, 1903, they culminated three years of trials with the 12-second 120-foot flight of the *Flyer,* reported in this jubilant telegram home: "Success four flights thursday morning all against twenty one mile wind started from Level with engine power alone average speed though air thirty one miles longest 57 seconds inform Press home Christmas."

The Wright Brothers Memorial is a simple monument near their campsite and the takeoff point of their flight. A reproduction of the *Flyer* is at the Visitor Center. Since the Memorial is just off the main road, it's an easy stop; the Park Service's programs bring the place and time to life.

If you arrive at Pea Island from the west on U.S. 64, you will have passed the Fort Raleigh National Historic Site on Roanoke Island, where the first two English Colonies in America were planted in 1585 and 1587. Both of these early Colonies failed, in part because of the hostility between the settlers and the Indian inhabitants. Here, in 1587, Virginia Dare made history as the first English child to be born in the New World. Between then and 1590 the colony of over 100 men, women, and children was lost. The Colonial leaders who returned to Virginia to reestablish contact found only the word "Croatoan," the name of a nearby island, carved onto a palisade post. Even today no one knows exactly what happened.

Fort Raleigh National Historic Site offers visitors a chance to stroll through a lovely Elizabethan garden and see exhibits on the life and art of the period, including copies of illustrations made by John White, Virginia Dare's grandfather, which show Indian life then. There is also a short film about the settlement. The Waterside Theatre features outdoor performances of *The Lost Colony,* a play about this historic colony. A nature trail winds around the site and a restoration of the original "Newe Fort" helps visitors understand the defensive nature of the first settlements, their vulnerability and smallness in the wilderness where they tried to settle.

From Fort Raleigh, head back to the coast road and turn south on State Highway 12 to the Pea Island Refuge Headquarters, where you can pick up information about the four-mile walk around the North Pond Impoundment. Pea Island is just over 5,900 acres and extends for 12 miles. The walk around the North Pond affords an opportunity to view a variety of bird species up close. (There are more than 265 different species that regularly spend time on the island.)

Whenever you decide to visit Pea Island (named for the dune peas that grow in the dunes), you will be able to see an abundance of birds and wildlife as you follow this trail. In the spring and summer, ibises, egrets, and herons nest here, and in summer and fall brown pelicans can be seen. Summer nights are witness to the loggerhead sea turtles that come ashore nearby to lay their eggs in the sand. Winter months bring waterfowl to the island; and if you visit then, you can see snow and Canada geese plus about 25 different kinds of duck. Otter, muskrat, and pheasant are among the wildlife that lives here.

For further information about Pea Island, write: Refuge Manager, Pea Island National Wildlife Refuge, P.O. Box 150, Rodanthe, NC 27968, or call (919) 987-2394. Because there is so much to do and see in all of Cape Hatteras National Seashore, especially in the summer, Robert Woody, Chief of Interpretation, recommends that visitors call or write the Headquarters for information about special activities. The number is (919) 473-2111; the address is Route 1, Box 675, Manteo, NC 27954. "We have a schedule of over 200 activities provided every week during the summer months," says Woody. "There are birding walks, beach walks, island forest trail walks, and living history programs. On some programs, such as snorkeling, canoe trips, fishing trips, etc., we have to limit group size for safety reasons, so if people want to partake, they should reserve a place 24 hours in advance between mid-June and Labor Day."

South Carolina

CAESAR'S HEAD STATE PARK

Directions: Caesar's Head State Park is located on Route 276, in the northeast corner of South Carolina, near the North Carolina border. The closest city is Greenville. Route 276 continues northward to intersect the Blue Ridge Parkway, so Caesar's Head is convenient to other areas of remarkable natural beauty.

Best Season: Mark Dutton, who nominated this walk, calls Caesar's Head "just a beautiful place . . . it exudes good feeling." He recommends it in every season, except the hottest days of summer. Spring is particularly wonderful, when there is a profusion of wildflowers — bloodroot, serviceberry, bellwort, and more.

Length: The walk most favored by nominator Dutton is the 4½-mile, round-trip trail to Raven Cliff Falls. If you bring the whole family, plan on a full day, with picnic lunch.

Degree of Difficulty: Moderate. Be careful not to disturb the animals or remove any vegetation.

Raven Cliff Falls Trail

Begin by driving to the Overlook on Route 276. A country store is there, if you need supplies for the walk. The Overlook is more than 3,000 feet above sea level and on a clear day the views of the mountains in Georgia, North Carolina, and South Carolina are spectacular. Caesar's Head is the natural rock formation within 500 feet of the store. (The origin of the name is the subject of some controversy. Some say the jutting rock cliff resembles the head of Julius Caesar. Others believe "Caesar" is a corruption of the Indian word, "Sachem," meaning chieftain; still others think Caesar was the name of a hunting dog who leapt over the cliff to his death.)

A quarter mile past the store and the Overlook is a parking lot on your right. Leading from the parking lot are two trails, the Jones Gap Trail, a 10-mile walk round trip, and the Cold Spring Trail, which has a 5.6-mile loop that branches back to the road near the Jones Gap trailhead, offering the walker a number of options regarding the length and time of the walk. These two trails intersect along the course of the Middle Saluda River, the first designated and protected scenic river in South Carolina.

To get to the Raven Cliff Falls trailhead, cross the street from the parking lot. Raven Cliff Falls is a beautiful trail. It leads to an observation platform overlooking the 420-foot falls, a perfect spot for a picnic.

This was Cherokee country two centuries ago. Now it's part of the 10,000-acre Mountain Bridge Recreation and Wilderness Area, and it's remarkably unchanged. "What I like best about Caesar's Head," says Dutton, "is that it's a very young park, and the trail system is still relatively fresh and wild-looking."

The park is a favorite of birders because its warm mountain updrafts attract hawks and turkey vultures. You'll have an unusual opportunity to see them flying over the treetops from your point of view *above* them. Animals in the park include black bear, whitetail deer, fox, raccoon, skunk and bobcat, among others. Some people have even seen a cougar!

Park naturalists conduct wildflower walks, birding walks, and overnight backpacking trips into the remote areas of the park. To make a reservation, or for information about dates and times, call (803) 836-6115.

CHARLESTON

Directions: Charleston is on the southern Atlantic coast of South Carolina, about 85 miles northeast of Savannah, as the crow flies. I–95, either northbound or southbound, picks up I–26 South to Charleston; or, for a little more local color, try U.S. 17, which runs along the coast.

Best Season: Spring, fall, and winter are all fine. Charleston's southern coastal climate is temperate year round. Avoid July and August.

Length: The walk described here is about 3 miles long, with stops along the way. All of Charleston is an historic site, though, so don't plan to breeze through it.

Degree of Difficulty: Easy.

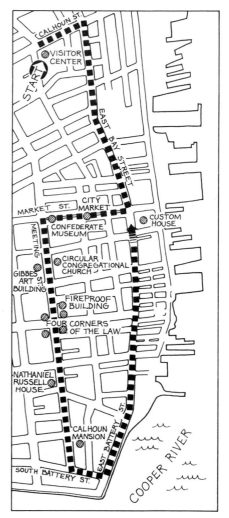

Charleston: A Vision of the Old South

Charleston has a history of being at the center of things — war, trade, politics. It was established in 1670 and named Albemarle, after George Monck, Duke of Albemarle. Within a year the name was changed to Charles Towne after England's King Charles II. Indian trade from the west and European and American trade from the coast made the town rich. Rice, indigo, and cotton poured over her docks.

The British held the city for two years during the Revolutionary War. After their occupation ended, the name was changed to Charleston. Coastal pirates plagued her shipping. The Civil War began here with the rebel bombardment of Fort Sumter in Charleston Harbor; the city was evacuated during William Tecumseh Sherman's march to the sea.

Today's Charleston is as ornate and as romantic as an old-style Christmas tree. The peninsula between the Ashley and Cooper rivers is famous for its old homes and buildings: 73 pre-Revolutionary, 136 late 18th-century, and over 600 pre-1840 structures.

Needless to say, this brief walk only scratches the surface of this gracious and elegant city. To get a real feeling for Charleston, you'll want to spend a couple of days enjoying its easy southern charm, its quiet side streets, its big porches, and the elaborate ironwork of its pastel homes. Take it slowly. Charleston is a city of details. Look for the firemarks on the outsides of the houses — they used to tell insurance companies whether the household subscribed to their firefighting service — and the "earthquake bolts" that stick out of some front walls (ever since the big quake of 1886). Enjoy the many gardens next to private homes. Look for "single houses," such as the Thomas Elfe Workshop at 54 Queen Street. It's just one room wide, with the entrance turned away from the street into a garden so that greenery-cooled breezes drift through the living quarters.

Begin at the Charleston Visitor Information Center at 85 Calhoun Street. This restored pre-Revolutionary building is operated by the Charleston Trident Chamber of Commerce, whose maps and orientation materials offer you the best introduction to Charleston. The 30-minute presentation "Charleston Adventure" is a multi-image sound and light show introducing visitors to the delights of the city.

From the Center, take a right onto Calhoun and another right to East Bay Street. The Cooper River will be on your left.

At 200 East Bay is the U.S. Custom House, completed in 1879. The marker there gives some history of the building and the site it occupies. Opposite the Custom House is City Market, which extends along Market Street from East Bay to Meeting Street. Dating from the turn of the 19th century, the Market includes shops, an open-air flea market, 19th-century homes, and the Museum of the Confederacy at 188 Meeting Street, in Market Hall. Walk slowly along Market Street, savoring its atmosphere, before turning left onto Meeting Street.

Past Cumberland Street on the left is the circular Congregational Church, the "meeting house" that first gave the street its name. The congregation here dates from 1681; this building was built in 1891. Just past it, also on the left, is the marker designating the site of Institute Hall, where the Order of Secession was signed signaling South Carolina's departure from the Union on December 20, 1860. Across the street is Gibbs Memorial Art Gallery, home of the Carolina Art Association, exhibiting paintings and special exhibitions.

On the left, past Queen Street, is the "Fireproof Building," the first in the country, now housing the South Carolina Historical Society. Just past that is the "Four Corners of the Law" commemorated in Ripley's "Believe It or Not." Each corner represents a different legal authority: City Hall for municipal law; the 1790 County Courthouse for county law; the Post Office and Federal Court for federal law, and St. Michael's Protestant Episcopal Church for ecclesiastical law. Washington and Lafayette both worshipped at St. Michael's on visits to Charleston.

51 Meeting Street is the Nathaniel Russell House, famous for an astonishing flying spiral staircase. At 16 Meeting is the fabulous Calhoun Mansion, *circa* 1876, embodying the most ornate and gracious Victorian sensibility. And now, within sight as you look toward the water, is White Point Gardens, where those pirates who robbed the coastal shipping were hanged.

A left on South Battery and another on East Battery will take you back to East Bay Street and the Visitor Information Center via the riverfront, where wharves and alleys recall the days of the cotton trade.

After your tour of Charleston, plan a visit to Drayton Hall for a vision of plantation life. Drive across town and over the Ashley River Bridge to Route 61; Drayton Hall is about nine miles from Charleston, off Route 61. This stately red-brick plantation home was built between 1738 and 1742. Surrounded by beautiful grounds and bordered by live oak, Drayton Hall is an excellent example of 18th-century architecture and southern life-style.

Also recommended is a stop at Middleton Place, just west of Drayton Hall, also off Route 61. Here you can wander through the oldest and certainly one of the most beautifully landscaped gardens in America. A self-guided walking tour takes you past sunken gardens, lakes shaped like butterflies, and camellia-lined *allées*. Designed in 1741, it is believed the gardens took 100 slaves 10 years to complete. After the Civil War the grounds were left unattended, but in 1916, a descendant of Henry Middleton began their restoration.

Tennessee

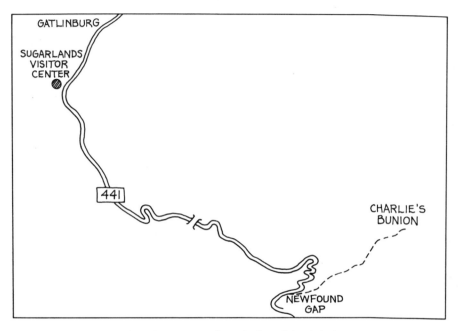

CHARLIE'S BUNION
Great Smoky Mountains National Park

Directions: Great Smoky Mountains National Park is located on the Tennessee/North Carolina border, south of Knoxville. The Appalachian Trail runs through the park and follows the border most of the way. To get to the park from Knoxville, take I–40 east to 66 and 441 to park headquarters at Gatlinburg bypass road. Stop in at the Sugarlands Visitor Center for information on weather conditions and for a short film about the park. There are exhibits there, too, depicting the history of the Smokies. From the Visitor Center, Route 441 continues up the mountain, following the Little Pigeon River, into the evergreen forested peaks. Along the roadside you may see a family of black bear. Don't share your food with them; they may look friendly, but they can be very dangerous. The twin peaks off to your right as you ascend are called "Chimney Tops," and beyond them is Newfound Gap, over 5,000 feet high, where you park and begin the walk.

Best Season: Autumn is the best for the foliage. From November through March the weather is extremely changeable, usually for the worse, and it can be very cold. Dona Diftler, who nominated this walk, says that even in summer it can be cool at the higher elevations. Unless you've had plenty of experience, stick to the warmer months.

Length: 8 miles round trip. Leave early in the morning and allow a full day. If you decide to spend the night, backcountry campsites are available, but permits are required. You can get a permit (which is free) at Sugarlands Visitor Center or at several campground offices throughout the park. You can also write for a permit to Backcountry Reservations, Great Smoky National Park, Gatlinburg, TN 37738 or call (615) 436-9564.

Degree of Difficulty: The 800 plus miles of trail in Great Smoky Mountains National Park range from easy-walking trails to demanding backcountry hikes requiring wilderness expertise. Step one of any walk in the park should be toward a ranger who can advise you on conditions, regulations, weather, wildlife, and so on. The walk to Charlie's Bunion can be moderate to moderately difficult, or even difficult, depending upon weather conditions and your own degree of fitness. What does wilderness walking demand from you? Sensitivity to the surroundings, for one thing; for another, courtesy to the hiker who will follow you, whether next week or 10 years from now. Experiencing the virgin forest depends on seeing no trace of human abuse: no trash, no fires, no carved tree trunks, no graffiti. Follow the trails; don't start one of your own. Be respectful and *very careful* of wildlife. Up here, that means bears, as well as the raccoons and chipmunks you might take for granted.

The mountains will also test your alertness and savvy. Don't invite trouble. Don't try to be daring when caution is required. Cross moving water with extreme care. Keep dry and warm. Pack the right equipment.

The Walk to Charlie's Bunion

Dona Diftler of Knoxville shared her firsthand account of a walk to Charlie's Bunion with us, and we share it here with you:

"Most all walks have their own personality, and certainly all have at least some characteristics of a great walk. But I suppose that a great walk, by definition, must begin by stuffing the traditional peanut butter and jelly sandwiches in day packs just as the sun is peeking through the windows.

"As we drive up Highway 441 to Newfound Gap, it's almost impossible to describe how the mountain air feels, or how pretty the streams look as the sun bathes them. I never tire of seeing the pines reaching toward the sky. At the first clearing the mountains seem to be waiting for me. Time and again their strength and beauty seem to anticipate my return and to greet me.

"We climb 5,000 feet to Newfound Gap, the trailhead for Charlie's Bunion. We walk through a forest of red spruce and fir. Looking down the slopes brings sights of wildflowers, ferns, mosses, and blackberries. Charlie's Bunion has the most spectacular views in the park, with sheer cliffs dropping more than 1,000 feet into the Greenbrier section.

"My favorite point in the walk is the ridge at about 5,400 feet elevation. The view in either direction is endless. The rolling mountains look so close you feel you could reach out and touch them. About a half mile ahead the bare rock knob called Charlie's Bunion is visible.

"We climb the rock and unpack the (now smashed) peanut butter sandwiches and fruit. The temperature back in town is nearly 90, but up here it feels like winter. We have the best seats in the house, and the show is spectacular: mountains surrounding us, sweeping to the valley below, the dark clouds rolling in so gracefully, as if to music, with the sound of the wind as our orchestra. We are fortunate to be there alone. It's not that I wouldn't share this with others, but the sights and the deafening quiet capture my attention in a way that the city never does, never could. I feel part of the sights around me, and so appreciative. It begins to rain. Suddenly it's quarter-inch hail. We awake from our trance, and we have to laugh.

"A great walk lasts in your mind and heart for days, weeks, even months after it's over. . . ."

Virgin Islands

VIRGIN ISLANDS NATIONAL PARK
St. John

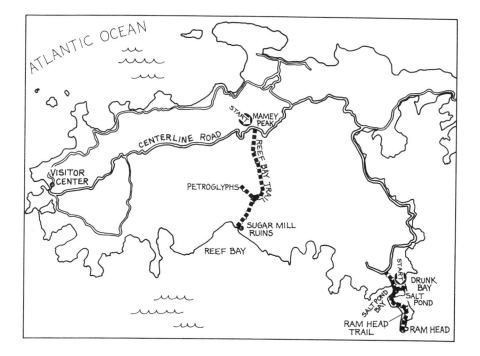

Directions: St. John is the smallest of the American Virgin Islands, located just east of St. Thomas, about 80 miles east of San Juan, Puerto Rico. There is air access via both cities and also by sea. A ferry runs from St. Thomas at Redhook to St. John.

Best Season: Park Ranger Richard Jones recommends the fall, when tourist traffic is light. "It's dead here," he says, "so you'll have the place all to yourself. The water's wonderful, clear, and warm, and when the crowds aren't in, the prices for food and shopping are a little more reasonable than usual."

Length: St. John has trails of varying length, from as short as ¹⁄₁₀ mile to 6 miles, mostly over clear paths that rise and fall with the island's rugged topography. The two trails recommended here, Ram Head and Reef Bay, are 1 mile and 3 miles one-way, respectively.

Degree of Difficulty: Moderate to strenuous, depending on the trail you choose. Consult the trail guide that's available at the park Visitor Center on Cruz Bay, or call ahead while planning your trip: (809) 776-6201. The Reef Bay and Ram Head trails are moderately easy, but you need to watch your footing, especially on the Ram Head Trail, which climbs to a cliff 200 feet above the Caribbean Sea. Wherever you walk on St. John, follow the standard precautions: don't hike alone, don't eat fruits or berries you can't identify, stay on the trails, and wear suitably sturdy footwear. Make sure to outfit yourself with a good canteen and keep it full. Fresh water does not occur naturally on St. John; what you need, you carry.

Ram Head and Reef Bay Trails

St. John is one of the loveliest islands in the Caribbean, partly because it's relatively free of the standard tourist amenities that have transformed so many other islands into resorts. Columbus discovered it in 1493. It was settled permanently by the Danes in 1717 and became a prosperous sugar and cotton colony — until 1848 when the Danish emancipation of the slaves and the perfection of sugar beets undercut the economy. St. John settled into being extremely beautiful and of no particular use. This makes it an especially wonderful place for walking. In an unspoiled island setting, St. John offers rugged hiking, silky beaches, and wonderful scenery, both above and below sea level; beneath the surface of the clear Caribbean are some great opportunities for snorkeling.

Getting around St. John requires a little work and some thinking. The trailheads are scattered. Rental cars are available but may be expensive. Taxicabs can take you to a trailhead, and the 25 miles of paved road are easy to walk or hitch.

Ram Head Trail, suggested by Park Ranger Richard Jones, covers the little peninsula on the southeast corner of the island, starting on Salt Pond Bay Beach, a good swimming spot. A side spur leads to the rough rubble beach on Drunk Bay, where you might find some interesting junk or driftwood tossed up by the surf. The Ram Head Trail continues to a sheer cliff, 200 feet above the sea, with a dazzling view of the island's south shore and the ocean. Ranger Jones notes that the cliff offers "a long drop and a short stop," so be careful.

Ranger Jones also recommends the Reef Bay Trail and the Petroglyph Spur, which begins about 1.7 miles down the Reef Bay Trail. The Reef Bay trailhead is near Mamey Peak on Centerline Road, close to the middle of the island. It descends through the forest past the remains of old sugar factories. The Petroglyph Trail leads to carvings in the stone above some jungle pools. Are the carvings prehistoric? West African? No one is certain. Some attribute them to the early Arawak Indians. The Petroglyph Trail loops back to the Reef Bay Trail, which continues past the ruins of yet another sugar mill and ends on Reef Bay Beach. The park service offers guided hikes around many other trails, and one especially delightful tour: an underwater trail in Trunk Bay, which provides an opportunity to see some of the most beautiful aquatic life on earth.

Walking the Central States

WHEN YOU EXPLORE an area on foot, you establish a connection with it. You leave a mark on the place, and it leaves a mark on you. This is undoubtedly at the heart of the tremendous appeal that walking has in an age when too many experiences are impersonal or come prepackaged. You also form a kind of kinship with the walkers in whose footsteps you travel; in the Central States, these walkers and their trails trace the history of the country.

Formed primarily by the forces of retreating glaciers and erosion, the comparatively gentle land of the Central States has been walked, over and over again, ever since prehistoric times when Asian tribes, having crossed the Bering Strait, migrated over this land on their trek south. They left behind here their pottery, their tools, and those mysterious geometric and animal-shaped mounds such as are found around the Wyalusing Ridges walk in Wisconsin. Then American Indians crossed these plains, lakes, and mountains, followed by European explorers and settlers. The marks of leather boots replaced the footsteps of moccasins, and cattle roamed in the tracks of the buffalo. Today, the on-foot traveler can walk the Indian Trail of Tears; and, in the soft sandstone paths of places like Kanopolis State Park, the old buffalo tracks can still be seen.

The Central States continue to record our history. During the Civil War, soldiers from both sides trudged, fought, advanced, and retreated through these hills and valleys. And, even though the automobile has become our primary means of transportation, care is taken in each of these states to preserve the old and well-worn trails for walking, and to create new ones. Even in the cities, quiet walks — like those along the Chicago lakefront and on Belle Isle in Detroit — are protected and treasured.

The variety of walks in the Central States region is enormous. There are beautiful dune walks along the Great Lakes and the Gulf of Mexico, like the one up Mt. Tom in Indiana Dunes State Park; awesome mountain walks, like the climb up South Dakota's Bear Butte, the sacred mountain of the Cheyenne and Sioux; walks through the historic, architectural, and cultural sections of cities like New Orleans or along the sidewalks and through the alleys of small towns like Perrysburg, Ohio. There are cave walks and walks by waterfalls and quiet rivers; walks through deep forests and over wild prairies, around hot springs and along island paths. There are deserts here, too, and bitter winters, bear and buffalo, tremendous bird migrations, exotic tropical flowers, and stands of pine, along with cactus and sagebrush.

Among the walks presented here is a peaceful three-mile stretch of wilderness area in the Cuyahoga River Valley of Ohio, a walk that traces what was once the western boundary of the United States. Easily accessible from the highway, it is a perfect example of the ease with which automobile travel and travel by foot can be combined. By getting out of your car and discovering the area up close, you establish a special connection with it, and you share something with the people who live there now and with those who lived there long ago. These walks were nominated proudly by people who love them and walk them as often as they can. As you follow these walking trails into the Central States, America's heart in more than just a literary sense, imagine the footsteps of those who went before you, and think too of those yet to come.

Part 1

THE SOUTH CENTRAL REGION
Arkansas, Kansas, Louisiana, Missouri, Oklahoma, Texas

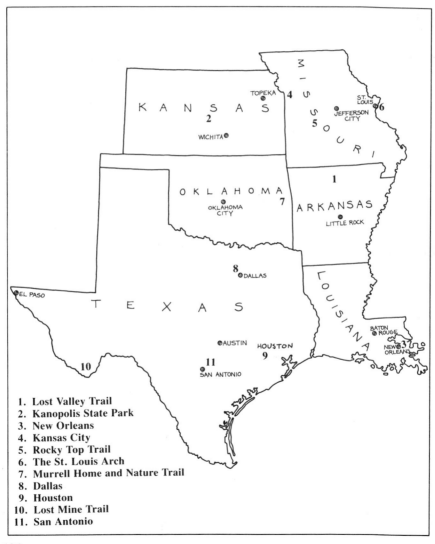

1. Lost Valley Trail
2. Kanopolis State Park
3. New Orleans
4. Kansas City
5. Rocky Top Trail
6. The St. Louis Arch
7. Murrell Home and Nature Trail
8. Dallas
9. Houston
10. Lost Mine Trail
11. San Antonio

BUFFALO NATIONAL RIVER
Lost Valley Trail

Directions: Take Highway 43 southwest from Harrison through Ponca, which borders the Buffalo River. Continue on Highway 43 to the short turnoff to Lost Valley campgrounds (about 35 miles from Harrison). The campground parking area provides excellent parking at the trailhead.

Best Season: Richard McCamant nominated this walk. He describes the trail as delightful any time of the year, from blooming flowers in spring to lush summer greenery, superb fall foliage, and finally frozen waterfalls and icicles hanging from the cliffs in winter. There is good fishing on the river, and park naturalists conduct programs at Lost Valley at intervals throughout the summer. Check at any information station in the park for schedules, or call (501) 741-5443.

Length: This is a two-loop trail of about 3½ miles. Allow two to three hours for the walk. Bring a flashlight if you want to explore the small cave at the end of the trail.

Degree of Difficulty: The first half of the walk is easy. The last portion is quite steep; be especially careful as you descend.

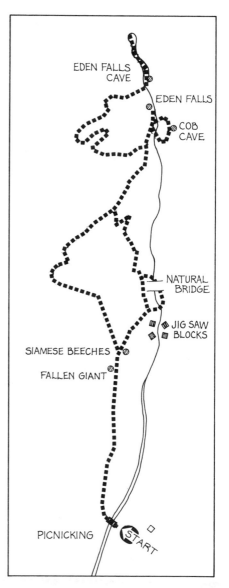

EDEN FALLS CAVE

EDEN FALLS

COB CAVE

NATURAL BRIDGE

JIG SAW BLOCKS

SIAMESE BEECHES

FALLEN GIANT

PICNICKING

START

Lost Valley Trail

The Buffalo is an unusual river. It is surrounded by civilization, yet it remains unspoiled. This is in part because, in 1972, it became the first stream in the country to be designated as a national river. The Buffalo winds through the Ozark Mountains for about 148 miles, passing stark limestone cliffs whose caves once provided shelter to the Indians. There are huge numbers and varieties of plants in the area — nearly 1,000 flowering varieties alone. The bluffs along the Buffalo are the highest in the Ozarks, rising up to 500 feet. They are formed from uplifted sea beds. The river, as if bent on revenge, relentlessly erodes them.

The Lost Valley Trail begins at the picnic area along Clark Creek, named for Abraham Clark, an early pioneer. Cross the footbridge and enjoy the steep, dramatic creek, which pours down the bluffs and over a series of waterfalls during wet weather. The clearing on the left may have been a pioneer homesite or a field for crops.

The trail continues past some magnificent trees, including the eastern red cedar, once heavily logged for use in pencil manufacture. The precise rows of holes in the trunks were made by the yellow-bellied sapsucker, a species of woodpecker that drills the holes and returns later to drink the escaping sap.

In this region, where the eastern woodlands meet the Great Plains, you'll find both eastern beech trees and sweet gum growing along the trail. One enormous tree will certainly catch your eye: it is called the Fallen Giant and is a graphic illustration of the last phase of a tree's life cycle. Bacteria and fungi are working on the hollow trunk, and termites, ants, and other insects feast on it. Birds find the insects in the soft interior, and mice and woodrats seek shelter in its hollows. Moss, mushroom, and other fungi grow in the rich decaying wood, which took its nutrients from the soil and now gives them back.

High above, where the trail forks, you'll see the Siamese Beeches, which have grown together in an X-shape. Naturalists assume that the two trees rubbed together until the bark was worn through and the growth cells underneath touched. Then natural growth took over and grafted them together.

Follow the right fork and you will see, along the course of Clark Creek, three massive stone blocks dubbed the "Jig Saw Blocks." They got their name because they resemble leftover bits of a jigsaw puzzle that had been scattered about; actually, of course, they fell from the bluff behind them. Any jigsaw these came from would have to have been pretty formidable; the largest block is 28 feet long, 20 feet wide, and 11 feet high and weighs more than 300 tons. The Fallen Giant shows the last stage of a tree's cycle; and the Jig Saw Blocks illustrate the first growth of the soil cycle. Lichens, made up of algae and fungi, grow on the rocks; the algae produce food, while the fungi absorb water and minerals. Their acid secretions help dissolve the rock surface, and cracks made by the lichens are widened further by freezing and thawing. When enough soil is worn from the rock, spores from moss and fern grow and reproduce.

The trail leads on to a natural bridge, carved through 50 feet of limestone by the violence of Clark Creek. This is really the gateway to the hidden gorge called Lost Valley. You can either take the trail to your left around the natural bridge, or you can climb through the bridge and walk up the creek bed. Both routes lead to Cob Cave, but be careful if you choose to go through the natural bridge. The opening is 10 feet wide, and there is a dry ledge above the stream, but you will have to step from rock to rock to get to the ledge. As you emerge on the far side, you will understand how the valley got its name.

If you wish to take only the first half of the trail, you can turn left instead of right at the fork, and follow the loop back to the Siamese beeches, where you rejoin the original route to the picnic area.

Cob Cave is located at the base of a 200-foot bluff, and has served as a shelter for man for perhaps 2,000 years. Archaic Indians lived here and left behind the corn cobs that give the cave its name. Walk to the back of the cave (carefully) to really appreciate its dimensions: 50 feet in height, 150 feet deep, 260 feet from end to end.

Just a bit farther up the trail Clark Creek makes its dramatic entrance into Lost Valley through four waterfalls, totaling 170 feet. These are known as Eden Falls, and the pool fed by them is in a romantic and beautiful spot. In dry weather the falls become a delicate trickle, revealing their own beauty as they expose the mossy ledges.

Return now to the main trail and continue your climb to Eden Falls Cave. A stream, beginning spectacularly 200 feet deep in the cave, flows from an opening at the top of a circular room and drops 35 feet to a small pool at the floor of the cavern. From there it pours out of the cave through a low passageway. Again, use caution exploring the depths of the cave and be sure to have a flashlight.

To return, retrace your steps to the fork in the trail between Cob Cave and the natural bridge, and bear right on the loop back to the Siamese Beeches. From there you return along the same trail to the picnic area.

Nominator Richard McCamant calls this walk "one of the most varied and romantic trails in the country." He suggests visitors may want to make time for a canoe float down the Buffalo, available at about 25 park concessions along the river; the half-day float is a nice complement to the trail walk.

Kansas

KANOPOLIS STATE PARK

Directions: Near Salina, Kansas, Kanopolis State Park is approximately 20 miles south of I–70, or 25 miles west of I–135.

Best Season: Late spring through early autumn.

Length: ¾ mile; about 30 to 45 minutes.

Degree of Difficulty: Moderately difficult, due to the ruggedness of the physical environment. Bring an ample supply of water and, during the summer months, watch out for snakes and poison ivy.

Kanopolis State Park Nature Trail

The rewards of this walk through the Smoky Hill region of Kansas are numerous. It takes you along rolling hills and sandy bottoms, among native wildflowers and yucca, past magnificent rock formations and caves, by fish ponds, and over old buffalo trails. You are likely to see hawks, owls, gopher burrows, and occasionally turkey buzzards.

Although there is no drinking water on the trail, it was water that created the beautiful sculpture of the walk. The pestle and mortar rock formations in the upper reaches were produced by the carving action of the water and the grinding of harder rocks, forming the bowl (or mortar) at the base holding its own pestle. Buffalo tracks are still visible in the soft sandstone path. Herds of buffalo used to come here for precious water, and water seepage formed the caves along the trail. Several of these caves (now drowned in the lake created by Kanopolis Dam) were used by early homesteaders as residences and schoolrooms sometime after 1870. Even the great canyons were formed by water draining across the soft Dakota sandstone into the Smoky Hill River. The steepest of the box canyons were once used to trap wild horses or to hold cattle in the days of the Old West, and the rock ledges on the canyon walls support the nests of hawks and owls. These pink cliffs are colored with hematite, an iron oxide.

Besides the great birds, there is plenty of life on the trail. The green, sharp-pointed plants that abound on the walk are yucca, used as basket fibers by the Indians. Their roots furnished a kind of shampoo. The blue-stem grass provides food for the animals, and the gopher burrows, in addition to furnishing safety from predators, are a food line in winter when the gophers' main menu item is roots. In the spring, catfish, perch, and bass swim upstream from Kanopolis Lake to lay their eggs in the fish

ponds; this is one of the old Indian fishing grounds, where nets were spread to capture the bass and crappie that dominated the waters.

Views along the hiking trail are wonderfully varied according to the time of day. Brilliant sunsets add a reddened haze to the already pink cliffs; the bright sun of midday softens the colors; and the slanting rays of twilight awaken new images on the canyon walls. Chris Stanfield nominated this walk. He recalls dramatic sunsets when "The sun seemed to be swallowed up by the dark, rich soil, giving it an abundance of colors that were reflected more brightly by the cumulus clouds overhead."

Sudden storms come from the Southwest, there are tremendous winds and spring rains, and in fall the walk lies in the path of migrating birds: whooping cranes, sand cranes, Canada snow geese, teals, and mallards all pass over on crisp fall days when you need a sweater to feel comfortable. "No matter how often I walk this trail," enthused Chris Stanfield, "I always think at the end that I've got to come back, because I didn't have enough time to look at the new parts: a special kind of wildflower might have just bloomed or erosion might have revealed new rock formations or new crystals. It's always new."

Louisiana

NEW ORLEANS
The French Quarter

Directions: Begin this walk at the New Orleans Police Department, Vieux Carré District, 334 Royal Street.

Best Season: Spring and fall are best; summers are hot, but okay, and winters are usually mild. Plan to take this walk during the day.

Length: Anywhere from a half hour to two days.

Degree of Difficulty: Easy; there are no hazards other than what happens to your waistline when you eat the deliciously rich food.

Exploring the Vieux Carré

One of the most delightful walks on earth is through the 12-block area of New Orleans' Vieux Carré, or French Quarter, nicknamed "America's European masterpiece." Much of the Quarter is designed for walkers who share it with the St. Charles streetcars and horse-drawn carriages. 334 Royal Street, where this walk begins, is a beautiful old building, which was completed in 1826 to house the old Bank of Louisiana and was for many years home to the Visitor Information Center. The Information Center has recently moved to 529 St. Ann Street, but you can still find material on virtually every house and alley in the French Quarter at 334 Royal.

As you walk out the door of this historic building, you are in what used to be the financial hub of the city, the corner of Conti and Royal, where three great banks of the early 1800s stand on three corners. Turn left on Royal toward Canal Street and note the house at 127 Royal. Here the secret society, the Mistick Krewe of Comus, was set up to save the Mardi Gras, which was in danger of being prohibited because of the violence that surrounded the celebrations. Strolling back along Royal Street toward Jackson Square, the heart of the French Quarter, you are walking along the route once taken by Tennessee Williams' "Streetcar Named Desire," now in retirement at the Old United States Mint, which stands on the site of Fort San Carlos in the 400 block of Esplanade. You can shop for bits of the past on your way to the Square; Royal Street is best known for its antique shops.

If you're getting an early start on your walk, you may want to fortify yourself at Brennan's at 417 Royal, where New Orleans' most famous breakfasts are served in a mansion built in 1801 for Degas' grandfather. Cocktails were born at a drugstore at 437 Royal in the early 19th century, when drinks were served in egg cups after the meetings of the local Masonic Lodge.

Merieult House at 533 Royal Street was one of the few buildings that escaped the terrible fire of 1794. It was built in 1792 by Jean François Merieult, whose beautiful wife was offered a castle by Napoleon in exchange for her glorious head of red hair. Madame turned down the castle and kept her hair. The famous Court of the Two Sisters is at 615 Royal. You should definitely visit it for a meal, or at least a refreshing drink on the lovely patio, complete with wishing well.

At the corner of St. Peter Street is the Maison LeMonnier, frequently called the first skyscraper, built in 1811 by Dr. Yves LeMonnier. His third-floor study is considered to be the most beautiful room (architecturally) in the city. In 1869 Antoine Alciatoire operated it as a boarding house. Here he served such magnificent dishes that he opened the restaurant that gave him his international fame. Antoine's is still operated on St. Louis Street by his descendants.

At the next corner is Pirates Alley. Here, according to legend, Major-General Jackson conferred with the freebooting Lafitte brothers concerning the defense of New Orleans against the British in 1814. From Pirates Alley you emerge onto Jackson Square, between the St. Louis Cathedral and the Cabildo. Dedicated on Christmas Eve, 1794, the Cathedral is the oldest in the United States. Two churches stood on this spot; the first destroyed by a hurricane; the second burned on Good Friday, 1788. The bells were kept silent for religious reasons, and the alarm was sounded too late to save the 850 buildings in the Quarter that burned. Spain donated the stained-glass windows that show the period of Spanish colonialism in New Orleans.

On the other side of Pirates Alley is the Cabildo, also a replacement of a building that burned in the 1788 fire. It was used as a guardhouse and police station by the French in the 1750s. During the Spanish occupation it was the center of government. Now it is a museum. Here are exhibits of plantations and riverboats and Napoleon's death mask. The Emperor's personal physician, who moved to New Orleans, donated it to the city.

By this time the sights and the scents of Jackson Square will have tempted you to stay awhile. You will want to spend quite a bit of time here, watching the musicians, mimes, pavement artists, and magicians. Established in 1721 as a military drill field, the Square changed names as it changed nationalities; it became the Place d'Armes under the French, then the Plaza de Armas when Spain took over the colony; the flag has changed colors seven times.

Decatur Street, on the other side of the Square, used to be right on the Mississippi, before the levees. Where St. Peter and Decatur meet you'll find the Jackson Brewery, converted (it was home of Jax Beer) into a complex of restaurants, shopping, and entertainment, all with a New Orleans flair. As soon as you are able to extract yourself from the Brewery, head past the Moon Walk (named for Mayor "Moon" Landrieu), across St. Ann from the French Market. Stop at the Café du Monde. At an outdoor table you can enjoy the pleasant odor of coffee, chickory, and freshly made donuts which drifts across the Market and over Jackson Square. The French Market's graceful arcades and colonnades are crammed with delicacies: pralines and spices, fresh breads, wonderful cheeses. The Farmer's Market, attached to this, is an animated place of bargaining and conversation and beautifully arranged fresh fruits and flowers. On weekends there is a famous flea market here, where Barracks Street crosses Decatur, behind the French Market itself.

Walk over to Gov. Nicholls Street, past the many 19th-century historic homes, and up to Royal again. On the corner (1140) is the LaLaurie House, the city's most famous private home. It is believed by many to be haunted. A ghostly young black child reportedly walks the balcony, and moans are said to emanate from the place after dark. The story behind all this is a terrible one. The house was built by Louis Berthelemy de MacCarthy. One of his five children, the beautiful Delphine LaLaurie, made it a brilliant center of New Orleans society. There was, however, persistent gossip about her. Her servants were said to be mistreated; in 1833 she was taken to court on the testimony of a neighbor who had seen her mercilessly lashing a young slave. The slave fell from the rooftop soon after and died in the courtyard below. Delphine was merely fined. The climax came on April 10, 1834, when a fire broke out in the LaLaurie house. Neighbors, attempting to save the furniture, broke through a locked door and found seven starving slaves chained in painful positions. A crowd of outraged citizens formed outside the house, but Delphine broke through in her carriage and escaped to Europe. After her body was secretly brought back to New Orleans for burial the haunting began.

Continue now a block up Gov. Nicholls to Bourbon Street and turn left. On the corner of St. Phillip is Lafitte's Blacksmith Shop, at #941. This cottage, now a bar, supposedly served as a cover for the piratical enterprises of the swashbuckling brothers Lafitte. Continuing along Bourbon Street, you enter the heart of New Orleans' hottest bars, nightclubs, and restaurants. Bourbon Street leaps into life after dark (although it's not exactly "asleep" by day). Toward the Canal Street end, at 238 Bour-

115

bon Street, is the Old Absinthe House, built in 1806. Leave your calling card on the wall with the thousands of others and enjoy a cooling drink (not absinthe, though; it's illegal).

You may want to slip up to 813 Bienville Street, Arnaud's, and enjoy some of the most magnificent food on earth; or wander back along St. Peter, from which you can detour to Burgundy Street. At #721 Burgundy you can wallow in red beans, rice, and gumbo, along with some extraordinary fried chicken at Buster Homes's famous place.

"The European atmosphere and Southern ambience of the French Quarter, bordered by the Mississippi River and containing numerous architecturally and historically significant buildings, make it one of America's first National Historic Districts," says Dawson Corley, who submitted the walk. We couldn't agree more.

Missouri

KANSAS CITY

Directions: Kansas City is the "Heart of America," located near the geographic center of the continental United States. It is in northwest Missouri, on the Kansas border. Kansas City, Kansas, is just across the Missouri River. Take I–70 west from St. Louis or east from Topeka, Kansas. Follow the signs downtown.

Best Season: For outdoor walking spring and summer; for indoor walking choose winter or late summer.

Length: Indoor walks offer hundreds of route variations, although it's best to keep them under 3 miles or one hour's worth of walking. The Crown Center Walk is approximately 2 miles round trip.

Degree of Difficulty: Easy, although you can make it more difficult by going from level to level using the stairs instead of the escalator.

America's Mall Walking Capitol

From Nebraska, Iowa, Oklahoma, and even Mexico travelers come to Kansas City for shopping. And the best shopping is done on foot in Kansas City's malls where mall exercise walking has also become the rage. From the downtown shopping centers to the outlying malls like

Ward Parkway, mall walkers turn out by the hundreds, so many that they have restricted "mall walking" to off peak shopping hours. However if you mix shopping with your walking you should be safe from any prohibitions.

The jewel of the seven mall walking areas is Kansas City's Crown Center. It is owned by a subsidiary of Hallmark Cards and consists of two hotels, shopping areas, a 10-acre Center Square, and a residential apartment complex already covering half the 85-acre site, which has been described as a "city within a city." The Center is also near one of Kansas City's prettiest parks, Penn Valley Park, which includes a five-mile fitness trail winding through its 175 acres.

You can walk or drive to Crown Center from Kansas City. Follow Main Street or Grand Avenue South to Pershing Road. The Center's Westin Hotel is on Pershing between Grand and Main.

Start your walk by entering the lobby of the Westin Crown Center. The Hotel is a 20-story structure built by Chicago Architect Harry Weese. Proceed to the back of the lobby until you see a seventy-foot landscaped hill which rises out of the back of the lobby. This is Signboard Hill, a ten-million-year-old outcrop made of limestone. Shaped originally by the Missouri River, it was reshaped in the early 1970s and incorporated into the lobby of the Westin Hotel. Take the Grand Staircase up to the Mezzanine floor of the hotel. Walk up the wooden stairway and walkway which takes you up to the bluff of the hill. The hill is five stories high and has been elaborately landscaped with weeping fig trees, boulders, and flowering plants. It is not a scene you would expect to find in a hotel lobby but it is really the highpoint of this walking tour. As you climb Signboard Hill you see a series of waterfalls which flow into the 50-foot pool below. The sound of running water is very soothing and creates a feeling of detachment from the business world that this hotel was built to serve. Some executives attending business conferences walk this route in jogging clothes every morning during their stay at the hotel, according to Sales Manager Patricia Wyatt.

At the top of the bluff you can enter the Hotel Health Club and Pool Area. From there you can either return to the lobby the way you came or take the stairs on the left down to the fourth floor Game Deck. From there you can see Kansas City's Union Station, where Hemingway arrived to do his six-month journalist's tour for the Kansas City *Star*. Walk to the west side of the game room by the bluff side of the hotel and descend the stairway on the outside of the building to the ground floor. From this staircase you have a spectacular view of all Kansas City below. On the ground floor re-enter the lobby and go left on the passageway connecting the hotel to the shopping center.

If you want to do some brisk walking, choose the early morning period from 6 to 8 a.m. when the shops are not open. Many residents, like John Cox, owner of Robinson's Shoe Store chain, take their morning constitutional in this area before going to work. The escalators are still turned off; you can walk up and down them.

The shopping center itself stretches out for a one-half mile walking distance on three separate floors containing restaurants, art galleries, toy and card shops. If you combine shopping with your walk, enter Hall's Department Store from the third level. Go through the store and find the escalator and stairs at the other end to go down two flights where you can exit onto the Crown Center Square. Walk the half mile distance once around the Square and return into Hall's on the third level, cross back into the shopping center, down its stairs, and back into the Westin Hotel lobby.

ROCKY TOP TRAIL
Lake of the Ozarks State Park

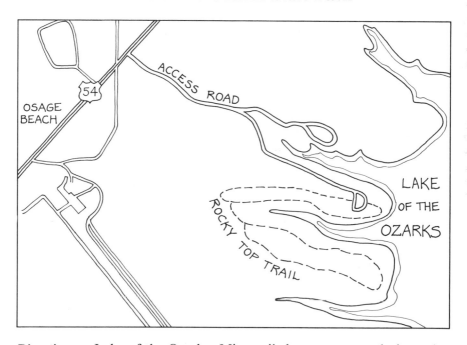

Directions: Lake of the Ozarks, Missouri's largest state park, is on the eastern border of the Lake of the Ozarks, sometimes called the "Missouri Dragon" because of its twisting shoreline of 1,375 miles. Rocky Top Trail begins at Grand Glaize Beach, about two and a half miles southwest of the Grand Glaize Bridge on Highway 54 in Osage Beach. The trailhead is across the road from the picnic shelter, where there is ample parking.

Best Season: This is an interesting walk at any time of the year, with a special bonus from early October to mid-March. That's when you can see the bald eagles that winter on the high bluffs at the end of the trail.

Length: The route is made up of two 1½-mile loops, which form a figure 8. With pauses to enjoy the scenery and wildlife along the trail, a leisurely walk takes about an hour and a quarter. A beach and boat ramp are nearby, so there is enough diversion for a full day's pleasure.

Degree of Difficulty: The walk is a moderate one; the second half of the trail winds to the top of a 100-foot-high bluff.

Rocky Top Trail

Tom Nagel, who nominated this walk, says, "This is my favorite trail at Lake of the Ozarks State Park because varied plant and animal communities, as well as rock outcroppings along the way, provide continually changing scenery." As you walk the three miles of trail, you will pass through a desert-like environment, an oak woods, along the shores of a man-made lake, and into a rich forest of flowering dogwood, hardwoods, and ferns, with wild turkey and deer and other forest animals.

"Rocky Top Glade is the most prominent natural feature on the first loop of the trail," explains Nagel. "In the Ozarks, glades are natural, rocky openings in the forest and, during the hot summer months, the closest we get to desert in Missouri. Tarantulas and scorpions (neither species is dangerous in Missouri) are seldom seen by hikers since they take refuge beneath rocks and burrows by day and come out at night. Fence lizards and six-lined race-runners (another type of lizard) live on the glades. The showy Indian paint brush and yellow coneflower are also found here. The latter species is found only in Missouri and extreme Southern Arkansas. Also, on the first loop, a dry forest of post oak and black jack oak is predominant on a south-facing slope. About 300 yards of the first loop trail parallels the lake shore."

The second loop takes you into a lush forest, and up to a really spectacular view of the park. "This second loop," says Nagel, "traverses a rich north-facing slope dominated by sugar maple and white oak with Missouri's state tree, the flowering dogwood, in the understory. In places, maidenhair and Christmas ferns cover the forest floor. Whitetail deer and wild turkey can sometimes be seen here. This portion of the trail offers a rich tapestry of fall color and a variety of spring wildflower, including bellwort and bloodroot. The trail winds to the top of a 100-foot-high bluff offering a scenic view down the Grand Glaize Arm into Lake of the Ozarks State Park." The lakeview is particularly beautiful because of the twisting, irregular shoreline and the narrowness of the lake, more like a great river. Long fingers of land extend into the water, and the high bluffs are colored with columbine in the spring. The bluffs are the nesting places of turkey buzzards and cliff swallows.

Lake of the Ozarks State Park has eight other walking trails, one of which allows backpacking. Another permits horseback riding as well. All the trails, like Rocky Top, are identified with entrance signs and have directional arrows and colored markers. A map with trail descriptions is available at the park office, where you can also pick up a self-guiding booklet that describes a unique water trail for boaters, marked by buoys. A Trail Center with additional information on sights to see along other park trails is on Highway 134, one mile from the park entrance, at the intersection of Highways 42 and 134. For further information, write: Lake of the Ozarks State Park, Kaiser, MO 65047.

THE ST. LOUIS ARCH

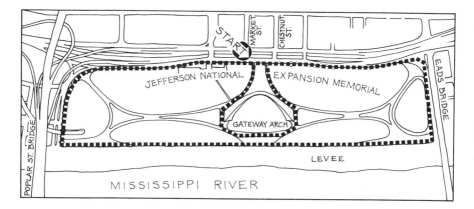

Directions: The walk starts at Market Street and Memorial Drive, just east of I–70 at the western edge of Jefferson National Expansion Memorial Park.

Best Season: This walk can be enjoyed any time of year; choose the season you like best.

Length: 1½ miles.

Degree of Difficulty: Easy, except for two sets of steps, which can be avoided by taking a different route at that point. The paths are well lit and reasonably safe during the day. Avoid this walk at night.

Around the St. Louis Arch

St. Louis's signature is, of course, the stainless steel Gateway Arch designed by Eero Saarinen as a symbol of the city's role as gateway to the West. One of the most visited tourist attractions in the country, the arch is amazing from every perspective; the best way to appreciate it is to walk around it.

From the park, follow the path on its curving route south, past the arch. Turn right where the path ends and continue to the southeast plaza. There you can step up to a raised deck and enjoy the panorama of the Mississippi as it rounds the St. Louis bend, laced with bridges to the south.

Now, turn around and go straight ahead to the long flight of steps down to the street, where you'll find another flight up to the opposite end of the park. To avoid the steps, bear left at the plaza and retrace the path part way. This time continue to the right where the original path swings left. This takes you directly past the arch on the river side and over to the plaza at the other end of the park.

As you pass the arch you'll see charming restaurants along the levee, built on the riverboats directly in front of the arch. You may want to pause for a bite and a leisurely chance to enjoy the view, before you approach the raised platform at the northwest corner. From here you can see the Eads Bridge, which literally took the steam out of the steamboats; before this bridge was built, the boats held a monopoly on traffic crossing the Mississippi.

Turning away from the plaza, return by the easy route, taking the dogleg to the right. This brings you back behind the arch (away from the river) to the path that takes you out of the park, between Market and Chestnut streets, just north of the one by which you entered.

Oklahoma

MURRELL HOME AND NATURE TRAIL

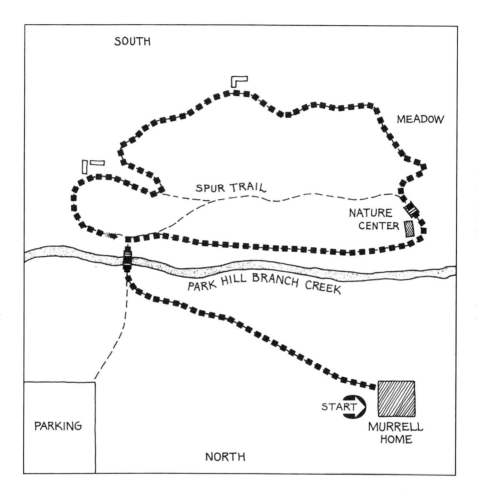

Directions: From Tahlequah, take State Highway 82 south for three miles, then follow it east for one mile to the Murrell Home. From I–40, take Highway 82 north, toward Tahlequah. Watch for signs and stop for a self-guided description of the walk before you begin. For additional information call (918) 456-2751. The Murrell Home is closed on Thanksgiving and Christmas.

Best Season: Spring and fall, when temperatures are less severe. Trees and flowers are in bloom in spring, and the fall colors are beautiful.

Length: The Nature Trail is a half mile to a mile, depending on the spurs you decide to take. You can walk it in a half hour to an hour, but you'll want to leave plenty of time to explore the Murrell Home. There is enough to do in the surrounding area to spend a whole day.

Degree of Difficulty: Easy.

Murrell Home and Nature Trail

The Murrell Home, a beautiful example of antebellum style, was built around 1845 by George Murrell, who imported furnishings from France and Italy for his splendid new home. At one time a room on the first floor was an indoor aviary, filled with flowering plants and exotic birds.

Murrell himself was colorful. The Cherokee Indians, forced west from their homes, had arrived in Oklahoma across the "Trail of Tears." Murrell was closely allied to the Cherokee; in fact, he married the niece of Cherokee Chief John Ross. When she died, he married her sister. Murrell's home was the scene of many social gatherings for both the Cherokee and the soldiers of nearby Fort Gibson, until the Civil War. Then Murrell left his home to fight for the Confederate Army, never to return. "Hunter's Home," as Murrell dubbed his mansion, survived the raids and looting after the war; and, in 1948, the State of Oklahoma purchased and restored the mansion and its grounds.

Exploration of the house complements the walk along the Nature Trail, once a part of the Murrell grounds. The trail passes through what had been an imposing orchard during the heyday of the Murrell Home, when carriages full of hoopskirted ladies drew up to the door and candles lit the elegant windows. Now the old orchard is a woodland haven for blue herons, belted kingfishers, chipmunks, and deer. The round nests of squirrels are clearly visible high in the trees, and black-eyed Susans, brilliant sumac, and delicate wildflowers edge the trail. Woodpeckers drum on the trees along the path as harmless snakes slip along in search of mice; and you can hear the songs of the cedar waxwing, the tufted titmouse, and the crested flycatcher, that curious bird that decorates its nest with abandoned snakeskin. Frogs and box turtles live in the creek that runs through the area, and rabbits and raccoons come there to drink. The place is a paradise of lush ferns. Among them you'll find evergreen Christmas fern and the rattlesnake fern.

Kris Marek, who nominated this walk, explains that visitors frequently combine the various activities for a daylong stay. "Since it is located adjacent to an historic site and recreation facilities," she says, "it provides an interesting and diverse day's outing."

DALLAS
White Rock Lake Park

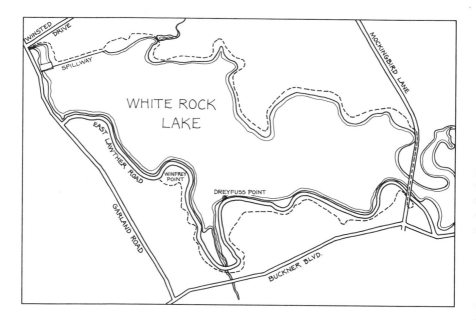

Directions: To get to White Rock Lake Park from downtown Dallas, take I–30 east. Exit on Winslow, turn left, and continue until you reach East Grand. Turn right. East Grand becomes Garland Road. Turn left on East Lawther to enter the park. Follow signs for parking.

Best Season: Year round. The trail is used by joggers, bicyclists, and walkers all year and at all times of day. If you are walking, take care to stay out of the way of bikers and joggers. (Olympic bicyclists use the course for training; signs are posted to keep the bicyclists on certain parts of the path and on the streets of the park, separate from the jogging trail.) Exercise stations are located all along the path.

Length: The Bike and Hike Trail is 11.8 miles. It is well marked, so you can choose the distance for which you have the time and/or inclination. If you plan to walk the entire 11.8 miles at a leisurely pace, count on about five hours. Water and restrooms are available; bring a picnic lunch.

Degree of Difficulty: Easy. The almost 1,000-acre White Rock Lake Park is patroled by police on horseback and on bicycles, but nighttime strolling is not recommended.

White Rock Lake Bike and Hike Trail

Man-made White Rock Lake was scooped out of brittle Texas white rock in the 1900s. It has long been a recreation focus for Dallasites; and the Bike and Hike Trail, which loops around the lake and was completed in 1973, is a particularly popular place. The paved path curves around the lake in an open area; near the lake large, graceful willow trees thrive.

White Rock Lake is used for sailing regattas, motorboats, and waterskiing, so there is a lot to see while tooling along the path. A bicycle festival is held each March, and the fireworks festivals and Christmas flotilla of trees and lights attract crowds of often over 100,000 people.

Many of the pavilions, shelters, and buildings at White Rock Lake were built by the WPA in the 1930s and '40s when the recreation area was in its heyday. Around the turn of the century, when the lake was built, some of the huge mansions were built by the Texas wealthy. The Hunt mansion, for example, still occupied by Bunker Hunt, was constructed then.

HOUSTON
A Walk through the Underground Network

Directions: Central Houston is accessible from the north or south via I-45, and from the east or west via I-10. This walk begins at the Central Public Library downtown between Bagby and Smith on Lamar (you will find ample parking in the second basement).

Best Season: Because this entire walk is underground it can be taken at any time of the year. However, many of the tunnels are closed on weekends, so you should try this route during the week.

Length: This walk can be completed in about two and a half hours, but because you'll want to spend time shopping and refreshing yourself at the arcades and cafes, you might want to make a day of it.

Degree of Difficulty: Quite easy (to walk, not necessarily to find your way through).

An Unusual View of Houston

This unusual, indoor walk was nominated by Douglas Milburn and Eli Zal, ardent walkers and writers. From the Library parking garage cross Bagby at Lamar to enter Sam Houston Park, where you'll find the key to Houston's past. The long Row to your left is a replica of the first block of commercial buildings in the city. The Yesteryear Shop in the Row offers a free brochure on the park. On the other side of the Row there are several 19th-century houses including the oldest house in the county, a log cabin built around 1824 and known as the "Old Place." Guided tours are available for the historic homes.

Turn south on Bagby at Lamar to Dallas Street; turn left on Dallas and go one block to the Allen Cen-

ter, where you can enter the downtown tunnel system and enjoy the huge tapestry, "Angelstone." Take the escalator down one level, double back, take a quick right and left; at the end of the hallway turn left through the glass doors, then right at a set of curving mirrors. If you stand at the center of the group and speak, you get both visual and sound echoes. Continue down the beige tunnel to another set of the curving mirrors and turn right; make another right turn at the red wall. Go through the glass doors and up the long escalator to the lobby of the Hyatt Regency Hotel which has an enormous atrium, glass elevators, and a revolving Spindletop.

Cross the lobby to the escalator for the mezzanine, which leads you to the skywalk. There you will have an excellent view of the 54-story First International Plaza, the heavily mirrored Entex Building, and the Shamrock Hilton to the south. Continue across the skywalk to the mezzanine of the Milam Building, and walk around the corner diagonally opposite, over the intersection of Milam and Lamar. Take the escalator to the ground level, walk straight ahead 50 feet, then turn right, still inside the building; after 75 feet turn right onto the down escalator, back into the tunnels.

Stepping off the escalator you'll find a shopping plaza. Turn right, then left into the short wide tunnel. At the end turn right into the white tile tunnel. Turn right at the Tenneco Building sign into a mint green tunnel. Keep going; turn left into another mint green tunnel and go through the wood-paneled underground lobby. Turn right toward the Ten-ten Parking garage, and at the end of the tunnel turn left through the glass doors toward the Bank of the Southwest.

Go on down the gray tunnel past the large window on your left and turn right by the Bank of the Southwest mall. Pass the double escalators and, in the far left corner of the mall, enter the tunnel to the Commerce Building. Travis Street is above you. Bear right, past another escalator on the left and enter the brown tunnel toward Woolworth's. Turn right through a short tunnel, then left toward the Southern National Bank. Go up four steps and keep walking (Corrigan's Jewelers on the right is an indication that you are still with us). Jog right, then left, passing the escalators on the left. Bend left, then right, and go down a short slope; ascend nine steps and a curving staircase into Houston Center.

Take the escalator up one flight, as Peter Fonda did in the 1976 film *Futureworld*. The view here is of the Esperson Buildings, the Old Gulf Building, and James Coney Island at ground level on Walker Street, where you can devour hotdogs in the atmosphere of the 1930s. Turn right up the short escalator and continue straight ahead past the elevators to the vast lobby, where photographers are vehemently forbidden to take advantage of the view.

Go out the glass doors, onto the plaza above San Jacinto Street, turn right to the south railing, where you'll see the Texas Medical Center and the spire of the First Presbyterian Church.

Go back to the fountain on the plaza and enter the door to the right. Turn right, passing a stainless steel wall sculpture, one of three you will pass by the same sculptor. Continue past the escalators to the 28-star Watmough Flag which dates from 1845. Go down the escalators to the ground level and leave the building onto McKinney. Turn west and continue across San Jacinto and Fannin and turn south on Fannin. Turn into Sakowitz, which the authors say "is to Nieman's what Seville is to Rolls Royce. Or maybe what Avis is to Hertz." You can shop your way through the store to Main Street on the west side, and cross to Foley's where "you go to have your faith in American consumerism revived." Turn south on Main, passing the old Humble Building, the original home office of the company that later became Esso, then Exxon. Turn west when you get to Clay and proceed to Milam, where you'll see the red and yellow 15-story YMCA; cross Louisiana and continue west past the Hyatt Garage. Cross Smith to the R. E. "Bob" Smith Fountain, which the nominators simply describe as "a plaster and Plexiglass undertaking of some volume." Two blocks southwest you'll see the Antioch Baptist Church, one of the oldest churches in the city; turn south on Smith Street and continue past the "High Plains Drifter," winner of a national sculpture contest, to Lamar, where you can turn west and find your car at the Public Library.

For more walks in Houston, see Doug Milburn's book, *The Last American City: An Intrepid Guide to Houston.*

128

LOST MINE TRAIL
Big Bend National Park

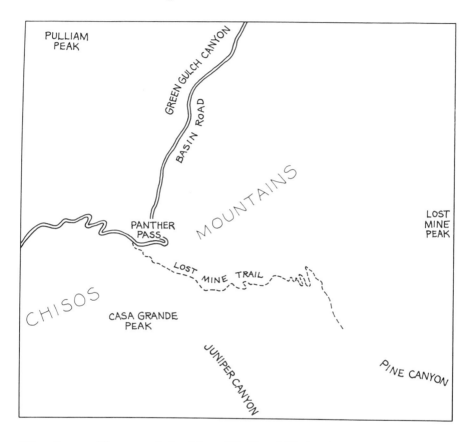

Directions: Three roads lead into Big Bend National Park, located in the southern tip of West Texas: U.S. 385, State Highway 118, and Route 170. From Marathon, take U.S. 385; from Alpine, take State Highway 118; from Marfa, take U.S. 67 south to Presidio and Route 170 east to the park. Highways 67, 118, and 385 all turn south from U.S. 90. There is no entrance fee for the park; lodgings and restaurants are in the Chisos Basin, near the start of the walk. Campgrounds and grocery stores, showers, and laundry facilities are scattered throughout the park.

Best Season: Year round. In summer an occasional thunderstorm can add to the drama of the landscape, and fall colors heighten contrasts in autumn.

Length: 5 miles round trip. Allow about four hours.

Degree of Difficulty: The National Park Service rates this walk as moderate, steep in spots, but with benches along the way for rest stops.
 The trail rises gradually up a gentle slope to a saddle between two peaks, then climbs over switchbacks to a high ridge separating Pine and Juniper canyons. For an easy walk, take only the first mile of the trail. Stop at the Juniper Canyon Overlook at the saddle, where you'll find a bench for enjoying the view. Be sure to carry ample water with you; don't drink untreated spring water. Lost Mine Trail may be walked at specified times with a naturalist guide. To arrange a guided walk, check the naturalist activity schedules posted throughout the park.

Lost Mine Trail
 The Lost Mine Trail starts at Panther Pass on the way to the Chisos Basin and proceeds through the spectacular scenery of the Chisos Mountains, a green island surrounded by desert. In the mountains the evergreen pinyon pine grows above a 4,800-foot elevation; since the trail goes from about 5,600 feet to 6,580 feet, the pines grow thickly on the slopes, providing food for birds and rodents, who are kept in check by the fox and cougar that inhabit this region. There are also whitetailed deer and hundreds of species of birds. Juniper and oak line the trail, as well as Mexican Drooping Juniper. This curious tree, which in the United States grows only in the Chisos Mountains, always looks wilted, but is not lacking water. Ash, with sweet-smelling blossoms, decorate the slopes in spring; and blooming plants such as asters, daisies, and sunflowers add their own bits of color to the mountains.
 The contrasts in Big Bend National Park are remarkable. Below the lush green mountains lies the Chihuahuan Desert. Here there are more than 60 species of cacti, as well as numerous other plants whose development is devoted to survival in the desert: the ocotillo, for example, which sheds its leaves in drought and bears bright red flowers that attract hummingbirds; and the lechuguilla, a small agave with dagger-sharp leaves to protect it against both man and beast.
 As you walk up the gentle slope of the first mile of the trail, you get a good view of Green Gulch, where the road enters the mountains. The high point on the left of the gulch is Pulliam Bluff, named for a pioneer ranching family; further to the left is the great dome of Vernon Bailey Peak. The high rocky cliff to the right of Green Gulch is the end of Lost Mine Peak. The hills visible between Pulliam Bluff and the rocky cliff on the right are the Rosillos, just outside the park.
 When you arrive at the saddle, a little over a mile along the trail, you can rest, and look out over Juniper Canyon, before undertaking the switchbacks beyond. The canyon was formed by millions of years of erosion on an uplifted inland sea bed. The trees, skyscapes, and sharp sculpture of Juniper Canyon, and the distant mountains softening and merging

with the clouds, provide pleasant vistas at this half-way stop along the trail. If the steep section looks too formidable, this is the place to turn back.

After climbing up the switchbacks for about two miles, look back at the narrow ridge extending toward Casa Grande. This ridge top divides the pine woodland from the dry, warm slopes to the south. At the top of the ridge, the trail runs nearly level with a bench, where you can enjoy the views of Pine and Juniper canyons and Lost Mine Peak, the rocky summit directly across the canyon.

Nobody seems to know whether the Lost Mine really existed or whether it is merely a campfire story worthy of Indiana Jones. The early Spanish explorers developed many mines in the Southwest; and legend tells of a rich ore strike near the summit of Lost Mine Peak, where prisoners were brought blindfolded from Presidio San Vicente to work the mines. The ruins of the presidio exist, about 20 miles southeast of the peak, across the Rio Grande in Mexico. The Indians are said to have killed all the Spaniards and sealed the mine entrance to block further development; but the legend states that if a man stands at the door of the chapel at Presidio San Vicente on Easter morning, he can see the sun's first rays strike the peak at the entrance to the mine.

There are many trails of varying length in the park but the Lost Mine route is special, combining the desert with the woodlands, and giving some wonderful views of the mountains and canyons of this part of the country.

SAN ANTONIO

Directions: This walk begins at Alamo Plaza in downtown San Antonio, easily accessible from Route 37. Park your car in one of the lots behind the Alamo.

Best Season: Spring, fall, and winter.

Length: About 1½ miles; the time span is flexible, depending on how many stops you make in the little cafés and boutiques and on how long you linger in the Alamo section.

Degree of Difficulty: Easy.

Paseo del Rio

Before you begin your walk along the river, stop to "remember the Alamo." But don't enter the fortress-like chapel just yet. From the parking lot, turn left and enter through the gate that leads into the gardens,

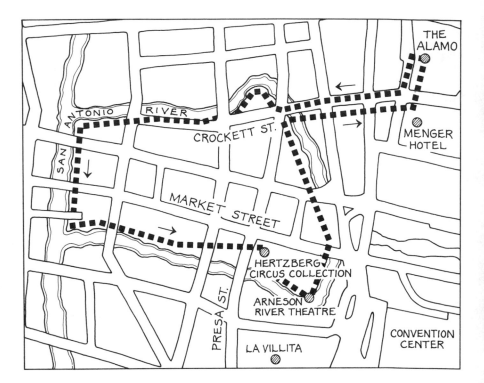

then into a courtyard with an ancient oak and wishing well. Turn left and face the Long Barracks, the only remaining part of the original fortification. Step across to the Alamo Theater and Museum. Here you can see a very moving sight and sound show on the hopeless battle in which Davy Crockett and 187 other Americans died for Texas independence. The museum exhibits are poignant reminders that real people were involved in this struggle, not remote historical figures.

Built in the 1740s, the Alamo, which stands on the site of a Spanish mission established in 1718, is considered the "Cradle of Texas Liberty." Near the flagpole on the lawn is the spot where Davy Crockett was killed in the battle, following a 13-day siege. To the right, where a Japanese yew grows today, is where Jim Bowie died. Colonel William Travis was shot where the post office now stands. His small group of men tried in vain to stop the 4,000 men led by Santa Anna. A month and a half later, independence fighters, inspired by the battle cry "Remember the Alamo!," surprised the Mexican ruler at San Jacinto. Under the leadership of Sam Houston, 783 men, victorious against the Mexican forces, won independence for Texas.

From the Alamo, walk next door to the Menger Hotel. Here, at the Victorian bar, Theodore Roosevelt recruited his Rough Riders, primed with fiery spirits of both varieties. From the Menger, continue west on Crockett Street; walk down the steps at the corner of Presa and Crockett to begin your walk along the Paseo del Rio.

Fifty years ago concerned citizens blocked an attempt to change the course of the winding San Antonio River, which was creating havoc (especially at flood) with the rapidly expanding city. Old San Antonio was rescued from decay; and the Paseo del Rio, or River Walk, was established one level below the busy downtown streets. The scent of spicy food competes with that of flowers, and music and conversation replace the traffic and noise of the city above. You can, if you wish, cruise the Paseo del Rio Circle. Rent a boat near the Market Street Bridge. Paddleboats are also available for rent, so you can design your own boat tour. Brightly painted barges seem barely able to navigate the narrow river, made all the more charming by the stone bridges, hotels, restaurants, shops, and clubs along the way, balanced by open areas with many sidewalk cafés.

In addition to the beautiful cypress, oak, and willow trees that shade the walk, the Paseo del Rio is sprinkled with eccentric characters, none more famous than Bongo Joe, on the Crockett Street Bridge. Evenings Bongo Joe beats out his amplified rhythms on 55-gallon oil drums, while whistling and keeping up a rich line of patter.

There are other delights along the Paseo del Rio: a wonderful little church surrounded by Joske's Department Store, a waterfall, a statue of St. Anthony, and several restaurants — the tempting smell of broiling steaks fills the air on both sides of the water. There is the Arneson River Theatre and the Convention Center area for sports; a statue of an elephant guards the entrance of the Hertzberg Circus Collection at the corner of South Presa and West Market. Here Tom Thumb's carriage holds its place among 20,000 relics of circus life.

Return slowly to your car. La Villita, the little village that was San Antonio 250 years ago, opens from the River Walk two blocks from the Alamo. It is now a maze of artisans' shops and studios, a wild mixture of junk and magnificently executed crafts. If you find something you admire — a piece of jewelry, perhaps — stop to chat with the artist who created it. It's that sort of place.

The remains of HemisFair make another delightful side trip. Ascend to the street level at the Palacio del Rio Hilton and enjoy the Tower of the Americas, where an elevator shoots up through a 579-foot glass shaft to carry you to an observation deck, revolving restaurant, and disco at the top. From there you can return to the pleasures of the Paseo del Rio, or go back to your car.

Part 2

THE GREAT LAKES AREA
Illinois, Indiana, Michigan, Ohio, Wisconsin

1. Chicago
2. Indiana Dunes
3. Belle Isle
4. Mackinac Island
5. Cuyahoga River Valley
6. Eden Park
7. Perrysburg
8. The Wyalusing Ridges

Illinois

CHICAGO
The Lakefront

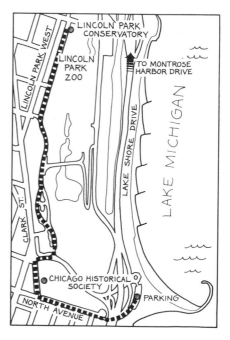

Directions: From Lake Shore Drive in Chicago, take the North Avenue/LaSalle Drive exit and park in the North Avenue Beach parking lot.

Best Season: Year round. In spring the trees are in bloom; in summertime the beaches are packed with people; in fall the crisp autumn weather produces bright, clear days; and in winter the serene lakefront features breathtaking natural ice sculptures. (It's cold, though. Michael Teuschler, who nominated this walk, recommends a winter walk only for the hale and hearty.)

Length: 5 miles round trip. Allow as much as a full day; there are many attractions and distractions along the way.

Degree of Difficulty: Walking almost anywhere in Chicago is easy. There are no hills (just small rises here and there), and the streets are laid out in a checkerboard pattern. Michael Teuschler offers a cautionary note, however: "One of my favorite times of day to take this walk is in the pre-dawn twilight, in anticipation of a glorious sunrise; however, I would suggest, for safety's sake, that this activity be undertaken only by city dwellers, or at least by those who are 'street-wise.' Naiveté can be dangerous in the dark in the city."

Chicago's Lakefront — The North Walk to Montrose Harbor
This walk winds through parkland and offers some magnificent views of both the city and the lake. Michael Teuschler nominated the walk be-

cause it combines the serenity of a beachwalk with the stimulation of a city walk. You'll stroll past yacht harbors that look like pocket resorts, the Lincoln Park Zoo, the Conservatory and gardens, graceful outdoor sculpture and fountains along the paths, sandy beaches, and archers shooting at targets. The paved walkway leads past tennis courts and golf courses, through formal gardens and clustered seats, where you can stop, relax, and enjoy the spectacular architecture of both man and nature.

From the very beginning there are tempting detours. From the parking lot, take North Avenue west for four blocks to where it meets Clark Street. The Chicago Historical Society, on your right, will give you an unusually lively picture of the Chicago area's history. From there you enter Lincoln Park, crammed with attractions, including its own physical beauty and the views of the city and beaches it provides. The Lincoln Park Zoo is being transformed, with special environments such as the Ape House where chimpanzees and orangutans prosper in their own rain forest. Be sure to stop at the delightful Farm-in-the-Zoo, the Reptile House, and the Zoo Rookery.

Next, in Lincoln Park's Conservatory, you'll find four acres of exotic plants, with magnificent formal gardens filling the block in front. Pause at the Storks at Play Fountain, just for the sheer pleasure of it; and you'll want to detour again between Stockton and Lincoln Park West for a visit to Grandmother's Garden, filled with gorgeous, old-fashioned flowers. If that doesn't satisfy your horticultural cravings, the Bates Fountain is surrounded by 25,000 flowering plants.

From the conservatory, Lincoln Park continues north along the lakefront another four miles. All the park makes for good walking, but at least one other of its sights is a must. Montrose Harbor Drive, about two miles from the conservatory, offers what Michael Teuschler calls "probably the most breathtaking view of Chicago."

The fascination of this walk is the opportunity it affords to see up close the interrelationship between the city and the lake. They are constantly changing and reflecting each other; fog turns the skyscrapers into soft silhouettes and mutes the sounds from the lake; both the water and the buildings take on new colors with the angle of the sun; city lights glisten at night causing myriad dazzling reflections on the lake. Michael Teuschler sums it up when he says, "Chicago's multi-faceted personality is featured in a remarkable showcase along this rewarding and marvelous pathway."

INDIANA DUNES
The Mt. Tom Trail

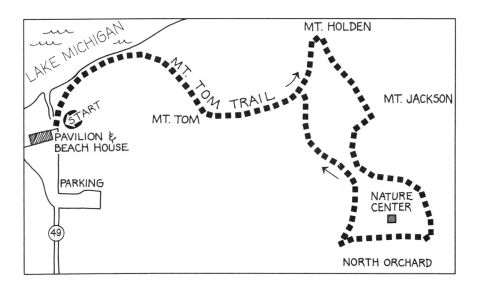

Directions: Located on the glittering shoreline of Lake Michigan, Indiana Dunes State Park is accessible from Route 49. From Chicago, take I–94 to Route 49. The park entrance is two miles north of the Interstate. The Mt. Tom Trail begins at the Pavilion and Beach House. There is an entrance fee of $1.50 per car.

Best Season: All year. In the warmer months, the swimming and water-skiing are excellent. In winter, there is fine downhill and cross-country skiing in the area and good ice fishing.

Length: The Mt. Tom Trail (Trail 8) is just under 3 miles.

Degree of Difficulty: Moderately difficult. The trail takes you up the three highest dunes in the park: Mt. Tom (192 feet), Mt. Holden (184 feet), and Mt. Jackson (176 feet).

The Mt. Tom Trail

Indiana Dunes State Park is a walker's dream. The paths are lined with wildflowers; constantly changing vistas across beautiful Lake Michigan provide endless joy; and the perfectly formed sand dunes offer just the right challenge.

There are 27 miles of trail among the park's 2,182 acres. Of these, the Mt. Tom Trail is the most challenging. To begin the walk, take the trail northeast from the Pavilion and Beach House, along the swimming beach. Trail 8 to the right leads you to Mount Tom, standing broad and gigantic on his enormous bed.

From here, the trail leads over the landward side of the great dune and across to Mount Holden. Here you can stand at the top and view the lake, dotted with swimmers and sailboats in the summer.

Continue south on the trail to Mount Jackson, which overlooks a glacial moraine and the bed of ancient "Lake Chicago." From here you slip downward (your shoes full of sand) to the intersection of Trails 8 and 9. You can follow Trail 8 to the inland marsh or turn right to the Nature Center. From there, take Trail 7 north to the beach, crossing your original path. For a different perspective of Mount Tom, follow the trail around the lake. You can follow the beach back to the Pavilion, or reward yourself with a refreshing swim and rest on the sand. For an even more rigorous hike, try walking this in reverse order.

Michigan

BELLE ISLE

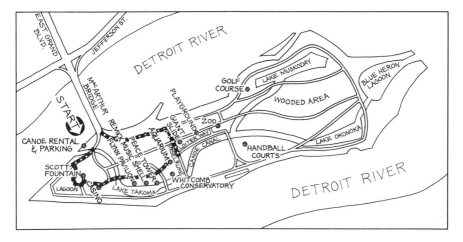

Directions: Belle Isle is located just across MacArthur Bridge from downtown Detroit, a surprise so near the industrial city. Fork right as you come across MacArthur Bridge to the thousand-acre island park. You can leave your car near the canoe rental on the right.

Best Season: Belle Isle is a wonderful place to walk any time of year. Spring flowers and summer swimming and water sports give way to fall color and then to sleigh rides, a 30-foot ice sculpture on the beach, and skating in winter.

Length: Just under 2½ miles.

Degree of Difficulty: The walk is on the sidewalk or on the grass area along the road, and is quite easy. The route is well lit, but make this walk during the day. It may be unsafe at night.

Belle Isle Walk

Belle Isle was developed by Frederick Law Olmsted, the designer of New York's Central Park. The island went through several name changes and several owners before it became the property of the city of Detroit. The Indians knew it as Wah-na-be-zee (White Swan); the French called it Isle au St. Claire. The first settlers in the area secured their hogs on it for safety, and it was dubbed for a while "L'Isle à Cochon." In 1752, the

French governor granted title of the island to a Douville Dequindre, but the title was later revoked because settlers were vehement about its remaining in public domain. A Lt. McDougall was more successful. He purchased it from the Ojibwa and Ottawa Indians. The price: three rolls of tobacco, five barrels of rum, three pounds of red paint, and a wampum belt. It was McDougall's heirs who gained the first clear title to the land, and they sold it to William Macomb; Macomb's sons sold the island in 1817 to Barnabas Campau, whose descendants sold it to Detroit in 1879 for $200,000. (Some of the city's residents complained bitterly about the price, which they considered ridiculously high. It is hard to imagine what they would have thought about the $10-million renovation program begun in 1974.)

Begin this walk at Scott Fountain, across the street from your car, at the end of the island. You'll be looking toward downtown Detroit, two and a half miles to the southwest. The enormous marble fountain, 38 feet above its lagoon, is a kind of Noah's Ark, with 109 water outlets in the shape of dolphins, human heads, turtles, lionesses, animal horns, and so forth.

A very short walk from the mountain on Loiter Way takes you to the Casino, not really a gambling den, but a recreation building and the site of countless parties and dances since its construction in 1908. Through the windows and great arcade you can see the north shore of the city of Windsor, on the Canadian side of the Detroit River, plus a great view of the river itself. It's a good place to relax, or stop for something to eat.

Continue on Loiter Way across Lake Tacoma, enjoyed by canoeists in summer and skaters in winter. Between the lake and the road are the Flynn Pavilion (for skating); the Remick Music Shell, which has free concerts during the summer; and the 85-foot Peace Tower, with a carillon that fills the air shortly after noon and 3 o'clock.

Past the intersection with Picnic Way is the nation's oldest freshwater aquarium, opened in 1904 and a Detroit institution. The Aquarium has about 5,000 live fish — 155 species from both salt and freshwater environments, although the Great Lakes varieties dominate. It is open all year and you can stop to see the piranhas and sharks, as well as the lake fish, between 10 and 5:30. Just south of the glass-domed Aquarium is the Whitcomb Conservatory, with more than a quarter of a million plants, and surrounded by formal gardens. You can pause at the Conservatory at any time from 9 in the morning until dusk.

Turn left on Inselruhe and go around the large statue of Major General Altheus Williams on his horse. Head for Riverbank Road. Follow the waterfront to the bridge and continue past it to pick up your car. If you want to extend your walk, keep going on Loiter Way instead of turning on Inselruhe. Here you'll find a giant slide, a zoo, handball courts, the beach, a golf course, and a playground, all within a half mile.

MACKINAC ISLAND

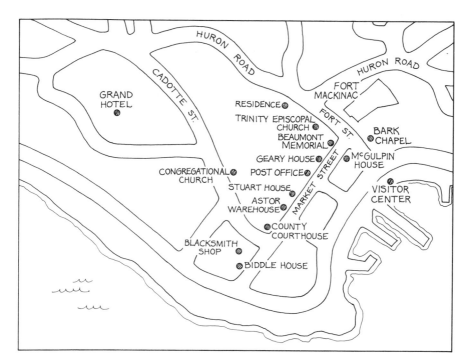

Directions: Located in the Straits of Mackinac between Michigan's Upper and Lower peninsulas, Mackinac Island is accessible via ferry service from St. Ignace and from Mackinaw City, both off of I–75. From October to May the ferry service is offered only from St. Ignace.

Best Season: May through October.

Length: 1½ miles. Allow at least 45 minutes for the walk; much more than that to enjoy the whole island. If you plan to spend the night, there are several places to stay. The elegant Grand Hotel is one of the great Victorian showplaces in the country.

Degree of Difficulty: Easy to moderate; there is a gentle uphill grade along part of the route.

Historic Mackinac Island

Just two by three miles, Mackinac Island is packed full with delights. The walk described here was nominated by Phil Porter, who says, "It takes one through the unique environment of the island where the horse is king and cars are prohibited. It also includes breathtaking views and fascinating history."

Before starting out on the walk, stop at the Visitor Center at the foot of Fort Street, by the harbor. Here you can pick up a self-guided brochure to the island as well as an Historic Mackinac Island Ticket, which allows entrance to many of the sites along the route.

From the Visitor Center, walk up Fort Street and turn left onto Market Street, where the American Fur Company presided over the profitable fur trade during its heyday in the late 18th and early 19th centuries. On the corner of Fort and Market is the Beaumont Memorial, named for William Beaumont, an army doctor who was involved in one of the most bizarre episodes in medical history. On June 6, 1822, a young man named Alexis St. Martin was accidentally shot in the stomach by a friend who stood just three feet away. Although Dr. Beaumont managed to keep St. Martin alive, the wound never healed completely, and the doctor was able to observe and record the digestive process through the hole. His observations led to an understanding of digestion that was new to medicine. Today the Beaumont Memorial has four dioramas which dramatize this event and show that Dr. Beaumont's relationship with his unusual patient wasn't all clear sailing.

Next to the Beaumont Memorial is the Matthew Geary House, typical of 19th-century Mackinac architecture. On the other side of the post office is the imposing home of Robert Stuart, manager of John Jacob Astor's multimillion-dollar fur interest on the island. Astor, who became America's first millionaire, arrived in the country penniless. At his death in 1848 he left an estate of around $20 million.

Convenient to Stuart's home is the Astor Warehouse next door, where a large group of clerks for the American Fur Company processed the pelts brought in by the Indians and *couriers de bois* each spring when the ice broke. Furs were the rage of the East as well as England in the mid-19th century.

Next to the warehouse is the Michilimackinac County Courthouse, where the landmark case of *The People* v. *Pond* was tried. Pond was first convicted of murder here for killing a man who was destroying one of his outbuildings. This decision was overturned by the Michigan Supreme Court on the basis that "A man's home is his castle."

Half a block farther down Market Street, set well back from the street, is the blacksmith shop of William E. Benjamin, who worked the forge until his death in 1968 when his family donated the shop and its contents to the state park. The shop has been kept active; today the smith produces horseshoes, wagon rims, and street light brackets from the hot iron. Next door is Edward Biddle's home, one of the oldest structures in the downtown area. Biddle, of the prominent Philadelphia family, established his fortune in the fur trade. His restored home, fitted out in the style of the 1820s, provides an intimate look at domestic life during that era.

The rest of Market Street is private homes and tempting shops, many of which sell the famous Mackinac Island fudge (local residents often call visitors to the island "fudgies").

Turn right off Market onto Cadotte Street; beyond a group of private homes on the right is the Stone Congregational Church, its stained glass windows showing scenes of Mackinac's history. Just beyond it, across the Grand Hotel Golf Course, you can see the governor's summer residence. On the left is the famous Grand Hotel. It was built by two railroad companies in 1887 in the heyday of the trains. This brought wealthy midwesterners to Mackinaw City and from there to the Island. The 660-foot porch, studded with columns, is thought to be the longest in the world. The teatime promenade along this porch is no more, but the atmosphere is still fairly formal, and the hotel retains its Victorian elegance. There is an admission fee for nonregistered guests to enter the grounds.

Beyond the hotel, the hill leads to Four Corners. Make the extreme right turn here past the Governor's Residence, then walk down Fort Hill. At the corner of Huron Road and Fort Street is Trinity Episcopal Church, built in 1882; across Fort Street is the Bark Chapel. In 1670 Father Claude Dablon spent the winter on the island in a bark building like this reproduction, and the following year Father Jacques Marquette left a small settlement at Sault St. Marie and established his mission near present-day St. Ignace. A statue of the great explorer and priest stands near the chapel.

The last stop on the walk, not far from the Visitor Center where you started, is Fort Mackinac, on the bluff above the Bark Chapel. The Fort was built to protect the British fur trading interests in 1779 during the Revolution. The ramp leading up looks more taxing than it is; walk it slowly, enjoy the view. It becomes most impressive as you approach the 150-foot-high South Sally Port. Nearby is the Commissary, with weapon displays, dioramas showing the War of 1812, artifacts used by the soldiers and their families, and a 1781 deed in which local Ojibwa chiefs "acknowledge to have received on His Majesties' behalf the sum of five thousand pounds Sterling being the adequate and compleat value of the Island of Michilimackinac."

At the Fort's administrative buildings, barracks, and officers' quarters you can get a detailed and fascinating picture of military life through the latter part of the 19th century. On the parade ground colorfully dressed guides fire muskets and offer tours, while at the Tea Room in the old officers' quarters you can enjoy the wonderful view as well as American apple pie, English tea, and French onion soup.

Ohio

CUYAHOGA RIVER VALLEY

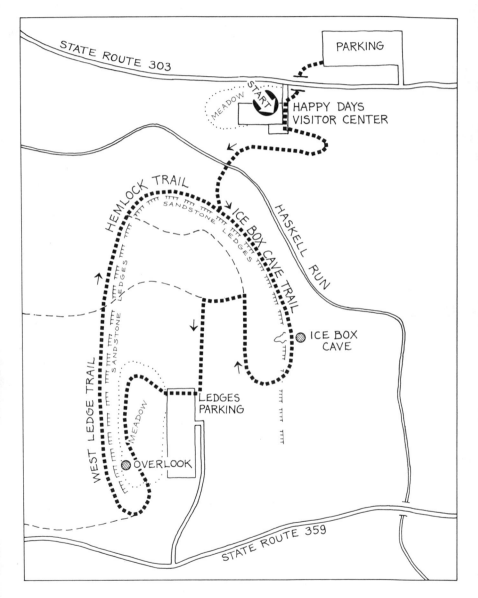

Directions: Located between the metropolitan areas of Akron and Cleveland, Cuyahoga Valley National Recreation Area is accessible from State Route 303. From I–77, go east through Peninsula to "Happy Days," the park headquarters, open daily from 8 a.m. to 5 p.m. year round. Or take Route 303 west from State Route 8 to "Happy Days."

Best Season: Spring for wildflowers; fall for color.

Length: About 2½ miles. Allow at least two hours.

Degree of Difficulty: Moderate. There are a few steep hills, but the ground is mostly level.

The Cuyahoga Valley Trail

Once the western boundary of the United States, the Cuyahoga River Valley is an interesting geological formation as well as historically significant. Along the trail you'll pass sandstone ledges and "Ice Box Cave" and go through meadows and a hemlock forest to glorious views of the valley. Marian Zehnder, who submitted this walk, describes the progression of the trail: "From Happy Days, the trail descends to Haskell Run, then climbs back up to the hemlock covered Ritchie Ledges. These sandstone cliffs, studded with quartz pebbles, contain many cracks and crevices. The largest, Ice Box Cave, will cool you in summer, for the temperature remains in the 50s all year.

"Then the trail climbs up to the top of the cliffs and turns west, crossing the road to the Ledges parking and picnic area. Skirt the meadow with its picnic tables on the western side, until you find the marvelous lookout point with the lovely Cuyahoga River Valley below you. The color here is spectacular in October.

"A short distance past the lookout point is the West Ledges Trail, which follows the bottom of the sandstone cliffs, meeting Hemlock Trail and ending the loop which began near the stone staircase just past Haskell Run. An alternate route back to Happy Days completes the walk."

EDEN PARK AND MT. ADAMS

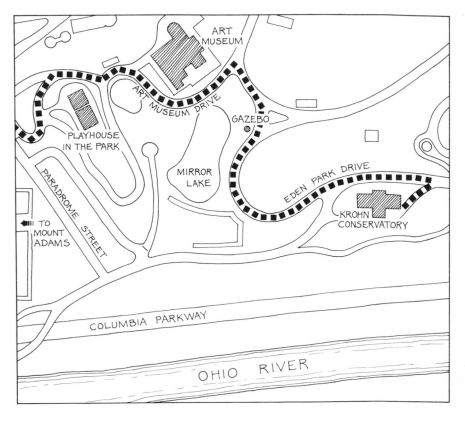

Directions: Begin at the Krohn Conservatory, in Eden Park, in the center of downtown Cincinnati.

Best Season: Summer, spring, and fall.

Length: 1.2 miles; the amount of time it takes to walk is determined by the number of stops you make. Walked straight through, it wouldn't take more than half an hour, but nobody does it that way.

146

Degree of Difficulty: Easy.

The Cincinnati Eden Park/Mt. Adams Walk

This surprising combination park and village walk, in the heart of Cincinnati, offers spectacular views of the Ohio River and the Kentucky hills, as well as the downtown area. It rolls (no exaggeration) by some of the most charming restaurants and cultural centers in the city, past restored Victorian homes and shops trimmed with flowers, sculptures, and banners.

It's a short walk, but most people spend a long time taking it. If you can resist the waterfall, exotic forest, and orchidarium of the Krohn Conservatory, you'll probably give in to the frisbee games and swimming dogs around Mirror Lake, or pause for a concert in the band shell near the Victorian gazebo. Across the street is the Cincinnati Art Museum, with more than a hundred galleries and a charming restaurant. The city's major theater, Playhouse in the Park, is on the hill overlooking the band shell and the museum.

Across Paradrome Street from the Playhouse is the village of Mt. Adams, named in the 1840s when John Quincy Adams, then in his seventies, made the difficult trip from New England to lay the cornerstone for the nation's greatest observatory. Walk up St. Gregory Street, dotted with little restaurants and a few craft studios, and turn left at Pavillion Street. At the end of Pavillion is the Church of the Immaculate Conception, known as the Church of the Steps since 1860. That was the year the custom of praying each of the steps up the side of Mt. Adams on Good Friday began. Here is a comfortable bench overlooking the downtown area, the river traffic, and the bridges that disappear into the hills of Kentucky. From the serenity of Mt. Adams, the whole bustling panorama looks like a stage set.

Downtown, take Central Parkway east (it will turn into Reading Road and swing north) for about a mile, then turn left on Elsinore. Follow Elsinore one block to Gilbert Avenue, where you turn left to the next light, Eden Park Drive. Turn right here, and follow the winding drive to the Krohn Conservatory parking lot.

PERRYSBURG

Directions: Perrysburg is about five miles up the Maumee River from Toledo. Take I–75 south from Toledo, to State Route 20. Follow 20 north to the intersection with Route 65 (Louisiana Avenue and Front streets) where the walk begins.

Best Season: Spring, summer, and fall.

Length: 4 miles. Allow about an hour and a half, with another 20 minutes thrown in to enjoy the views.

Degree of Difficulty: Easy. There is a short climb (25 yards) up the ramparts of Fort Meigs.

A Walk through Small-Town America

John Hamel, a resident of Perrysburg, nominated this walk through his town. "I suppose there are other walks," he explains, "that are more awesome in their natural grandeur, or more important in their historical significance, but I believe there are few which can so well capture the serenity and solidity — the feeling of small-town America that I want to share with others."

The walk begins at Louisiana Avenue and Front Street, at the monument to Commodore Perry. From there, walk west along the river side of Front Street. A particularly good view of the river is from the monument to Perrysburg's men of World War I. Continue along Front Street, bearing right at the stop light marking the intersections of Routes 20, 25, and 65. You'll get another perspective of the river as

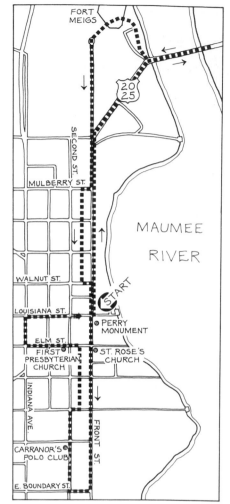

you walk the bridge across the county line to the city of Maumee.

Cross the street at the first stop light in Maumee and walk back across the other side of the bridge, stopping halfway to look at Fort Meigs on the far bank. The Fort was built in 1813 by William Henry Harrison to prevent the British from invading the territories of the Northwest. "Imagine how formidable it must have looked to the British," says John Hamel. "And to their Indian allies 172 years ago. There was no bridge and the canoe ride across was often precarious." Circle the base of the ramparts before taking a well-worn path up to an opening in the stockade wall. This brings you to Croghan's Battery, where the cannon was placed to fire against the British.

Following the stockade wall to the east, you come to Woods Battery. Walk down the rampart on your left, through the meadow along Front Street. Cross at the light and go one block to Mulberry. This brings you to the Historic District. Its elegant homes range from 1850 to the turn of the century.

In the Historic District, turn left for a walk through the Perrysburg alleys. Much more active in horse-and-buggy days, today the alleys provide the best vantage point for viewing the lovely backyard gardens of Perrysburg residents. Continue on to Walnut Street and turn left, returning to Front. Note the great Victorian on the corner, with its tree-shaded gazebo. Walk along Front, passing by St. Rose's Church, as well as several more strikingly handsome Victorians, and turn right on East Boundary. Go one block and turn right again on East Second. Across the street is the vast lawn of Carranor's Polo Club (now slowly giving way to tennis courts) and the clubhouse, a veteran of the twenties when polo mounts and horses ridden to the hounds filled the grounds.

Continue along Second Street from the Polo Club and wind through another set of serene houses and garden-trimmed alleys before reaching Elm Street, where you turn left, past the First Presbyterian Church with its square tower and wood filigree. Turn right on Indiana Street and walk one block to Louisiana Avenue. Turn right at the Library and walk along Louisiana to the railroad tracks. Here several presidents made whistle-stops; standing on the rear platform of their campaign trains, arms flailing, voices raised, they delivered their campaign speeches to the people of Perrysburg. The Commodore Perry monument where you started the walk is just a few steps away.

You won't be lonely walking in Perrysburg; walks are a part of the life of the town: after-dinner walks, for example, taken by strolling couples or families. "People are friendly," says John Hamel, "and there is always someone around, if you have questions or simply want to talk."

Wisconsin

THE WYALUSING RIDGES

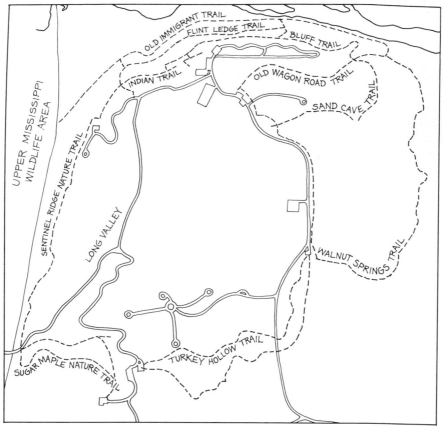

Directions: Take Highway 18 west to county Highway C and go south-west one mile to the Wyalusing State Park entrance. Stop at the park office for a trail map. From there drive along the park road to the parking lot. From your car follow the signs to the Sentinel Ridge Trail.

Best Season: Late spring; summer and fall.

Length: 14 miles, if the entire trail is walked. Plan about six hours, with a stop for a picnic lunch.

Degree of Difficulty: Moderate. The trail is fairly level, with slight contours.

Sentinel Ridge Trail

The Wyalusing Ridges, along the southwestern edge of Wisconsin, offer one of the most varied and beautiful walks in the state. Sentinel Ridge Trail follows the high ridge overlooking the confluence of the Mississippi and Wisconsin rivers. It served as a point of vigilance (thus the name Sentinel) for both the Indians and the French, offering wide views of the plains below. The trail goes through forest and along bluffs, with several spectacular lookout points. From one you have a clear view of Prairie du Chien, the second oldest city in Wisconsin, about five miles away. The name Prairie du Chien commemorates a proud Indian chief, Chief Dog, who once roamed the plains beneath Sentinal Ridge.

Walkers hundreds and thousands of years ago left their signs here: the prehistoric effigy mounds, in the shapes of animals, that line parts of the trail were built by Asian tribes on their slow migration from the Bering Strait to South America; and fossil hunting has yielded the images of plants and animals long extinct.

The present life of the Ridges is equally fascinating: hawks and blue herons soar over the bluffs; deer, raccoons, and squirrels slip among the trees, and the rush of tiny waterfalls and streams accompanies the bird calls. Ronda Allen, from the Wisconsin Department of Development, Division of Tourism, submitted the Wyalusing Ridges walk. "It's a favorite walk for naturalists, birders, those who enjoy photography, and anyone who likes quiet natural beauty," she says. "It's also a good 'walking workout' for both the novice and veteran walker."

Part 3

THE NORTH CENTRAL REGION
Iowa, Minnesota, Nebraska, North Dakota, South Dakota

1. **Starr's Cave**
2. **Three Lakes Walk**
3. **Fontenelle Forest**
4. **Lincoln**
5. **Caprock Coulee Nature Trail**
6. **Bear Butte**

Iowa

STARR'S CAVE

Directions: From Highway 61 on the north side of Burlington, go east four blocks on Sunnyside, then north on Irish Ridge Road to the scenic overlook pull-off.

Best Season: Summer, but it's open all year.

Length: One and a half hours.

Degree of Difficulty: Moderate, due to hilly terrain and number of steps.

Starr's Cave Park and Preserve's Scenic and Cave Walk

In Burlington, Iowa, Starr's Cave Park and Preserve has a combined scenic and cave walk that is an unusual treat. The walk features a scenic overlook on a 100-foot limestone cliff above Flint Creek. From there the trail follows the top of the bluff and then drops through Devil's Kitchen, a small, two-entrance cave. It then continues below to the entrance of Starr's Cave. The three-quarter-mile trail runs through short-grass prairie, lush bottomland woods, and oak-hickory woodlands, along the slopes and upland ridges.

Starr's Cave is a natural 250-foot, single-passage, limestone cave, and you'll need flashlights to see it. Guided tours are available, but the trail and cave are open for unguided tours as well. Guided tours should be scheduled well in advance. Write or call: Des Moines County Naturalist, Starr's Cave Nature Center, 3299 Irish Ridge, Burlington, IA 52601; (319) 753-5808.

Minnesota

MINNEAPOLIS
Three Lakes Walk

Directions: Take I–94 to the Hennepin Avenue exit in Minneapolis. Go south to the first light (Franklin) and turn right to Kenwood Park (eight blocks). The walk begins at the north end of Lake of the Isles, right by Kenwood Park.

Best Season: Year round this walk is pleasant, but for the flowers and swimming summer is best. The trail is religiously plowed during winter; in summer you can swim or canoe, and in nice weather any time of the year you can picnic outside or lunch in the restaurant at the Calhoun Beach Club. There is a bandstand at the Lake Harriet Pavilion, where band concerts are offered free every night during the summer.

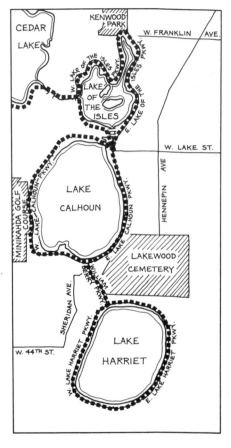

Length: This walk has three components, so the length varies, depending on the time and ambition of the walker. You can walk around one lake or two without retracing your steps, or do the complete route, again always on new ground. The first lake is Lake of the Isles, 3 miles around (about an hour to an hour and a quarter); the second is Lake Calhoun, 5 miles in circumference (about two to two and a half hours); the third is Lake Harriet, 2½ miles of walking, an additional hour. A walk around all three lakes totals about 10½ miles.

Degree of Difficulty: Easy. The route is well paved, and, according to Carla Waldemar who nominated it, it is very safe.

A Three Lakes Walk in the Land of Lakes

This is a particularly appropriate walk for this part of the country, since Minneapolis got its name from the Sioux word for "water." The first water on the walk is Lake of the Isles. The two heavily wooded, man-made islands you see out in the lake are wildlife preserves; they gave the lake its name. Nominator Carla Waldemar says the lake is just as popular with ducks and geese as it is with walkers and joggers. The residential neighborhood across the boulevard is one of the most beautiful in Minneapolis, and the great trees add to the peacefulness of the setting.

Halfway around Lake of the Isles you must decide whether you want to extend your walk around Lake Calhoun or continue around the remaining one-and-a-half miles of Lake of the Isles. If you choose to add the five-mile Lake Calhoun walk, you can stop for a breather at the Calhoun Beach Club. Here you can rent canoes or relax in Calhoun's Restaurant. Fortified, you can then continue your walk along the largest of the three lakes, watching the windsurfers as you go. There is a more open-air atmosphere to Lake Calhoun, fewer trees, and more grassy parkland. There are beaches all around the lake, so swimmers are everywhere in the warmer months.

You have another decision to make when you reach the halfway point here. You can continue around Lake Calhoun and finish the walk around the other side of Lake of the Isles, or you can walk an additional two and a half miles around Lake Harriet. If you have the time and energy, Lake Harriet is worth it. Flowers line the shore, and there are picnic tables along the way. During the summer plan a stop here in the evening to hear a free concert at the Lake Harriet Pavilion. On the northeast shore of Lake Harriet is the Lake Harriet Garden Center. Roses, tulips, and numerous other flowers, as well as exotic trees, are displayed here.

"I walk or run at least part of this trail every day of my life," says nominator Waldemar, "and it has simply become more and more beautiful with repetition."

Nebraska

FONTENELLE FOREST

Directions: From Omaha, take I–80 to the Highway 73–75 exit and travel south four miles to the Southroads Shopping Center, where there is a sign to Fontenelle Forest; turn left.

Best Season: Fall and spring.

Length: About 90 minutes.

Degree of Difficulty: Moderately difficult, due to the up-and-down-hill nature of the forest.

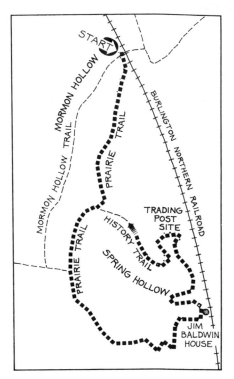

Fontenelle Forest's Self-Guided Wilderness Walk

Fontenelle Forest is four miles south of Omaha in Bellevue, Nebraska's oldest community. Here you'll find a two-mile, self-guided walk that covers a century of history. You'll pass prehistoric Indian earth lodge sites, the Trading Post Road (older than the Oregon Trail), and the original trading post of Logan Fontenelle. This half-French, half-Indian "Omaha Chief" tried by example to show the Indians how to adapt to the white man's way of life. He lived in a house, not in a lodge or tepee, and dressed in white man's clothes. It's not clear whether Fontenelle was actually a chief of the Omahas, but it is certain he had unusual prominence in the tribe.

In the forest itself, along the Missouri River, connecting foot trails pass through a 1,200-acre nature area. Here wild ravines and high ridges overlook the Missouri floodplain and the Iowa bluffs. Gentle springs at the bottoms of these ridges feed the slow streams, which broaden in places to form marshes. Stately bur oak, shagbark hickory, black walnut, mulberry, and cottonwood cover the ridges; opossum, mink, beaver, whitetail deer, raccoon, coyote, fox, and 200 species of birds thrive in the forest.

The first stop on this winning guided tour — submitted by the Division of Travel and Tourism of the Nebraska Department of Economic Development — is Mormon Hollow. According to legend, this is the place where 10,000 Mormons, led by Brigham Young, set up dwellings from the summer of 1846 until spring, 1848. Continuing from Mormon Hollow toward Prairie Trail, turn left to a cleared area and the Trading Post Road. Barely visible now, it was once the main route for fur traders, Indians, and early settlers to and from Bellevue. The Trading Post itself is farther down the trail; it began operation in 1823 when the Missouri River flowed closer to this site.

Following along the trail you come to the home of Jim Baldwin, the forest hermit. Jim lived in the forest until 1960, telling stories and reciting poetry from memory to all who walked by. His tales about hoop snakes racing one another downhill and then swallowing each other whole have become a local legend. A lovely locust grove has spread from a line of trees he planted; you can smell the sweet scented flowers far along the trail in May.

LINCOLN

Directions: From I–80, exit at 9th Street in Lincoln and park near 14th and O streets.

Best Season: Spring and fall are best; but any day is good if it's not too cold, too hot, rainy, or snowy.

Length: 17 blocks. Allow from 35 to 45 minutes for the walk itself, but much more time for exploring.

Degree of Difficulty: Easy.

A Stroll through Lincoln's Capitol Area
This self-guided historic tour of Lincoln, Nebraska, was nominated by Barbara Steinfeld of the Nebraska Division of Travel and Tourism. The walk begins on the southeast corner of 14th and O streets. A plaque on

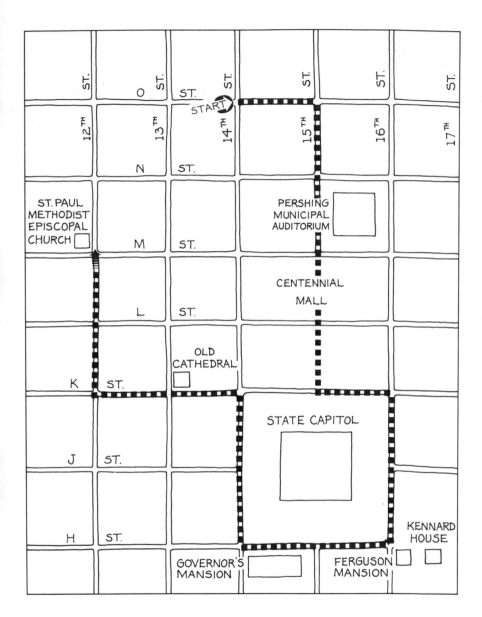

the west wall of the Chapin building (now a McDonald's) claims this as the site of Lincoln's first cabin, built in 1864 by Luke Lavender, the "highway robber." Lavender owned 80 acres in the area, including four square blocks needed for a new state capitol. All the other landowners donated land to the state; Lavender alone demanded — and got — an acre-for-acre replacement, along with $1,000. Since he had paid only 60 cents per acre in the first place, his shrewd dealings were considered "highway robbery."

As you walk from 14th to 15th Street, between M and N, you will approach an enormous 763,000-piece mosaic mural, which depicts the activities inside the Pershing Auditorium; 38 by 140 feet, it is the largest mural of its type in the United States. The auditorium is named after the World War I hero, John "Black Jack" Pershing, who was a Nebraska University military instructor before the war. The ground you stand on as you view the mural was once a school. At that time (1873) it was so far out of town that parents refused to let their children attend in winter for fear of wolves.

From the auditorium, continue across M Street to the award-winning Centennial Mall, a six-block stretch of walkways, gardens, sculpture, and fountains connecting the Capitol to the university area. Gracious trees shelter picnickers and people just relaxing on benches or watching the imposing fountains, so beautifully illuminated at night. When festivals fill the mall, there are bicycle races and music performances to watch, and craft booths dot the sidewalk.

The Capitol, occupying the four square blocks between K and H and 14th and 16th streets (formerly the property of "highway robber" Luke Lavender), is unique. Barbara Steinfeld tells us it was voted the fourth architectural wonder of the world in a nationwide poll of architects; it is an Art Deco masterpiece, the result of a contest in 1919 when the existing Capitol threatened to collapse. The design is a complex one; you step into the great hall, its dome so far above you that it is practically invisible. Here there are six huge mosaics on themes of Nebraska history: surveying the land, homesteading, and milestones in the settlement and development of the state. The offices of the Capitol are arranged in four small squares, each surrounding an open courtyard. It is more like a little world of its own, a complex, than a single building. From outside you can see the giant statue on the dome, The Sower, with his bag of seed on his shoulder; and near the Capitol's west entrance there is an imposing sculpture of Lincoln by Daniel Chester French, the sculptor of the famous statue in Washington, D.C.'s Lincoln Memorial.

When the Nebraska legislature chose the tiny village of Lancaster (population 30) to be the state capital in 1867 and renamed it Lincoln, the three capital commissioners each showed his faith in the future of the town by purchasing a lot and building an imposing house. Only one of these homes remains, that of Thomas Kennard, who later became Nebraska's secretary of state. His charming Italianate house at 17th and H streets, crowned with a cupola, is open to the public daily.

Next door, on 16th Street, is the mansion of William Ferguson, a wealthy businessman who built a house that looks as if it had been removed from Embassy Row in Washington, D.C. Like the Kennard House, it is now operated as a free museum. You can explore both the main house and the carriage house daily.

Walking a block and a half west on H Street, you'll find the Governor's Mansion, filled with mementos from the state's history. Tours include the Nebraska Authors' Library and the First Ladies' Doll Collection.

As you stroll back north and west of the Capitol, you'll pass a number of churches. The Old Cathedral at 13th and K streets is a fine example of Gothic Revival architecture. The St. Paul Methodist Episcopal Church, at M and 12th streets, is the only church still standing on the free property offered by the city to 10 religious denominations as an incentive to build churches in Lincoln.

At some point during your walk, look (or sniff) around 14th and N streets for the Corn Popper, a wonderful place for snacks. Behind it is the Foundation Gardens, a haven for tired people. Relax among its pools and fountain or stop and listen to the live concerts.

The Tourist Information Center in Lincoln is open every day from June to mid-September; it is located on the corner of O and 9th streets. Stop by for information about other walking tours of the "Star City."

North Dakota

CAPROCK COULEE NATURE TRAIL
Theodore Roosevelt National Park

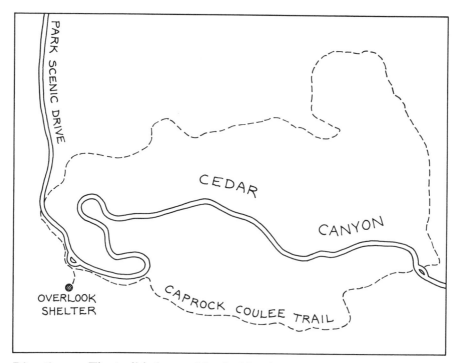

Directions: The trail is located in the North Unit of Theodore Roosevelt National Park. From I–94, take Highway 85 north, toward Watford City. The North Unit, accessible from Highway 85, is 52 miles from the Interstate.

Best Season: Beth McCauley, who nominated the Caprock Coulee Nature Trail, suggests late spring and early summer "when the temperatures are tolerable, the breeding birds have arrived, and the blooming wildflowers are most diverse."

Length: Caprock Coulee is a loop trial of 4 miles. Allow at least three hours. For a shorter walk, have someone pick you up at the overlook shelter near the road, 2½ miles from the start of the trail.

Degree of Difficulty: Moderately difficult. The heat (temperatures can reach as high as 110 degrees) can make the walk strenuous, and the clay beds along the river canyon in the south section of the trail can be slippery. Beth McCauley suggests you bring at least a quart of water with you, and urges against climbing the badland slopes, which are unstable. She also warns walkers to use common sense with the wildlife on the trail. "All wild animals are dangerous," she says. "The bison may charge if you approach too close; yield the right of way. Prairie rattlesnakes are commonly seen along these trails. They prefer to avoid confrontations, but they may strike without warning if surprised."

Caprock Coulee Nature Walk

Beth McCauley, a seasonal intepreter at Theodore Roosevelt National Park, enthusiastically nominates the Caprock Coulee Nature Walk as one of America's greatest walks. "A walk in the badlands," she says, "instills a mysterious longing. I long to spend more time trying to read the stories revealed by the eroding formations, the scuffle of predator tracks, the changing wind direction, and the pattern of ancient tepee rings. The trail transports you into the past as you step up to the badlands buttes that expose layers of sandstone, mudstone, and siltstone, which were deposited 60 to 70 million years ago by ancient rivers and streams. As the trail booklet explains, clamshell fossils and fossilized plant material in the lignite coal testify to a time when rivers and swamps were prevalent. Petrified tree stumps, in association with bentonite clay beds (an altered form of volcanic ash), provoke images of violent earth grumblings during the formation of the Rocky Mountains."

This is a land of extremes. Prickly pear cacti grow among aromatic silver sagebrush and the delicate lavender shades of the harebell blossoms. The grunts of the bison bull during rutting season are heard over the lilting, vibrant song of a western meadowlark, one of Theodore Roosevelt's favorite birds.

The trail has several sections, running through a variety of habitats. A booklet describes the first three quarters of a mile, and outstanding features, such as the caprocks and petrified stumps, are marked with numbered posts.

The next one-and-three-quarter miles brings you from the base of the buttes to the high prairie. You pass first through a woody draw of juniper and ash that harbors many breeding birds and spring wildflowers. "If your eyes are sharp," says McCauley, "you may find a patch of wild strawberries, gooseberries, or June berries." Everything in the park is protected, but you may eat these. When you reach the top, you are high enough (2,400 feet) to see the stretch of the badlands along the Little Missouri River, far beyond the park boundary. As you follow the trail through the prairie grassland, watch for coyote and bobcat tracks.

The trail crosses the park road, to the outlook shelter, a structure built from native materials by the Civilian Conservation Corps in 1937. Huge logs make up the beams, and the base is quarried sandstone and scoria (a bricklike substance caused by lignite fires that bake the layers of clay). "This outlook point gives one of the finest dramatic views of the Little Missouri River badlands," says McCauley. "Often, bison herds are spotted in the river bottom, and birds of prey soar along the bluffs. Here you realize the magnetic magic that attracted Theodore Roosevelt and prompted him to say, 'I have always said I would not have been President had it not been for my experience in North Dakota.'"

The remaining one-and-a-half miles of trail follow the valley edge and skirt the rim of some of the most highly eroded formations in the park. Few varieties of plants grow here, but a small population of sagebrush lizard thrives. The trail passes through several juniper groves and ends back at the parking area.

There are 35 additional miles of trail in the 20,070-acre North Unit of the park, a state-designated scenic river for extended float trips, and a campground. A Visitor Center, located in the North Unit, is open during the summer months and offers interpretative programs. In addition, the 46,000-acre South Unit offers other hiking opportunities. For further information, call (701) 623-4466.

South Dakota

BEAR BUTTE
The Sacred Mountain

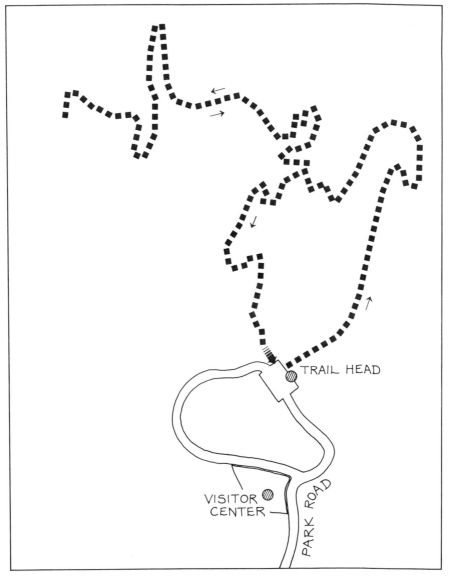

TRAIL HEAD

VISITOR
CENTER

PARK ROAD

Directions: Bear Butte State Park is located about eight miles northeast of Sturgis, South Dakota. From I–90, take Highway 34 east. Turn north on Highway 79 and right, into the park.

Best Season: Late spring and early fall. Summer temperatures on the bare rock can be intense, and in winter snow often forces park administrators to close the trail.

Length: 3 miles round trip. Allow about two hours for a full appreciation of the majesty of this sacred mountain.

Degree of Difficulty: Moderate. The trail is steep, but it winds around the mountain instead of going straight up, and steps have been added in places to keep the grade below 12 percent.

Walking Up the Sacred Mountain

Bear Butte is the sacred mountain of the Cheyenne and Sioux Indians. Both tribes return here in summer to fast and worship. The awesome 1,500-foot mountain is the place where the Indians' most famous medicine man received the word of the Great Spirit; and Tony Gullet, who nominated the walk, describes it as "a real spiritual experience, if you take the time to let the mountain and the surrounding country move you."

And there is plenty of surrounding countryside. From the summit you can see Wyoming, and you have a clear view of at least 70 miles, nearly to North Dakota. The Black Hills start around five miles over the prairie from Bear Butte. The park has made it easy for you to take in the panoramic view: there are two observation platforms on the way up, before you reach the big one at the top.

As you make your ascent, you will pass a few ponderosa pine; but, for the most part, the impressive structure of the mountain is bared to view. Gullet cautions that, unless a permit is issued for scientific reasons, visitors should stay on the trail and forgo shortcuts that can cause tremendous ecological damage. There is not really a butte but the remains of an ancient volcano that never erupted, although smoke is said to have streamed from the mountaintop at the hands of the Indians. A cave along the trail has a hole in its ceiling that pierces a 40-foot chimney, by legend the place where the Indians sent up smoke signals, signs that could be seen for miles and miles.

The walk to the summit of Bear Butte remains a unique, one-of-a-kind experience for all who take it. The cloudscapes from the top are stunning, especially when a thunderstorm is building, or as the sun sets. But most of all, the lasting impressions from this walk come from the mountain itself. "It's a feeling you won't forget," says Tony Gullet, "if you give it a chance to get hold of you."

Walking the Western States

THE WEST seems boundless. Boundless space, boundless sky, boundless panoramas that open to the most dramatic scenes in all America. And in the mountains of the West, in its valleys, canyons, lakes, streams, rivers, plains, and meadows, we can sense the boundlessness that is within us as well. As we stand amidst its scenic wonders, we can understand, for example, what biologist Steven Carothers meant when he wrote of the enchantment of the Grand Canyon as the "outgrowth of the human animal's response to being placed in its natural habitat, a sense of coming home." For in the fresh mountain air, in the silence of remote places, in the alpenglow, or in the depths of canyons, we experience a renewal of spirit. It is essential.

In the West, too, we can still be explorers and frontierspeople. We can search out the roots of history in its cities and towns, some virtually unchanged from the 1800s, and we can walk in wilderness few people have ever seen. And, of course, we can explore, within the limits of our abilities and interests, the great Western superlatives: the deepest lakes, highest waterfalls, biggest trees, tallest mountains, oldest rocks, steepest canyons, most European cities, longest-running cable cars, wettest countryside, most primitive beaches, hottest geysers.

The forces of nature responsible for these superlatives of the West are almost too incredible for us to comprehend. Crater Lake, for example, in southwestern Oregon, was formed within the last 6,000-plus years, making it a geologic youngster. It is the deepest lake (1,932 feet) in the United States; and the bowl containing its 22 square miles of water was formed with the collapse of a mighty volcano, Mt. Mazama. Pumice shot out of the crater with a force 100 times greater than an atomic bomb and filled all the valleys within the boundaries of what is now Crater Lake National Park; ash from the explosion covered all of northwestern America.

There is no better way to explore and observe the breathtaking beauty of an environment such as Crater Lake than on foot. Walkers can use all of their senses to experience the dramatic and varied regions of the West. Here is a sampling of Western walks — some of them well known and well traveled, many less known and less traveled. But all the walks were suggested by people who walked them and loved them. These people have discovered the beauty and serenity of the West, as well as its uniqueness. Nowhere else on earth is there a Grand Canyon, a wonder two billion years in the making, where the oldest rocks known can be seen and touched. There is nothing like it — anywhere. The Grand Canyon walk you'll find here is a tough one: down 10 miles in one day, up 10 very steep miles the next. But you'll never forget it.

The earth-shattering forces that so contributed to the awesome beauty of the West are seen in a different light at Point Reyes National Seashore in California. Jutting out to sea, the Point Reyes Peninsula is held aloft by the eastern ridge of the Pacific plate; it is earthquake country, continually affected by its location atop the San Andreas Fault. The Pierce Point Trail walk described here takes the walker to Tomales Point, an area that slid 16.4 feet northwestward during the 1906 earthquake. It continues to move three inches every year. It is a place of unique beauty, overlooking the crashing Pacific and the beaches of Tomales Bay.

San Francisco, too, is earthquake country. The 1906 quake and ensuing fires continue to live in the imagination of the City, as it is affectionately called by those who live there. They, of course, love their City and live there gladly (and gratefully), despite the threat of another shaking of the earth. Only this time hundreds of high rises will be tossed into the confrontation between the forces of nature and the tenaciousness of human beings. The two City walks included here are distinctive of San Francisco. One is along the Golden Gate Promenade, which leads to the Golden Gate Bridge, meeting place of city, bay, and ocean. One is an exploration of a favorite San Francisco hill, where the city meets the sky.

Alaska is truly the West's last frontier. Denali National Park is perhaps the most virgin area of all those we have covered. "Denali" is a melodic Indian word that means "the high one." It refers to the 20,320-foot Mount McKinley in south-central Alaska, the highest peak on the North American continent. At Denali there is a perfect opportunity to see the majestic beauty of The High One piercing the blue Western sky, only 250 miles south of the Arctic Circle. The vegetation above the timberline is so fragile that the keepers of Denali Park encourage walkers to scatter themselves around the environment. There are no trails.

These are just a few of the joys awaiting you in the West. As you continue to discover more, remember certain essentials. In the wilderness areas, you need to carry water and food, and you should wear appropriate clothing. We underscore this advice by urging you to first study the information about the environment in which you plan to walk. In that way not only you will be sufficiently prepared, you will know how to get the most out of the experience as well.

We hope you will have a wonderful time on these walks exploring the boundlessness of the West. We hope, too, that you will discover something new, something we forgot to mention perhaps or didn't even know about. Most of all, we hope you will discover something new about yourself.

Part 1

The Northwest Corner
Idaho, Montana, Oregon, Washington, Wyoming

1. Casino Lakes Trail
2. Danny On Trail
3. Mt. Scott Trail
4. Portland
5. Seattle
6. Shi Shi Beach
7. Cascade Canyon

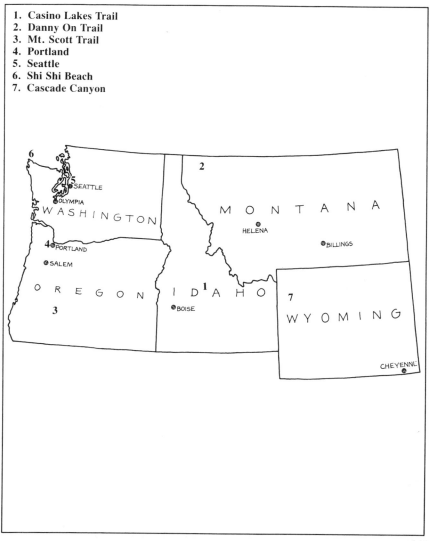

Idaho

CASINO LAKES TRAIL
White Cloud Mountains

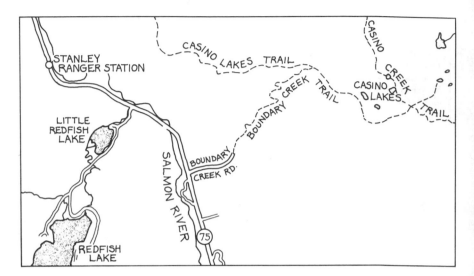

Directions: From a distance, even in summer, the White Clouds look snow-capped; hence their name. They are located in the Sawtooth National Recreation Area, north and west of Sun Valley. Traveling north from Sun Valley, take Highway 75 to a narrow dirt road marked "Boundary Creek," about 57 miles beyond Ketchum-Sun Valley. Take the road to the right for about a mile, until you see the Boundary Creek trailhead. Park and you are ready to take this hike. You won't see the White Clouds from the highway because of intervening foothills, but you'll see them from the trail.

Best Season: Mid-July to mid-September. On the upper reaches of the trail you will see lightning-killed trees; *do not hike this trail if a storm is threatening.*

Length: Approximately 11 miles round trip. Plan on an all-day walk.

Degree of Difficulty: You'll have to work hard in parts. At the trailhead, the elevation is 6,500 feet; at the crest of this walk, the elevation is about 9,500 feet. Nominator Elsie Adkins rates the trail "moderately difficult." In short, a challenge. Take your own water and food; neither is available on the trail. Make sure you have a jacket packed in your day-pack, too. Hypothermia can be a hazard in the summer, with sudden changes in temperature.

Casino Lakes Trail

The Casino Lakes Trail begins in the foothills of the White Cloud Mountains and passes through meadows and by trees. As you begin the ascent, you leave these for the open slopes, following fairly closely the path of Boundary Creek. As you get higher, you will be able to see behind you the Sawtooth Mountains and Red Fish Lake Drainage. "The most enticing thing about this trail," says Elsie Adkins, "is its wide-angle view."

It is on the ridge at the top that you'll see the lightning-struck trees. "This is a strange, yet interesting place," says Adkins. "The dead trees are exposed to the wind. They rub together and sound like an out-of-tune orchestra or a bad violin."

In the tree remnants you'll see cavity-nesting birds, and along the trail, deer and elk tracks, and grouse. On the ridge, you can get a great view of the White Clouds and across the Sawtooth Valley. Follow the Ridge Trail until you are above the lakes. This is the turning-around point. If you are a backpacker, you can go on forever.

The summers are short in this dramatic country. Take this walk as early as you can in the season. "There are gentler places," notes Elsie Adkins, "but I like this walk through rugged country." If you, too, like rugged country, the White Cloud Mountains are special.

Montana

DANNY ON TRAIL
Big Mountain Ski Resort, Whitefish

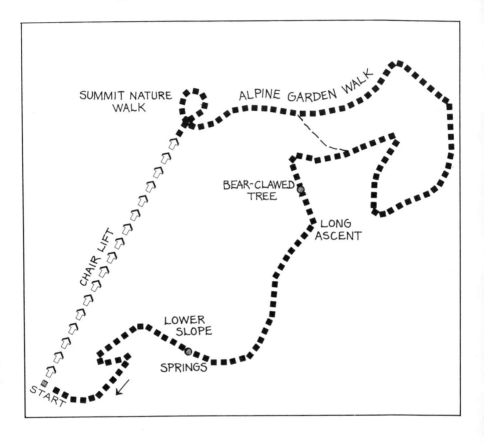

Directions: Big Mountain Ski Resort is located in the resort town of Whitefish, in the northeast corner of Montana, above Kalispell and 30 miles from the entrance to Glacier National Park. From Highway 93, follow signs to Whitefish. Drive through the town to the Big Mountain Ski and Summer Resort.

Best Season: This is a summer and early fall walk — July through October. The ski lift generally opens the third Friday in June and closes on

Labor Day. The chair lift runs every day from 11:00 a.m. to 6:30 p.m. (Accommodations are available at the resort.)

Length: The Danny On Trail ascends about 2,000 feet for 5 miles. It consists of four segments. Nominator Julie Davies says part of the beauty of the trail is that you can create a walk to suit your own desires and stamina. She suggests you ride the chair lift to the top and walk down, starting at Segment 4 of the trail, the Summit Nature Walk. This route takes about three hours and covers approximately a 4-mile descent.

Degree of Difficulty: Since you will be going downhill all the way, the walk is relatively moderate, but take care to watch your footing. Make sure you wear comfortable walking shoes or boots; dress in layers so that, if you get too warm, you can remove a few without risking exposure to the cold.

The Danny On Trail

Danny On was a U.S. Forest Service silviculturist (silvics is the study of the life history, characteristics, and ecology of forest trees), a well-known nature photographer, and a conservationist. He was killed on Big Mountain in a skiing accident at the age of 54, not far from the trail that bears his name. Danny On was known as a generous man, committed to his friends and to nature. The trail is his memorial.

The Summit Nature Walk begins near the top of the chair lift. About half a mile long, it is a loop trail around the summit. On your way up the mountain, in the chair lift, you will understand perfectly why Montana is called "Big Sky" country. On a clear day, from the top, you can see the mountains of Glacier National Park and the wide valley of the Flathead River. When the weather isn't clear, it will be obvious that you are in the Northern Rockies. Thick fog and bracing mists surround you. When this happens, it's like stepping into another dimension.

After finishing the loop, head east on the Alpine Garden Walk. You'll be in an alpine meadow for about a half mile, until you reach a "saddle," which crosses the trail. This is a pass used by wildlife. Take this cutoff over to Segment 2, the Long Ascent.

Along this part of the trail you'll find numerous flowering plants, including fireweed, with its spiky magenta flowers. Also known as the "healer" of land that has been devastated by fire, it blooms from mid-June to August. From July to late September, the white flowers of pearly everlasting and western yarrow, as well as lavender asters, are in bloom. Englemann spruce, whitebark pine, and subalpine fir are among the lush, full trees you will see.

The Long Ascent, actually your "long descent," passes by Haskill Slide, an area where avalanches were frequent before the mountain was used by skiers. (Skiing on the snow packs it down.) Near the cutoff,

"Bear-Clawed Tree" shows parallel marks made by bear claws. (If you have a cat, you'll notice the similarity between this tree and your furniture.)

Julie Davies tells how she recently gorged on juicy huckleberries near the springs on the Lower Slope at the end of the descent. They are the food of the grizzlies. "I had purple everywhere," she recalls.

Take the Forest Department's excellent brochure on the Danny On Memorial Trail with you. It is available at the Tally Lake Ranger Station in Whitefish; tel. (406) 862-1508. Wooden stakes along the trail are numbered so that walkers can take note of the area's plants and animals.

Oregon

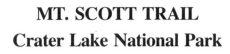
MT. SCOTT TRAIL
Crater Lake National Park

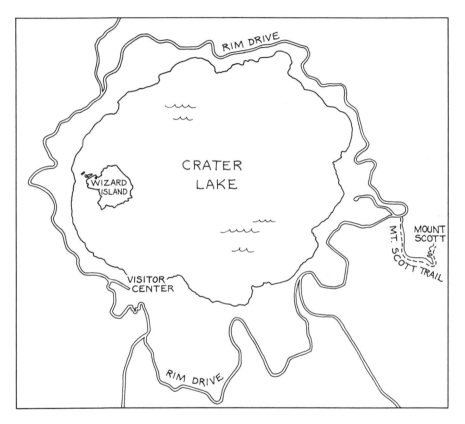

Directions: Crater Lake National Park is located in the southwest section of Oregon. To get there from Klamath Falls, take Highway 97, then Highway 62, to the park. From Medford, take I–5 to Highway 62. From Roseburg, Highway 138 leads east to Crater Lake. Once inside the park take Rim Drive to the base of Mt. Scott on the east side of the park. A sign, "Mt. Scott Trail," lets you know when you've reached the trailhead. The parking lot is actually just a pull-off along the side of the road, with room for four or five cars.

Best Season: The best time to take this walk is from July through September when the daytime highs are in the 70–75 degree range, the weather is clear, sunny, and warm, and the wildflowers light up the meadows. It is best to start out in the morning.

Length: Round trip on this steep trail is only about 5 miles, but allow at least four hours to complete the trip.

Degree of Difficulty: Moderately difficult; the rise in elevation is 1,500 feet to the Mt. Scott summit. The National Park Service staff says this trail is "no more dangerous than any other hiking trail on top of a mountain." Wear sturdy shoes, carry water and a lunch, and watch your footing at all times. Stay on the trail, and be careful of the precipitous areas.

Crater Lake — A National Wonder

Crater Lake, the deepest in the United States (1,932 feet), is also one of the most beautiful. But Klamath Indian legend warns against looking directly upon the lake, which was sacred to the spirits. Whatever spirits reside therein, though, seem to be of the restorative rather than the destructive kind.

The Mt. Scott Trail takes you through pine forest and into mountain meadows where, in July and August, profusions of mountain wildflowers are in bloom. You may see marmots, pikas, deer, and birds of prey (hawks and eagles) as you walk along.

When you reach the 8,926-foot summit, there is a tower lookout: "A good place to watch for migrating birds," says one member of the National Park Service staff, "and for the thousands of migrating California tortoise shell butterflies which fly up one side of Mt. Scott, over the top, and down the other side."

From this vantage point you can also see the intense blue of the 22-square-mile Crater Lake, contained within a 25-mile circle of volcanic cliffs. The lake was created more than 6,000 years ago when Mt. Mazama erupted and caved in. Over the centuries, the huge hole filled with rain and snow. Wizard Island, a tree-covered lava cone near the shore of Crater Lake, is also visible from the top of Mt. Scott.

When you enter Crater Lake National Park, you cross a section of the Pacific Crest National Scenic Trail, a 2,500-mile hiking route that follows West Coast mountain ranges from Canada to Mexico. Contact park officials at (503) 594-2211 for more information about hiking the Pacific Crest Trail, or pick up information at the park before you begin your walk up Mt. Scott. There is also a two-hour sightseeing boat trip on Crater Lake in the summer.

PORTLAND
Wildwood Trail

Directions: The Wildwood trailhead is located at the south end of the Hoyt Arboretum, next to the Western Forestry Center. (The Center has its roots in the Old Forestry Building, built for the 1905 Lewis and Clark Exposition.) Across the parking lot is the Washington Park Zoo. To get to the Arboretum (a 10-minute, nonrush-hour drive from downtown Portland), get on U.S. 26 (the Sunset Highway) and take the zoo exit. Drive to the top end of the zoo parking lot. The arboretum grounds are open every day from 5 a.m. until midnight. The Visitor Center is on Fairview Boulevard. It houses exhibits and a library and is open from 10 a.m. to 4 p.m. For additional information, call (503) 228-8732.

Best Season: The depth of winter excepted, this walk is pleasant all year. In Portland, snow falls six to ten times during the winter months, and snowfalls of three inches or more, snow sticking to the conifers, create a truly beautiful winter wonderland in the arboretum. Here the observant walker will often notice tiny flowers popping up through the snow. In the

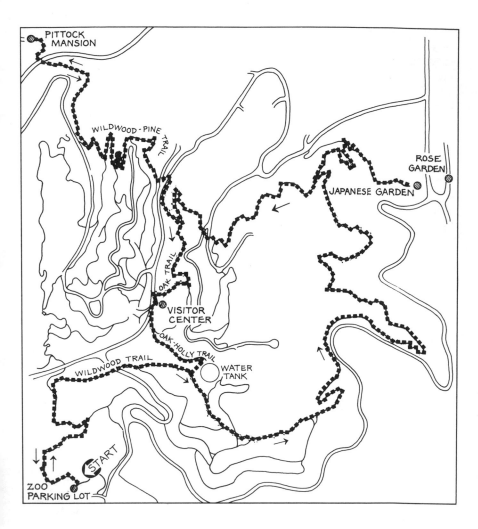

spring bloom magnolias, cherry trees, crabapples, and a beautiful carpet of wildflowers. Summer brings to life the dogwood collection, and in the fall the maple trees are at their spectacular best. Bring along an umbrella in spring and early summer, and then in late Sepember and October. The weather is usually dry during July, August, and the first part of September.

Length: The Wildwood Trail to Pittock Mansion is 4.7 miles; return by a zigzag route, which is about a mile and a half shorter, for a total of 7.9 miles round trip. Allow about four hours.

Degree of Difficulty: There are no hazards along this wide, well-maintained trail. Two people can walk side-by-side for most of the journey.

Wildwood Trail

An arboretum is a "tree museum," and the Hoyt Arboretum, established in 1922, is one of the best in the United States. More than 700 species of plants and shrubs, native to all but one continent, have been planted within its 200 acres. There are several ways to explore the arboretum. Guided tours are offered every Saturday and Sunday, except during the winter months, and self-guided tour books are available for the Redwood Trail and the Oak Trail. The Wildwood Trail, the longest in the arboretum, takes the walker past collections of dogwood, oak, and pine. The arboretum boasts 230 species of cone-bearing plants, the largest collection of conifers in the nation. For the knowledgeable are a number of rare specimen trees and shrubs, including the David's Maple (a small tree with green and white striped bark), the Dawn Redwood (considered to be a living fossil), Weeping Brewer's Spruce (an endangered tree native to Oregon), and Wilson's Magnolia, whose fragrant blossoms show themselves in May.

The Wildwood Trail leads from the zoo parking lot past the dogwoods and on to the Japanese Garden (located in Washington Park). Here, five separate gardens (5.5 acres in all) are maintained by the city in conjunction with the local chapter of the Japanese Garden Society.The Japanese garden is considered to be one of the most authentic outside Japan.

A favorite garden here is the Strolling Pond (Chisen-Kaiyu-Shiki), where poi fish swim and water lilies bloom. The Strolling Pond ends where the Tea Garden begins: the teahouse is for private ceremonial use only by bona fide tea masters. The Japanese Garden is open 10–4 daily from September 16 to April 14 and 10–6, April 15 to September 15. It is closed on New Year's, Thanksgiving, and Christmas days. The Garden may be closed during extremely wet weather when the paths become slippery. Admission is $2.50 for adults and $1.25 for seniors, students, and children ages six to seventeen. Children five and under are admitted free. Call (503) 223-4070 for additional information.

Portland is known as the City of Roses, an image cultivated carefully since the early 1900s, along with 8,000 rosebushes in the city's International Rose Test Garden, located adjacent to the Japanese Garden. It is the oldest official, continuously operating, public rose test garden in the United States. Should you wish to dally on your walk, stop here. The Rose Garden's "first flush" is in early June, and the blooming continues into the first half of July.

Follow Wildwood Trail from the Japanese Garden past the collection of pines to Pittock Mansion. Here you will find the best vantage point in the arboretum. You can see two states and the Willamette and Columbia rivers as well as five mountains to the north and east in the Cascade

Range: Rainier, St. Helens, Adams, Jefferson, and Hood. The view of Mt. Hood is spectacular. New York writer Rosemay Guiley (formerly of Portland) says the Pittock Mansion area is "very hilly and very serene. You feel like you're deep in a forest. The Pittock Mansion itself is sometimes rented out for dinners and other events, and when you're there you feel as if you've gone back in time." Her husband Bruce Trachtenberg agrees. He says that the area is the "jewel in the crown, so to speak, of the civic pride Portland has always had." The mansion, a 22-room restored landmark, was built in 1914 in the style of the French Renaissance. The builder was Henry L. Pittock, founder of the local newspaper, *The Oregonian*. The mansion is open to the public from 1–5 daily, except on major holidays, the first Monday and Tuesday of December, and the first two weeks in January.

To return to your car from the Pittock Mansion, take the Wildwood Trail back to where it intersects with the Oak Trail and follow Oak south, around the Visitor Center, where it becomes the Oak Holly Trail. Pick up Wildwood again by the water storage tank and follow it back to the parking lot.

Washington

SEATTLE
Burke-Gilman Trail

Directions: The Burke-Gilman Trail begins at Gas Works Park. The park is located on 34th Street on the north end of Lake Union. Parking is available.

Best Season: Although Seattle can be quite rainy, the Burke-Gilman Trail is popular for both recreation and commuting, no matter what the weather, no matter what season. If you wish to avoid crowds, try mid-morning. The trail can be crowded on weekends and on weekday early mornings and late afternoons. Since it cuts through the University of Washington, many students and staff people use it for commuting.

Length: 12.5 miles one way. If you want, you can go as far as Matthews Beach Park (about 5 miles) and stop there for a picnic. Then you have a choice. You can either continue on to the end of the trail, and walk back for a round trip of 25 miles; or you can return from Matthews Beach for a 10-mile, round-trip walk.

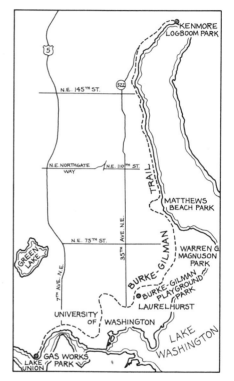

Degree of Difficulty: This is a long walk, but the trail is flat and hazard-free. Recently, though, some cyclists have been using it for triathlon training, so keep an eye out for them.

The Burke-Gilman Trail

The refreshing city of Seattle is surrounded by water on two sides: Puget Sound on the west and Lake Washington on the east. The views make Seattle a wonderful place to walk, and the creation of the urban

Burke-Gilman Trail has enhanced the pleasure of walking in this special city.

Burke and Gilman were community leaders in the 1880s. They headed a group of investors set on establishing a railroad based in Seattle. The trail named for them is the old railway line minus the tracks. Dedicated in August 1978, the trail is paved, closed to horses, and blissfully free of motorized vehicles.

Jane Harbison of Olympia, Washington, belongs to the "Tuesday Trotters." Despite its name, this is a group of 30 people who walk together on Thursdays. The group sets a walking goal each year. This year's "quest" is to walk from "sound to mountain." They do this in segments and recently completed the Burke-Gilman segment. "It's great for the average walker," Jane Harbison says, "and it is interesting, not boring. You can see so many areas of Seattle — the University of Washington, industrial and business areas, lakes, parks, and neighborhoods. It is fascinating to see people's homes and backyards."

From Gas Works Park, the trail roughly follows the ship canal, which connects Lake Union to the much larger Lake Washington. It passes through the University of Washington (about 2.6 miles along the trail) and lovely residential areas. The new Burke-Gilman Playground Park is next, and then the waterfront Warren G. Magnuson Park, where swimming, boating, and picnicking are enjoyed in mild weather. The trail continues to Matthews Beach Park, then north along the shore of Lake Washington to Sheridan Beach, and on to Kenmore Logboom Park, in King County.

Along the way you will have some magnificent views of mountains and lakes, beaches and parks. The trail is leafy and green most of the time, and trees along the trail's edge provide shade. In summer, keep an eye out for fat and tasty blackberries.

SHI SHI BEACH
Olympic National Park

Directions: Traveling west on the northern tip of the Olympic Peninsula, take Highway 112 to Neah Bay. You'll cross the Waatch River after passing an Air Force base. Take a left on the coastal gravel road; continue to the end of the road where the Shi Shi Beach trail begins.

Best Season: Summer is the best time to take this walk, although nominator Bryan Barrow, who was there in May, says it was sunny then, and beautiful. He suggests taking a daypack, with water and lunch.

Length: The trail is only about 1.5 miles. Plan to spend at least two hours covering the 3 round-trip miles, or even longer if you like to linger at the beach.

Degree of Difficulty: The walk is a moderate one, but the path will be muddy when it rains, which it often does.

The Olympic Peninsula and Shi Shi Beach

Olympic National Park, encompassing 1,400 square miles, is truly a national treasure. Majestic mountains, magical rain forests, and a 50-mile stretch of the wildest beaches in America combine to create a unique, magnificently beautiful area. The rain forests in the park result from moisture-filled clouds that blow in from the Pacific. They are truly extraordinary. The mountains form a barrier and force the clouds to rise. As they ascend they cool, and their moisture condenses into heavy rain or snow.

Abnormally high rainfall (as much as 200 inches a year) produces the only true rain forests outside of the tropics.

Bryan Barrow, who nominated the Shi Shi Beach walk, considers the park's coastline to be a backpacker's paradise. He should know. He recently walked the 3,300-mile U.S. Western coastline, from Canada to Mexico. It took him 13 months.

Shi Shi Beach is at the northernmost tip of Olympic National Park, where the forest meets the sea. The beach, which is only a mile long, lies beneath a lush, forested cliff. Bryan urges you to take advantage of low tides to explore rocky tidepools. "You might see a purple starfish," he says, "or large green sea anemones."

Just offshore, at the south end of the beach, is the Point of Arches — large rocks with arches sculpted by the sea. An occasional island is visible beyond the shoreline.

When Bryan was at Shi Shi Beach, he found an abandoned old squatter's cabin, which serves as a shelter for backpackers. It has a loft and wood-burning stove, but no plumbing. "This is the wilderness," he said, in response to our citified question.

CASCADE CANYON
Grand Teton National Park

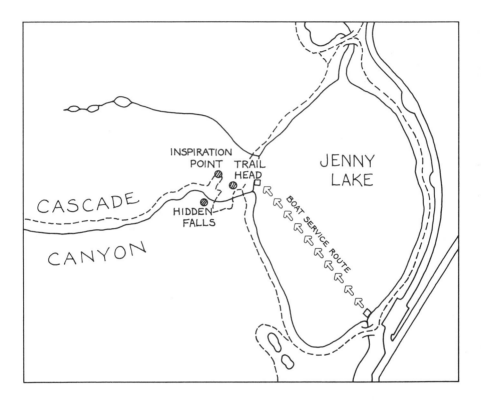

Directions: To get to Grand Teton National Park from the gateway city of Jackson, Wyoming, take Highway 89 north. From Yellowstone, head south on Highway 89, 191, or 287. The two parks interconnect.

Best Season: Mid-June to late September.

Length: To reach the trailhead, located on the west shore of Jenny Lake, you can walk the 2.5 miles around the lake or, from mid-June to mid-September, take the boat service. We recommend the boat trip; the Cascade Canyon Trail itself is 9 miles round trip. Allow a full day for this walk.

Degree of Difficulty: The trail, one of the most popular in the park, is an easy one, with spectacular views. Pack your own water and food, plus raingear. Afternoon thundershowers are as much a part of summer in the Grand Tetons as are the wildflowers. They come on fast and are of short duration. A sweater or jacket is essential; and make sure your footgear is appropriate — there are rocky areas. You might get a glimpse of a black bear so be forewarned. In the early morning you will likely see moose.

Cascade Canyon Trail

Companion-starved French-Canadian trappers gave the Grand Tetons their name in the 1800s. "Teton" is an archaic and crude French term for "breast." The park, much smaller than Yellowstone, contains a concentration of unsurpassed natural beauty, dominated by the mountains themselves. The 13,770-foot Grand Teton is often compared to the Matterhorn in Switzerland.

The Cascade Canyon Trail offers the walker a splendid opportunity to see the park's beauty up close. It passes through a variety of beautiful areas. Toward the beginning of the walk, a cascade of water called Hidden Falls beckons you. Then, after about a mile of walking up the gently ascending trail, you'll come to Inspiration Point, from which you can see the Jackson Hole valley floor ("hole" was the mountain man's word for "valley") and Jenny Lake.

Walk back into the Canyon, through spruce and fir forests, over rock slides, and out into views of the magnificent Grand Teton, as well as of Mt. Owen and Mt. Teewinot.

Nominator Linda Olson suggests you take this walk in mid- to late June. Then the lovely, cascading intermittent waterfalls are pouring out of the canyon walls, the result of still-melting snow. The blooming season for wildflowers, such as columbine and Indian paint brush, is July 1 through mid-August.

Part 2

THE SOUTHWEST
Arizona, Colorado, Nevada, New Mexico, Utah

1. Echo Canyon
2. Grand Canyon
3. Phoenix
4. Tucson
5. Grand Mesa
6. The Maroon Bells
7. Pike's Peak
8. Toiyabe National Forest
9. Frijoles Canyon
10. Santa Fe
11. Taos
12. Salt Lake City
13. Zion Narrows

THE CHIRICAHUA MOUNTAINS
Echo Canyon Loop Trail

Directions: From Phoenix, take I–10 to Willcox. Then follow Route 186 southeast of Willcox for 36 miles to the Chiricahua National Monument. Access to Echo Canyon Loop Trail is from the parking area at the end of a six-mile scenic drive.

Best Season: Spring through fall. Temperatures are generally mild then; however, thunderstorms are common from July through mid-September. The mean daily temperature for July is 74 degrees.

Length: The Loop Trail is 3.5 miles round trip and takes one and a half to two hours.

Degree of Difficulty: Moderately difficult. The trail descends approximately 500 feet, with a gradual climb back to the parking area. Although well maintained by the National Park Service, it is rough in parts. Take plenty of water and watch for loose rocks. Hiking boots are recommended. There are several varieties of snakes in the Monument. During the warm, wet months of July and August, be alert for occasional rattlesnakes.

Echo Canyon Loop Trail

The Echo Canyon Loop Trail, designed and built by the Civilian Conservation Corps between 1934 and 1940, is considered to be a masterpiece in trail engineering. Furthermore, it is perhaps the most beautiful trail in the Chiricahuas. Carolyn Dunn, who submitted the walk, and who works as a summer volunteer at Chiricahua National Monument, calls it "incredibly scenic. The rock formations are truly works of art."

In fact, the massive spires, turrets, and battlements make the rocks in the Chiricahuas among the most curious and unusual on earth. The rhyolite, or volcanic ash, formed what is called "welded tuff," creating banded pillars standing as high as 300 feet or more. Weaknesses in the rock, plus percolating water and erosion, formed, and continue to form, the balanced rocks for which the Chiricahua National Monument is so well known. As you begin your walk along the Echo Canyon Trail, you'll get an up-close view of the power of the geological forces that formed these massive "works of art." As you start down the trail, you'll see "Wall Street," where enormous rocks were split by faults. Many of the deep crevices and ravines have been "bridged" by the Civilian Conser-

vation Corps, permitting hikers to comfortably walk through the maze of spires, pinnacles, and balanced rocks.

After winding past the magnificent rock structures, the trail drops gently to a luxuriant wood and natural amphitheater called Echo Park. Here the towering rock formations are rivaled by towering ponderosa pine, Douglas fir, and Arizona cypress.

A portion of the return trail is strewn with "volcanic hailstones" from a ledge composed of marble-size pellets, apparently the result of wet conditions while the volcanic ash was descending through the atmosphere.

It is not unusual to see Arizona whitetail deer in the Chiricahuas, as well as coatis and peccaries. Also, it is sometimes possible to get a glimpse of bears, mountain lions, and nesting hawks in and around the canyon walls.

And once you would have seen Apache, for the Chiricahuas were Apache country, home to Cochise and Geronimo who fought the encroaching white man for more than 25 years. "Big Foot" Massai was another Chiricahua Apache who made a name for himself here, according to park superintendent Ted Scott. After the surrender of Geronimo in 1886, many of the Chiricahua Apache were transported to Ft. Sill, Oklahoma. Big Foot escaped from the train taking him east and walked hundreds of miles back home to his wife and child. He stole a horse from a local homesteader and disappeared with his little family into the Chiricahuas. They vanished without a trace near what is now known as Massai Point.

For further information on hiking in the Chiricahuas, call Chiricahua National Monument, (602) 824-3560, or write the park superintendent at: Chiricahua National Monument, Dos Cabezar Route, Box 6500, Willcox, AZ 85643.

GRAND CANYON NATIONAL PARK
Bright Angel Trail

Directions: The head of Bright Angel Trail is on the south rim of the Grand Canyon, in the heart of Grand Canyon Village. From Phoenix, head north on I–10 until you reach Flagstaff. From here, take I–80 north to the Grand Canyon. The drive is approximately four and a half hours. Clearly marked highway signs will lead you directly into Grand Canyon Village.

Best Season: Advice varies on the best time of year to descend into the Canyon. Unless you are the hardiest hiker, avoid the searing heat of summer. The rim of the Canyon is often cool in the summer months, but the bottom is hot and arid.

Best Time of Day: Starting down from the rim in the earliest morning is a necessity in any season, and it's a good idea to start up early the next morning, too. Hiker Chris Grace prefers to begin his ascent back to the rim around 3 a.m. by the full moon. "The clear light allows you to find your way," he says, "and the interplay of the soft light and the Canyon is pure enchantment."

Length: The trail is 20.6 miles round trip. Count on a four- to six-hour trek into the Canyon, twice that to return.

Degree of Difficulty: Seasoned hikers call Bright Angel Trail the easiest one into the Canyon; but, in the words of veteran Arizona hiker Bill Sewrey, "there is no easy trail." Be prepared. It's best to condition yourself a couple of months prior to the trip, and to walk the trail in two days. You'll be starting at approximately 6,900 feet in elevation; descending to 2,400 feet by the end of the day, and then up 4,500 feet the next. Use common sense along the trail; some areas are sheer drops into the pink-tinged Canyon below. Hikers warn of falling rocks, and almost anyone who has followed this path remembers the slick texture of the rocks. Bring water and some light (but direct-energy) food. A day-pack with a gallon or two of water is essential, although water is available seasonally at two locations in the first 3 miles, and year round at Indian Gardens oasis.

Places to Stay: If you plan to walk the trail in two days and want to backpack and camp at the bottom, you will need to make reservations in advance. Also, a National Park Service permit is necessary. Some may not take kindly to the idea of a 40-pound pack on such a long, steep, and rugged trail. They can stay at the privately owned Phantom Ranch, which provides dinner ("Steak or stew?" the reservationist will ask), breakfast the next morning, and a lunch to take along on the trail. The accommodations (dormitory style) and meals run under $100 for two people. (Phantom Ranch was called "Roosevelt's Camp" for many years after Teddy stayed there in 1908. It is also the only place in the Canyon where you can buy a beer.) Indian Gardens, an oasis 4.4 miles into the Canyon, is a good place to stay on your return trip out of the Canyon.

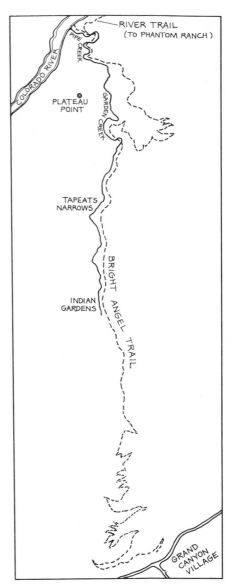

Walking the Bright Angel

The Canyon country and the wilderness it embraces was described by early Canyon explorer John Wesley Powell as "sublimity unequalled on the hither side of paradise." The Bright Angel Trail, which literally tumbles into the Canyon, is the best way to see this "unequalled sublim-

192

ity." A prehistoric Indian route to the inner Canyon, the trail was cultivated by old-time Canyon folk heroes in the 1890s who extracted a hefty $1 toll from anyone who attempted the descent. Today the trail is maintained by the National Park Service.

"There is nothing prettier than the Bright Angel Trail," says well-known walker and hiker Sid Hirsch, past State Chairman of the Sierra Club. Hirsch has seen big-horn sheep, deer, scrub jays, wrens, and a few snakes. ("Don't worry about them," he says. "They'll leave you alone, if you leave them be.")

About 4.4 miles after you begin your walk you'll come to the Indian Gardens oasis, a haven of lovely cottonwood trees; the area was cultivated by the Havasupai Indians centuries ago. Water is pumped through here to the south rim. From Indian Gardens, the trail forks. Here you can take a 1.4-mile additional excursion to Plateau Point and a breathtaking view of the Colorado River, 1,300 feet below. At Plateau Point look toward the north; you will see the formation known as Cheops Pyramid; you will also see Shiva Temple, Johnson Point, and Sturdevant Point from here and, to the northwest, Horn Creek Rapids.

After Indian Gardens, the trail follows Garden Creek for 1.2 miles (a good place to see wildflowers) and joins the River Trail, which parallels the Colorado River. Once you reach the river (cross it at the suspension bridge only), it is another 2.5 miles to Phantom Ranch.

The trip down Bright Angel is a journey through the varied life zones of Arizona; the view of the inner Canyon below and the play of rock, color, and space, underneath the canopy of Canyon sky, combine to create one of the most spectacular walks in the world.

PHOENIX
Squaw Peak

Directions: Squaw Peak (old maps will show it as "Phoenix Peak") is readily accessible from Lincoln Drive, a major Phoenix thoroughfare. Turn onto Squaw Peak Drive. The park is on the left, about 0.5 miles from the turnoff.

Best Season: From late October to April the trail can be hiked at any time of the day in relative comfort; by mid-April the afternoons are getting warm, and by June only the hardiest tackle the trail past 9:00 a.m.

Length: The trail to the top of Squaw Peak is 1.2 miles, with a rise in elevation from 1,400 to 2,608 feet. The 2.4 miles round trip can take as long as an hour and 45 minutes; or it can take just 40 minutes, for the fit and competitive.

Degree of Difficulty: The walk isn't easy; the steepest part is often compared to the last two miles of the Grand Canyon's Bright Angel Trail. But the glory of the Squaw Peak Trail is that you can approach it leisurely with plenty of stops to catch your breath. People young and old, fit and unfit, travel it daily. Local people walk the trail to get into shape for the Grand Canyon. If you get hooked on this trail, you can use it to improve your fitness, as you try to improve your time.

Squaw Peak Trail

This wonderful wilderness walk within a city has become a long-time friend to people who live in Phoenix. It is as well a special treat for visitors to Phoenix, the ninth-largest city in the United States. One Phoenix resident has been climbing Squaw Peak several times a week for 18 years; he first went to the top as a child in 1950. The rugged mountain path is classified as a "National Urban Trail" and is part of the U.S. Department of the Interior's National Trail System.

On weekends in the cooler months 1,000 people a day stream up and down Squaw Peak. Watch out for the terrifically fit running down; step aside. Dogs must be on a leash, and owners are required to clean up after them; but it's a good idea to watch your step. It pays to be cautious: avoid stepping on a snake or sliding on an occasional loose rock. You should have tread on your tennis shoes. Stay on the trail; "crosscutting" is frowned upon by the regulars, many of whom are volunteers who maintain the trail.

Always take water on any hike in Arizona, no matter what the time of year. Remember this is a desert environment; it is dry, rocky terrain, and its beauty is best appreciated in soft lights, not under the harsh, hot, midday sun. Early morning and late afternoon are the best times to see the light playing on the rock. (You can hear the well-modulated sounds of owls in the very early mornings, too.) The trail is fairly well traveled, even after dark, especially by people who head up after work. Be sure you have a flashlight at night, even if the moon is full.

On your way to the top of Squaw Peak you'll see the gamut of Arizona cacti: saguaros and prickly pears, for example, as well as barrel cacti and ocotillos. If there has been enough rainfall, you can see them all in bloom in early spring, clusters of white flowers crowning the ends of the saguaro branches, bright red painting the tips of the ocotillos. Palo Verde trees also abound; they are a delicate pale green, and — though not lush — they are richer than most of the vegetation along the walk.

The top of the mountain is a light gray, fractured, quartzite rock. From there you'll get a good panorama of Phoenix, as well as a view of the McDowell and Superstition mountains to the left and the White Tanks behind you, to the right.

194

About 100 people climb this trail every day, no matter what the weather: Some of them have been doing it for years. Charles Christiansen, deputy Phoenix city manager, has been walking up and down Squaw Peak for 20 years. He's walked it under Arizona's gentle rain, by moonlight, and in every season and all kinds of weather. "It's a marvelous recreational experience," he says; and he praises the walk for the physical and emotional well-being it provides.

Somewhere around mid-December, for the last few years, a group of hardy volunteers have placed luminaria (an Arizona Christmas tradition, borrowed from Mexico, of placing candles in sand in paper bags) every few feet all the way to the top of the peak. The 1984 Squaw Peak Luminaria and Caroling Walk attracted 3,500 people.

The top of Squaw Peak has been witness to weddings, business deals, new friendships, and even a hiking Santa Claus with presents on his back. It is a splendid place.

TUCSON
Seven Falls, Sabino Canyon

Directions: The Seven Falls Hike is located in the lower Catalina Mountains, north of Tucson. At the intersection of Tanque Verde and Sabino Canyon roads in Tucson, take Sabino Canyon Road for five miles. Note signs to Sabino Canyon parking lot. Directions to the Seven Falls trailhead may be found at the Information Kiosk or inside the Visitor Center.

Best Season: Arizona has a "monsoon" season, which begins around mid-July and can continue to the end of August. Bear Canyon and the Seven Falls Hike can be dangerous during this time; but if you are cautious and use common sense, it is also the time when Seven Falls is at its

loveliest, with the water running. January and February are also good months to take this walk.

Length: If you take the shuttle bus from the parking lot to the Seven Falls trailhead, it is 2.2 miles to the falls. (The shuttle bus runs on the hour from 9 a.m. until 4 p.m., seven days a week, except when there is flooding.) If you wish to walk to the trailhead, the trip to the falls is an extra 2 miles. Allow three to four hours for the 4.4-mile round trip, including the 20-minute shuttle.

Degree of Difficulty: The Seven Falls Hike is fairly easy. The creek is often dry, but even if it is not, take your own water, and don't drink the creek water unless you purify it first.

Seven Falls Hike
The creek in Bear Canyon, plunging down a series of shelves, forms seven waterfalls, interspersed by pools. To get to the base of the falls, take the lower path when the trail forks. Avoid the crowds by starting out on your walk early, and allow plenty of time for quiet contemplation of the varied desert vegetation and the sycamores, willows, and cottonwoods near the creek.

For a more challenging walk, you may want to hike to the 7,000-foot summit of the Catalinas. Here legend has it (according to seasoned hiker and Sabino Canyon booster Sid Hirsch) that 19th-century Apaches took livestock from a neighboring Sabino Canyon ranch and ran them right off the mountaintop, the U.S. Calvary in hot pursuit. It's 60 miles round trip up and down the mountain.

Call (602) 749-3223 for a recording of general information on Sabino Canyon, or (602) 629-5101 for more information from the U.S. Forest Service's Sabino Canyon Station.

Colorado

GRAND MESA
Crag Crest Trail

Directions: Located in western Colorado, the Crag Crest Trail is part of the Grand Mesa National Forest. Take Highway 65 from Grand Junction or Delta to Island Lake. Follow signs to West Trailhead.

Best Season: The trail is accessible only from mid-June until early September. Nominator Sandi Knudson urges you to try to arrange your walk in August. Plan to take the walk as early in the morning as you can. You'll need the time, and besides, elk and deer can be seen then.

Length: 10 miles; allow a full day.

Degree of Difficulty: Moderately difficult, due to the 11,000-foot altitude. Pack a good lunch and a snack (you might want to share some carrots or nuts with smaller animals). Water is a necessity. The weather may change without warning; shorts and a T-shirt are appropriate for this trip, but take a jacket or windbreaker along, and raingear.

The Crag Crest Trail

Sandi Knudson, of Grand Junction, calls the 10-mile circular Crag Crest Trail "the most spectacular I've ever seen, an absolutely fantastic day hike, which even the novice hiker can manage." The trail leads to magnificent panoramas from a flat-top vantage point, with views of mountain ranges in every direction. And, as you walk along the trail, you are witness to 10 million years of geologic history, including lava flows, slumping, and glacier movement.

The small animals you might befriend include snowshoe rabbits, pine squirrels, chipmunks, pocket gophers, pikas, and marmots. Porcupines are also found along the way, but you may not be as interested in sharing your trail mix with them. Black bears, mountain lions, and coyotes also live in the area but are rarely seen by walkers.

Parts of the trail on the top of the ridge along the crest portion are extremely narrow, only two feet in some areas. You'll have steep drop-offs on both sides, so be careful; the views here are the most spectacular.

On the way up you'll pass lakes and reservoirs (Wolverine Lake, Forrest Lake, Upper Eggleston Lake, Bullfinch Reservoir #1, Butts Lake, and Rockland Lake); and, if you happen to tote your fishing pole with you, the fishing (especially for trout) is excellent. Even in summer you may pass small snowdrifts, leftovers from winter; and you'll see wildflowers, including the delicately beautiful Colorado State Flower, the blue columbine. You may also see red columbine, Indian paintbrush, and many other flowers of summer.

There are restrictions on the number of people who can take this walk at one time. Check with the Grand Junction District Ranger at (303) 242-7006.

THE MAROON BELLS

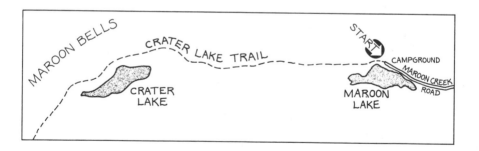

Directions: From Glenwood Springs, take the main road (Route 82) and turn right on Maroon Creek Road, just before coming into Aspen. Drive up to Maroon Lake Campground. Maroon Lake and the campground are at about a 9,000-foot altitude, and that's where you begin this walk, which follows Crater Lake Trail. At this height the sky is deep blue, the sun bright and warm, and the shadows of white clouds cool and fresh.

Best Season: Nominator Jim Powell recommends early fall (late August to mid-September) at this height, when the "landscape revels in a color display typical of much of the Rockies. The quaking aspen are turning in massive patches from their summer gray-green to clear yellow, then golden and finally to a tawny rust. You will not forget it."

Length: 4 miles round trip from Maroon Lake to the higher lake and back.

Degree of Difficulty: The trail is well marked and easy, except for a couple of short switchbacks over moraines left by the glacier that sculpted the peaks some ten thousand years ago in the last great Ice Age.

Crater Lake Trail

Have you ever turned to a new month on the calendar, only to imagine a scene from memory so strong you are almost there again? You can walk right into that perfect picture at the Maroon Bells in Colorado's Rockies. They appear as three perfectly arranged pyramids; indeed, maroon slab steps are projected against a deep blue sky at 14,000 feet altitude. Nearby is Aspen, a thriving winter and summer resort; once a rip-roaring silver mining town, it is now a skiers' gourmet paradise.

Crater Lake Trail heads upstream for most of the two miles to Crater Lake, above Maroon Lake. Crater Lake lies right at the base of the Bells in a lonely cirque almost at timberline. Stop a few times along the trail and step over to the stream. If you are a nimrod, try for a speckled or rainbow trout. Best of all, just relax and wonder about the tranquility, listen to the music of the brook tumbling over the rocks raised up in the Paleozoic Age in the Laramide Techtonic, a mere 60 million years earlier.

This area is different from most of the Rockies, which is composed of igneous rocks formed in the heat of the earth. The Bells were formed by layers of mud and sand from the bottom of an ancient sea. These layers of sediment were thrust up to their present heights, and their cracks became filled with molten rock, which contained the minerals sought by miners. Part of the Elk Mountains, the Maroon Bells are home to coyote, sheep, deer, moose, and elk.

When you reach the upper lake, you will want to relax in the rarified air at the timberline. If you have had a chance to acclimate a few days in the mountains, you can go for the steep, exhilarating climb over Buckskin Pass or opt for the less-strenuous hike over Maroon Pass — to see what is on the other side and to get even closer to the great Bells looming above. "For me," says Jim Powell, "it was fulfilling just to retrace the steps back down to the campground with the new aspect of the rocks, pines, aspens, and late wildflowers along the trail. In June you may cross snow on the path, and in August you will still see fields of snow against the peaks above timberline. In October have skis or snowshoes handy."

PIKE'S PEAK
Barr Trail

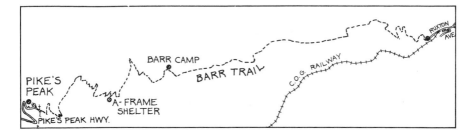

Directions: To reach Pike's Peak, travel south from Denver on I–25 to Colorado Springs. Then head west to Manitou Springs, to the foot of the Cog Railway, which travels to the top of Pike's Peak.

Best Season: August is the best month to take this challenging walk, for then the snow may have melted at the top of the trail.

Length: 13 miles to the top. Plan on an all-day walk, at least 10 hours. You can take the Cog Railway back down, or have someone meet you on top, at the Pike's Peak Highway. You need to make reservations on the railway by calling (303) 685-1045. Don't count on hitching a ride; it can't be done! There is a $4 toll per adult per car. For a much shorter walk, try taking the first section, the Mt. Manitou ascent, for 3 miles, and head back down for 6 miles round trip.

Degree of Difficulty: With a rise in elevation from 7,000 to 14,000 feet, this walk is a difficult one. The trail is well maintained, so follow signs and stay on the main path. There are some sheer cliffs and drop-offs near the top, but not on your pathway. Also, you need to be prepared for anything; after the timberline, about three miles from the summit, hail or snow can fall at any time. The temperature from the trailhead to the summit may vary as much as 40 degrees. Take a jacket or warm vest; hiking boots are essential. Carry your own water, even though you will see what look to be pristine mountain streams. The parasite whose infestation results in the serious "beaver fever" lurks in the clear waters.

Barr Trail
The Barr Trail to Pike's Peak is divided into three parts. The first, a brushy, ponderosa pine and Douglas fir area, climbs quickly and steeply for three miles. The second segment, seven or eight miles long, is fairly gentle and is marked by the rest area at Barr Camp. In case you run into bad weather, a few cots are available at Barr Camp. Refreshments are

sold here, too. (Call (303) 591-6120 for information.) Walk nominator Ronald Laird, however, never rests at Barr Camp. An accomplished race-walker, he has racewalked on four Olympic teams, was a National Racewalking coach for four years, and was named Outstanding U.S. Racewalker in six different years from 1963 to 1976. So, along with his recommendation for the walk up Pike's Peak comes the reminder that all 14 elite racewalkers from the Olympic Training Center in Colorado Springs used this walk for training. Four of them made the 1984 Olympic team.

The last section of Barr Trail begins at an A-frame shelter at the timberline. The terrain is quite steep again and very rocky. This is the toughest segment, a combination of high altitude and an extremely steep ascent.

The view along this trail is wonderful. In the distance you can see Colorado Springs and the surrounding mountains, including Colorado's Front Range and the Collegiates. From the summit you can see all the way to the Continental Divide. The up-close scenery is spectacular. You'll pass beautiful pines, clear mountain streams, golden aspens in the fall, blankets of wildflowers along the entire trail, and rugged rock formations. "If you're lucky," says Ron Laird, "you may see some big game, too, like mule deer, elk, and big-horn sheep."

Pike's Peak is the first high mountain you see when coming from the plains, and Colorado's most famous high peak. "Pike's Peak or Bust" was the slogan for many a hopeful 19th-century prospector. Today it is the slogan for many a hopeful walker, determined to reach the top.

Nevada

MT. ROSE TRAIL
Toiyabe National Forest, Reno

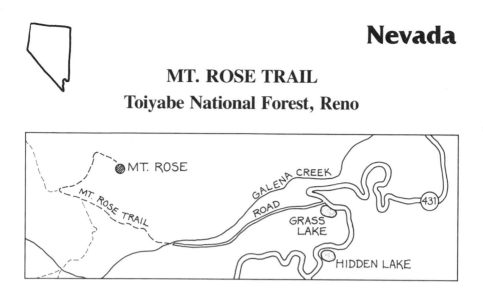

Directions: To get to the Mt. Rose trailhead, take Highway 431, the Mt. Rose Highway, south from U.S. 395 (toward Incline Village). It is approximately 14 miles from U.S. 395 to the trailhead. After passing the summit sign and the Forest Service campground, you'll see a small building on your right. Park here; signs will direct you up the road to the trailhead.

Best Season: The best time for this walk is between mid-July and early September; the snows usually start by mid-September. However, if you are an experienced hiker, a winter walk on snowshoes or on cross-country skis can be exhilarating. Neil Botts, of the Carson Ranger District, warns that trail signs are not visible in the snow; you have to be familiar with the route. If you plan a winter walk on the Mt. Rose Trail, call the "avalanche number" in Truckee: (916) 587-2158 for a recording, which is constantly being updated as weather conditions change. You can also call the Carson Ranger District: (703) 882-9211 for weather reports and further information.

Length: The all-day hike is 11 miles round trip; plan to take your time.

Degree of Difficulty: The rise in elevation is from 1,500 to 2,000 feet. The walk will be considered moderate by some, moderately difficult by others. Bring your own water and a picnic lunch. Prepare for cold weather; a warm jacket or windbreaker is a necessity.

The Mt. Rose Trail

Nevada conservationist, Sierra Club member, and avid walker and hiker Rose Strickland says that Mt. Rose's name is probably related to the form the mountain takes — a voluptuous reclining woman, long hair blowing in the wind.

Along the trail, you will be on the crest of the mighty Sierras; and on a clear day you can see forever, to Incline Village, Lake Tahoe's north shore, and glassy Emerald Bay. There is usually a register at the 10,778-foot summit where you can immortalize your feat by adding your name to those of other walkers who have made this trip.

Toiyabe National Forest is a wonderland of white bark and Jeffrey pine, willow, and sage. You'll see a small pond filled with frogs at the trailhead. Wildflowers line the path, and, farther on, you'll pass a mountain meadow where stout-bodied marmots play among the rocks. Above the tree line, the rocks become granite boulders.

Mt. Rose Trail was judged Reno's favorite high-altitude walk by a reader poll conducted by the *Reno Gazette-Journal,* according to Susan Lynn who nominated it. We urge you to consider walking the trail soon. On the lower reaches of Mt. Rose, construction is about to start on the Galena Creek Resort and ski area. Before long, ski-lift towers will loom above the Mt. Rose Trail.

New Mexico

FRIJOLES CANYON
Bandelier National Monument

Directions: To find Bandelier, New Mexico, head north from Santa Fe on U.S. 285. When you reach Pojoaque, turn left (west) on State Highway 4. The entrance to Bandelier National Monument is eight miles beyond the community of White Rock. It is essential to stop at the Visitors Center, since backcountry permits are required for day and overnight trips. Permits are free, although a $1-per-car entrance fee is charged. The Frijoles Canyon trailhead is six miles beyond the entrance station on Highway 4. Leave your car at the Ponderosa Campground. To return to your car, arrange for someone to pick you up at the Bandelier Visitors Center.

Best Season: The best time to go to Bandelier is during the summer season, May 1 to October 31. Although the trail is open in the winter and used by cross-country skiers, it is not maintained, and varying snow depths, up to three feet, make the area dangerous. Be prepared for heat in mid-summer. The temperature may rise to 90 degrees, and care should be taken to move slowly at the trailhead's 7,300-foot altitude. Start out early in the morning; the Visitors Center opens at 8:00 a.m. in the summer and closes at 6:00 p.m. During winter months, closing is at 4:30 p.m. July and August make up the monsoon season at Bandelier. You should be aware of the possibility of flash flooding and the risk of lightning. Carry light raingear.

Length: The trail is 6 miles into Frijoles Canyon to the Headquarters. Take your time to enjoy the walk; allow five to six hours for the trip.

Degree of Difficulty: The trail is moderate. Water and food are a necessity; allow at least a gallon of water per person, and pack a good lunch and a snack. You will cross Frijoles Creek about 22 times; many people carry tennis shoes in a day-pack to wear for the crossings, to keep hiking shoes and boots dry. Watch your step as you make the crossing; a twisted ankle would be a painful inconvenience. Rattlers and black bears are present in the canyon, but seldom seen. As in all wilderness areas, use your powers of observation to stay aware of what is around you.

Frijoles Canyon and Bandelier National Monument

Adolph Bandelier was a Swiss ethnologist, archaeologist, and author who settled in Santa Fe in 1880 to make an exhaustive study of the Pueblo Indians. Bandelier National Monument is on the Pajarito Plateau, an ash and lava remnant of a vanished, ancient volcano. It is surrounded by the Jemez Mountains. You will see rock with holes in it; this is tuff, petrified volcanic ash. Bandelier National Monument, established by Congress in 1916, protects 50 square miles and the ruined treasures of a civilization that flourished from the 9th to the 14th centuries.

Frijoles Canyon is a deep gorge cut by Frijoles Creek. It is a rare oasis in dry New Mexico. The canyon bottom was used as home for 300 years by the Anasazi people (Anasazi means "the ancient ones"), who most likely arrived here from the Four Corners area around 1250. In an "ethnohistorical" novel called *The Delight Makers,* Adolph Bandelier took as his inspiration the peaceful Anasazi who lived in the canyon centuries ago.

Dropping into the canyon, you will be traveling steep switchbacks but following a pleasant trail. You'll see cottonwood trees, box elder, water maples, ponderosa pine, rabbit brush, and New Mexico's State Flower, the spiny yucca. Mule deer are common; so are porcupines, and at night raccoons can be seen. There are many birds, from brown towhees to western tanagers. About twice a year there is a report of a mountain lion sighting.

Before you descend into the canyon, there is a ponderosa pine forest. The gentle descent will take you to the canyon floor's 6,000-foot elevation, a drop of 1,300 feet. The canyon is lush and beautiful; it is not difficult to understand why the ancients chose to live here. Lichens are found on the rocks of the shaded canyon. Rainfall is 12 inches per annum.

Near the Headquarters in the canyon is the Tyuonyi ruin, a word meaning "meeting place." The structure was once three stories high and contained 400 rooms.

A 10-minute slide presentation on the area and its history is shown on request at the Visitors Center. For further information write: Bandelier National Monument, Los Alamos, NM 87544, or call (505) 672-3861.

SANTA FE

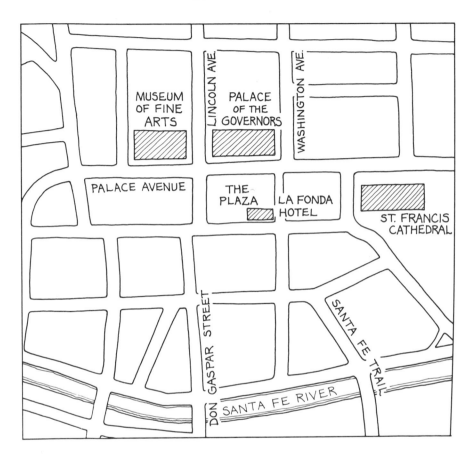

Directions: From Albuquerque, take U.S. 25 north and east to Santa Fe.

Best Season: The sun shines 300 days a year, but winters can be cold; dress warmly and wear boots to protect your feet from snow. If you can, take this walk early in the morning. Most shops will still be closed, but you can backtrack later. You need time to feel the town without too many distractions.

Length: You can meander around Santa Fe for about two hours, stop for lunch, and walk around for two hours more. The main downtown area covers several blocks; and Canyon Road, once a narrow burro trail connecting Santa Fe to Pecos, is lined with old adobes transformed into shops, galleries, and restaurants. It is 2 miles long.

Degree of Difficulty: Easy. There are no hazards along this walk, other than the danger of your becoming so intoxicated with Santa Fe that you quit your job to become a bartender in order to live here.

Experiencing Santa Fe

Legends are a part of the rarified air of Santa Fe's 7,000-foot elevation. One claims the town is on the site of an Indian village called, appropriately, "the place of the dancing ground of the sun." Even though people say Santa Fe is not what it was 40 years ago (and what is?), it is still a dream for the walker interested in history, culture, anthropology, and just about everything else.

Like a complicated organism, Santa Fe is multidimensional and not easily grasped with a cursory embrace. You might, for example, upon arriving in the downtown area, see a "gringa" — draped in a cut-silk-velvet, haute-couture version of traditional Navajo dress — stepping out of a maroon Rolls Royce. Santa Fe then looks like a playground for the ostentatious rich; shops abound with clothing and jewelry, retailing for thousands of dollars per item. But there's far more to this city: a history reaching back to the very roots of Southwestern civilization; architecture emerging from the primal ooze itself to embrace generations of people; artists and craftspeople creating beauty all around you; and the amalgamation of Anglo, Spanish, and Pueblo cultures.

Santa Fe is more than 400 years old. The Plaza, a good place to start your walk, is north of the Santa Fe River. It was laid out in 1610, following the colonial town plan of Spain's King Philip II. The plaque on the obelisk tells about the hard times white settlers had in northern New Mexico in the 1800s. On the north side of the Plaza is the Palace of the Governors, the oldest government building in the United States, built around 1612. One hundred governors have ruled here — Spanish, Indian, Mexican, and American. (Santa Fe is still the capital of New Mexico.) Old Zebulon Pike was nabbed by the Spanish and held prisoner here in the Palace of the Governors in 1807.

The street that fronts the Palace of the Governors is Palace Avenue. Turn left and cross Washington Avenue. You will shortly enter a portal which fronts some small stores. This is a site that was given to Arias DeQuiros by General Vargas in return for DeQuiros's role in helping to regain New Mexico from the Indians in 1693. Look around, then return to the Plaza.

The Museum of Fine Arts is on the northwest corner of the Plaza, at Lincoln Avenue. It was dedicated in 1917 and is a wonderful example of Spanish Pueblo-style architecture. On the southeast corner of the Plaza, at San Francisco Street, is La Fonda Hotel, likely the oldest hotel site in the United States. Billy the Kid supposedly worked in its kitchen. At the La Fonda newsstand you can purchase *The Santa Fe Guide* by Waite Thompson and Richard Gottlieb for $4.50. It's a wonderful guide to walking the city.

From La Fonda, cross San Francisco Street and walk up to Saint Francis Cathedral. Remodeled in 1869 under the supervision of Archbishop Lamy, this church is the most recent of numerous fine churches built on this site since 1610. Lamy, immortalized by Willa Cather in *Death Comes for the Archbishop,* is buried here.

Wander down the south side of San Francisco Street. After you cross Don Gaspar Avenue, San Francisco becomes West San Francisco. Here are some interesting shops and galleries you might enjoy browsing through.

Eating is another delight here. On Sunday morning, after a quiet walk, stop for brunch (which begins at 8:00 a.m.) at Café Pasqual's at 121 Don Gaspar. You will be soothed by the peaceful sounds of a lute being played by a young man perched on a chair set against a long wall with three hyperrealist murals. The first mural shows men building a brick wall, the mountains and sky of Santa Fe behind them. For dinner try The Pink Adobe, 406 Santa Fe Trail. Located in one of the oldest Santa Fe districts, this old restaurant is superb. New Mexican food is lighter than Old Mexican, and everything seems much fresher.

The Santa Fe described here is only the first course of a grand feast. Explore it for yourself, armed with *The Santa Fe Guide* or information from the Chamber of Commerce's Visitor's Bureau at (505) 983-7317. In the summer months there is a Visitors Information Booth under the portals of the First National Bank of Santa Fe at the Plaza.

To steep yourself in the ways of northern New Mexico and Santa Fe (as well as other parts of the Southwest), invest $14.95 in Robert L. Casey's incomparable *Journey to the High Southwest: A Traveler's Guide.*

TAOS
A Guided Walk

Directions: Taos is located 70 miles northeast of Santa Fe. From Santa Fe, take U.S. 68 and follow signs to Taos. This walk begins at Taos Inn, a half block from the Plaza on Paseo del Pueblo Norte.

Best Season: From November until June for the walk that leaves from Taos Inn. From June through October for both the walk that leaves from Taos Inn and the one beginning at Kachina Lodge on Paseo del Norte. The walks are conducted by Char Boie Graebner. For reservations or more information, call her at (505) 758-3861. The fee for the walk is $4 for adults. A discount is given for seniors, and children 16 and under are free.

Length: The walk takes from one-and-a-half to two hours, depending on the age of the people in the group and how acclimated they are to Taos's 7,000-foot altitude.

Degree of Difficulty: Relatively easy (level sidewalks, some stairs); but, again, it depends on the age and physical condition of those in the group.

Taos Walking Tour

Char Boie Graebner is an historical writer steeped in the folklore and history of Taos. She has lived here for 15 years and customizes her walking tours to the particular interests of each group. She surveys the people to determine their interests and their reasons for visiting Taos. Many people, she says, are interested in Taos's art colony and how its artists ended up here. The sound of the word "Taos" evokes the names of two great 20th-century artists, D. H. Lawrence and Georgia O'Keefe, as well as art maven Mabel Dodge Luhan, once a lover of Jack Reed (played by Warren Beatty in *Reds*) and later muse to artists and a driving force behind Taos's emergence as a haven for artists and writers.

Others, says Graebner, come to Taos to learn firsthand of its prehistoric and Indian origins or because they are interested in the Spanish, who used Taos as their northernmost colony in the 1600s or because they want to know more about the mountain men, who used it as an important out-fitting center. (There is actually an organization of mountain men in the U.S. today. They have taken this tour several times to pay homage to Kit Carson, only one of New Mexico's many colorful historical characters.)

"There are many aspects of the tour," Graebner says. "We are weaving in and out of three different cultures. Some people are interested in details of Taos architecture, for example; some in the great festivals of Taos."

One festival discussed on the tour is the San Geronimo Festival, which takes place in late September in Taos Pueblo, a traditional Indian village of 2,000 people, three miles northeast of Taos. The festival, which has its origins in prehistoric times, starts with a sundown dance and a dawn footrace the next morning. The men run barefoot, dressed in breechcloths.

The tour that leaves from the Taos Inn travels west on Bent Street and then weaves in and out of buildings toward the Plaza, the heart of Taos. Here, the American flag flies day and night, a tradition dating to the Civil War. Kit Carson and other pro-Union men who happened to be good with guns threatened to use them on anyone touching Old Glory. The flag stayed, and so has the tradition.

During the tour you'll sit on the Plaza, and Graebner will tell you about vanished buildings, destroyed by fire. One visible building, not far from Taos Plaza, is Las Palomas, the "big house," a 17-room adobe, once the home of Mabel Dodge Luhan. It now houses a nonprofit organization which provides courses in Southwestern culture.

Char Boie Graebner has taken Americans, Europeans, Japanese, American Indians, and many others on her tours of Taos. And she has taken them in all kinds of weather, including pouring spring rains with "water sweeping across our ankles" and in picturesque snowstorms. "If they're willing, I'm willing," she explains.

Utah

SALT LAKE CITY

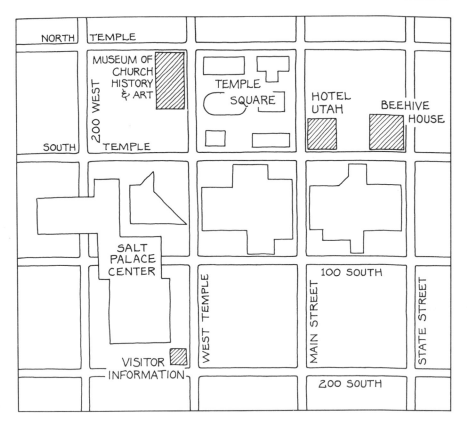

Directions: To get to Salt Lake City from the south, take I–15. The walking tour begins at the Salt Palace Center, five buildings owned by Salt Lake County. Start at the Visitor Information Station at 180 South West Temple Street. Summer hours for the Information Station are 8 a.m. to 6 p.m. on weekdays, Saturdays 9 a.m. until 6 p.m., and Sundays 10 a.m. until 2 p.m.

Best Season: This walk can be taken almost any time of year, although winter months may yield days too cold and snowy for some to enjoy a walking tour. Mid-morning is a good time to take the walk; museums and

212

other buildings are likely to be open. A brochure entitled "Salt Lake Walking and Driving Tours" is available at the Visitor Information Station, and will guide you to more than 18 points of interest in downtown Salt Lake City.

Length: 1.3 miles; about two hours.

Degree of Difficulty: This is an easy walk with many interesting things to see along the way.

Downtown Salt Lake City

With the exception of the Dead Sea, the Great Salt Lake is the saltiest body of water on earth, and the largest lake west of the Mississippi. The nearby city, which bears its name, has an elevation of 4,330 feet and is clean and wide and a good place to walk and explore. It is also the gateway to wonderful outdoor recreation areas, such as Alta, the second-oldest ski resort in the U.S., only 32 miles from Salt Lake International Airport.

Brigham Young himself was Salt Lake's first city planner. He was the second president of the Church of Jesus Christ of Latter-day Saints and the first territorial governor of Utah. Salt Lake City was laid out on a grid, originating at a meridian called Temple Square. The 10-acre square in the heart of Salt Lake City serves as the point of origin for the city's street numbering system. If you are there on a Thursday, you may want to attend a Mormon Tabernacle Choir rehearsal. They are open to the public and begin at 8 p.m. You can also attend the Sunday morning broadcast; plan to be there by 9:15.

As you cross Main Street from Temple Square, note the audible pedestrian signals for the blind ("chirps," for example, indicate a green light for north–south travel). The signals have been installed at 10 downtown intersections.

Among the places of historical interest on this walk is Beehive House, built by Young around 1854 as his home. It has been restored with furniture and artifacts of the era and is a National Historic Landmark. The Museum of Church History and Art displays memorabilia, documents, and sculpture dating from the early 1800s.

At Main and South Temple, near both the Mormon Temple and the Mormon Tabernacle, sits the 10-story white enamel brick building trimmed in terra cotta that is the Hotel Utah. At the center of Salt Lake City life since 1909, it is one of the finest hotels in the West. The restaurant on the 10th floor, called the Roof, serves excellent traditional French fare. Stop by in the afternoon for the tea and cakes served from rolling trays, a Salt Lake City tradition. (The phone number of the Hotel Utah is (901) 531-1000. The toll-free reservation number is (800) 453-3820.)

ZION NARROWS
Zion National Park

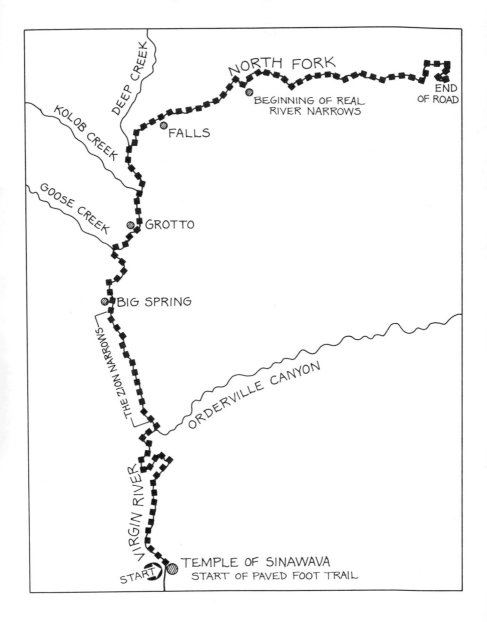

DEEP CREEK

NORTH FORK

END OF ROAD

BEGINNING OF REAL RIVER NARROWS

KOLOB CREEK

FALLS

GOOSE CREEK

GROTTO

BIG SPRING

THE ZION NARROWS

ORDERVILLE CANYON

VIRGIN RIVER

TEMPLE OF SINAWAVA
START OF PAVED FOOT TRAIL

START

Directions: Zion National Park is accessible from I–15 and Route 9 from the west and U.S. 89 and Route 9 from the east. The Zion Narrows walk begins at the north end of the Zion Canyon section of Zion National Park.

Best Season: The best time to walk the Narrows, in the opinion of nominator Nanette Larsen, is from June to mid-July and from September to early October. From mid-July to the second week in September, flash flooding may occur. Check the ranger station at (801) 772-3256 daily for weather conditions. The canyon is sometimes closed to walkers.

Length: The entire canyon is 13 miles long (and only for the hardy backpacker), but many people love the gorgeous, half-day, 2½-mile walk into the canyon and back. This round-trip, 5-mile walk into the Narrows ends at the intersection of Orderville Canyon. If you plan to take the entire 13-mile backpacking trek, special permits, available only 24 hours in advance, are required. They are issued at the Visitor Center at the south end of the canyon.

Degree of Difficulty: Overall, this walk must be classified as extremely difficult. It does, however, have its easier segments. The first paved mile is quite flat and actually an easy walk. It follows the Virgin River and offers views of the hanging gardens along the cliff edge. The walk begins at the natural amphitheater called the Temple of Sinawava. If you are not used to strenuous walking, turn around when the pavement ends. The next 1½ miles have some elevation rise and the path is uneven, with many rocks and some sandy areas. There will be spots where you will have to walk in water, sometimes up to your knees and even up to your waist in parts. The water temperature is about 60 degrees in June and about 66 degrees later in the summer. The canyon sometimes narrows to 75 feet; should you choose to go on another mile or two, it narrows to 25 feet in places, and you may encounter chest-high water. Carry drinking water and lunch in a day-pack; tennis shoes, cutoffs, and a sweatshirt tied around the waist or shoulders are the clothes of the day at Zion Canyon. You'll find a walking stick helpful as you ford the river, and bring a flashlight. It's easy to misjudge time in the Narrows. It may be dark before you know it.

Walking the Zion Narrows

Wind, rain, frost, and the Virgin River have cut through Navajo sandstone for millions of years to create breathtaking Zion Canyon. Mormons settling in Utah were the first non-Indians to find Zion; hence the Biblical names found throughout the canyon area. "Zion" means "heavenly resting place."

The rewards awaiting the walker in this "heavenly resting place" are immeasurable. The Virgin River winds through the canyon, and majestic sandstone walls (160 million years old) rise close to 2,000 feet on both sides. You'll pass a narrow corridor with hanging gardens of ferns and delightful swimming holes, where you can while away the hours in paradise.

Along the trail you'll also pass by an open area of pinyon-juniper woodland and short evergreens and oaks; and you'll see treasure coves, side canyons cut back into the walls of the main canyon. Take time to explore.

Part 3

THE GOLDEN WEST
California

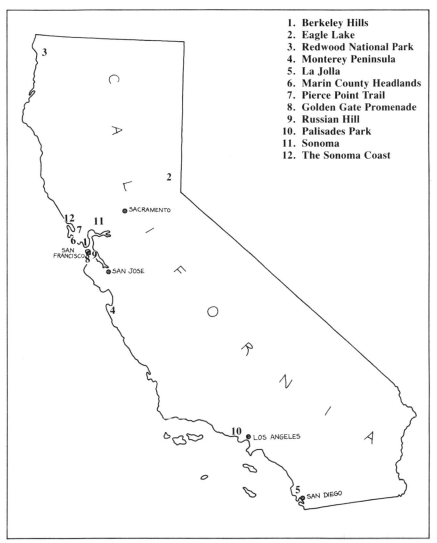

1. Berkeley Hills
2. Eagle Lake
3. Redwood National Park
4. Monterey Peninsula
5. La Jolla
6. Marin County Headlands
7. Pierce Point Trail
8. Golden Gate Promenade
9. Russian Hill
10. Palisades Park
11. Sonoma
12. The Sonoma Coast

California

BERKELEY HILLS

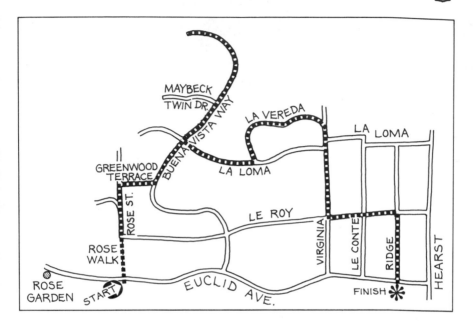

Directions: From San Francisco, take the East Bay Bridge to 17 north, which is also I–80. Follow this to the Berkeley exit marked University Avenue (about 4 miles from the toll plaza). Go east on University for about 2 miles and take a left on Oxford. Two blocks later, take a right on Hearst and continue for about ¾ mile. Go left on Euclid and drive ¾ mile until you see a street sign on your right that says Rose Walk. This is the starting point of the walk; park anywhere near here.

Best Season: September, or better still October, when the weather ranges from Indian summer mellow to invigorating autumnal crisp.

Length: You should allow one and a half to two hours for this leisurely 1½-mile walk.

Degree of Difficulty: Easy.

Art Follows Nature in the Berkeley Hills

"This walk will take you through a hillside neighborhood unlike any other," says Marilyn Wright Ford, who submitted it. "Where else could you encounter rustic rambling chalets, fanciful vine-draped cottages, commanding modern cliffhangers, and a Greek temple . . . all on the same street?"

Yet, for all the rich variety in architecture, most of the houses share an underlying design principle: the celebration and veneration of the natural environment. For this was one of the principles on which this neighborhood was built in the 1890s, when intellectuals, artists, architects, and aesthetes were first drawn to the hills' unspoiled serenity and the intellectual vigor of the nearby university.

In order to preserve the natural beauty of Berkeley, these early residents formed the Hillside Club. They published a pamphlet, "The Simple Home" (1904), prescribing the ideal Berkeley dwelling. It was to be loveingly crafted from natural materials to blend in with its natural setting: a tranquil, soul-sustaining sanctuary. "The Simple Home" was a hit. Berkeley was soon a forest of unassuming, unpainted redwood shingle houses, often with chimneys and walkways of irregularly shaped clinker bricks.

Devotees of the "simple home" were particularly influenced by the craftsmanlike homes built by their neighbor, architect Bernard Maybeck (1862–1957). His "chalets" were the beginning of a tradition in the regional architecture; but his work, as you'll see, was wonderfully diverse.

Let's begin. Stroll up Rose Walk, a picturesque development that looks like an idealized vision of a European hilltown. Maybeck designed the walkway in 1913 and was consultant to the houses' architect, Henry Gutterson, in 1923. At the end of Rose Walk, keep to the left and go up to the street.

To your right on the corner (#1401) is an imposing 1914 shingle house by John Galen Howard. It's a far cry from the grand classical buildings he designed for U.C. Berkeley as its supervising architect (1902–1924).

Continue straight up the hill and turn right on Greenwood Terrace. On the right side of the street you'll come upon Greenwood Common, a showcase for some of the Bay Area's architectural luminaries, created in 1950. Each house had a different architect, but all have a sleek modernism, softened by natural wood exteriors and a respectful restraint from upstaging their spectacular setting.

Take a left on Buena Vista. Coming up: a number of Maybecks, as well as his design legacies. #2704, on the southeast corner of Buena Vista and LaLoma, is a 1916 Maybeck, still fresh and contemporary today. Over its entrance on Buena Vista, note the iron Japanese-like lantern. Many of the houses here have handsome handcrafted details. #2711 was built by Maybeck in 1924, shortly after a fire destroyed many homes in these hills. The surface effect to the right of the front door came from

Maybeck's experiment: dipping flour sacks into a fireproof cementlike substance. (The 1924 fire dampened most Berkeley builders' enthusiasm for wood-sheathed houses for years to come.) #2717 is a Maybeck look-alike built in (surprise) 1968! Other Maybecks: #2733 and #2751 (on the northwest and northeast corners of Buena Vista and Maybeck Twin Drive) and #2780 (notice its unique "clapboard" concrete chimney).

Just before you reach #2800, look through the trees for a view of the Cal campus and Howard's tall, elegant Campanile (1914). #2800 is the Temple of the Wings (by A. R. Monroe, 1914). It was built as an open-air dance studio and house for Florence Boynton, whose childhood friend and inspiration was Isadora Duncan. Boynton's temple, her dance, and flowing robes expressed her passion for ancient Greek culture. Please respect the owner's privacy and just peek in from the driveway entrance.

Retrace your steps now down Buena Vista and walk left on LaLoma. #1515 LaLoma is a striking 1907 Maybeck. The concrete surface is unique in its scored, mosaic, and painted details. Note the trellises skirting the house. Maybeck often used them as a device to integrate indoors and outdoors.

Go left up LaVereda. Originally part of a rural stagecoach route, it still feels like a remote country lane. The Hillside Club lobbied to preserve the rural, trail-like character of these hill streets. LaVereda also contains an array of appealingly quirky architectural styles. Tucked away at the end of #1555's driveway is a turreted brick fantasy from 1914. #1651, an 1895 boarding house that looks like a Scandinavian dollhouse, is one of the neighborhood's oldest structures.

Where LaVereda forks, take the lower fork to the curve in the road and descend the far steps. #1705 was built in 1905 by an employee of Maybeck. All that's missing from this quintessential chalet is Heidi herself. Look across the divider to the high side of the street. Note the trio of classic "Berkeley brown shingles."

Descend the steps by #1705's driveway and walk left on the street below. #1709 is a 1910 Maybeck, which has been altered. Walk downhill and take a right on LeConte. #2669 is a 1905 brown shingle house whose "simple home" virtues are contradicted by the exotic later addition of an Islamic tower.

Walk left on LeRoy. #1772 (on the south side of the creek) was designed by Maybeck as a photographer's studio. Its contemporary classicism belies its birthdate: 1907. The mid-road tree stump was, until a few years ago, a magnificent oak. Maybeck's wife and her fellow Hillside Clubbers rescued it from destruction when this road was first put in.

Walk now to Ridge Road and take a right to Euclid. If you need a break here go to one of the coffeehouses and take in the college scene.

Eventually you want to grab a #7 bus on Euclid going north. Tell the driver you want to get off at the Rose Garden. (Its stop is right after Rose Walk, where you began.) If you have been revived by a cup of espresso, walk the uphill three quarters of a mile along Euclid instead.

220

The Rose Garden was created by the WPA and landscape architect V. M. Dean in 1933. It perfectly expresses the "ideal" garden, as set forth in "The Simple Home" years earlier: "Nature controlled by art . . . that will exhilarate our souls."

EAGLE LAKE
Near Tahoe City

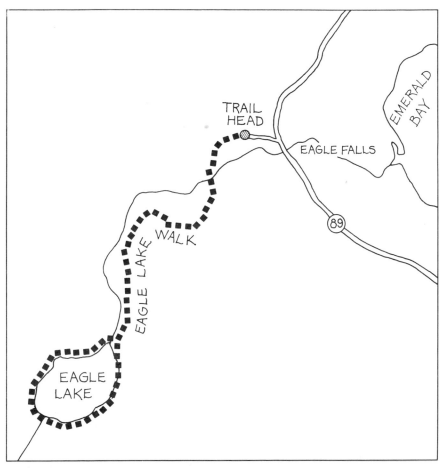

Directions: From Tahoe City, California, drive north to beautiful Emerald Bay, about 15 miles on Highway 89. Park on the west side of the highway at the Emerald Bay State Park parking lot. Cross the street to the Eagle Lake trailhead.

Best Season: Summer. The summer season at Lake Tahoe really doesn't begin until late June, but it continues until late September. Because of the crisp air even in summer you can take this walk at any time during the day. It's a fun walk, even when its foggy, although seeing the sun sparkle and dance on little Eagle Lake is preferable.

Length: The walk is only about 4 miles round trip, including a little exploration around Eagle Lake.

Degree of Difficulty: Easy. This is a walk you can take with school-age children. The only potential hazard is crossing a wooden footbridge about a quarter of a mile into the walk. After the footbridge, you must maneuver a few rocks as you finish crossing the rushing water of Eagle Falls. Take care, and assist the children with the crossing. This is a perfect, peaceful picnic spot; and, since the distance is short, you may want to sport a day-pack with a sumptuous lunch.

Eagle Lake Walk

Tahoe City was an old lumber camp. Today it is an expensive and trendy resort, both summer and winter — but it is still lovely. Magnificent Lake Tahoe, as long as the English Channel is wide (22 miles), is perfectly blue and, for the most part, perfectly clear. There are many places to walk and hike in the Sierras, but we suggest this walk to tiny Eagle Lake, a smaller image of the larger beauty of Lake Tahoe.

From the footbridge, observe the trail carefully. There are no posted signs, so you must use your powers of observation to judge where the trail goes. In most places, this is obvious, but it's a good idea to pay attention.

Soon you'll be in a delicious pine forest; and, even in late June, you'll find yourself stomping through good-sized snowdrifts, the warm sun a wonderful contrast to the icy snow.

After about a mile you'll see the tiny, jewel-like lake, surrounded by steep, pine-covered mountains. It is so peaceful and so beautiful, you'll want to pause for awhile, perhaps to contemplate the order of things, or just to let the beauty in.

If you take this walk to Eagle Lake in the morning and do not pack a picnic lunch, you may be ready to eat when you return to your car. Drive toward Tahoe City again and stop at Homewood, a tiny bend in the road. You'll see The Squirrel's Nest, a fascinating shop with pottery, glassware, and everything else imaginable for the kitchen. Behind the shop is a charming outdoor restaurant, open in the summer, called Soupçon. Its decor is wonderful, "surrealistic kitsch," and the food is fabulous. Try the sticky chewy chocolate pie. You'd better plan ahead for this stop by calling (916) 525-7944.

Lodging in Tahoe City is quite expensive; but there is a little 1940s motel, Lake Pines, with cottages tucked away in the old Lake Forest area of Tahoe City. Lake Pines is not fancy, but its prices aren't either. The North Lake Tahoe Visitors Bureau has a toll-free number for lodging reservations: (800) 824-8557.

ENDERTS BEACH
Redwood National Park

Directions: From Crescent City, take Highway 101 south to the Enderts Beach Road. Head west and park at the Enderts Beach overlook. Here you'll be about 200 feet above the beach. Walk south to the little trail used by bicyclists, which drops down to a tiny stream and a primitive campground.

Best Season: Spring, summer, and fall, although summer may be foggy. At any time of the year the weather is likely to be cool, favorable for the growth of the mighty redwoods; even on sunny days the giant trees shade the trail through the forest.

Length: Exploring Enderts Beach will take about half an hour; the sand stretches only 300 yards north and 300 yards south. To extend the walk into redwood country, go back up to the Enderts Beach overlook and walk for 5 miles along the California Coastal Trail. This 10-mile round-trip walk into the heavily forested redwoods will take the good part of a day.

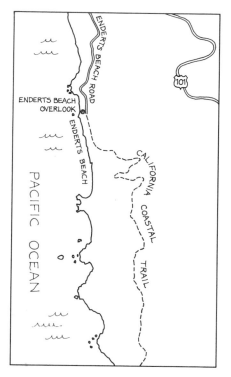

Degree of Difficulty: With the exception of a steep portion of the trail leading down to the beach, the walk is an easy one, with no hazards. Walk nominator Bryan Barrow says a child could walk along the path safely.

Enderts Beach and the Redwood Forest

The jewel of rugged Enderts Beach, where this walk begins, is the tidepool area found at the south end of the gravel and sand beach. It is a wonderful place to explore a microcosm of the sea. Be careful, though, not to disturb anything in the delicately balanced pools. Stay at the beach for as long as you like, before heading back up the pathway to the Coastal Trail and the redwoods.

What entrances Bryan Barrow (our intrepid friend who walked the western U.S. coastline in 13 months) about this northern California area is the dramatic and sudden change in the environment. "I experienced walking on windswept beach coves," he says, "and then, 10 minutes later, I was strolling through 300-foot-tall virgin redwods. Here was a rare chance to walk among the giants, some alive since the time of Christ."

At the start of the forest trail, you'll walk through densely compact second-growth trees. Then you'll see the big first-growth trees with massive trunks. The coast redwood (*Sequoia sempervirens*) is the California State Tree, and no living thing surpasses it in height. One tree, still alive and growing, measures almost 368 feet! Once part of a huge 2-million-acre forest, the remaining redwoods are lucky survivors of years of heedless exploitation. The timber industry still takes its toll of redwoods each year, but those in the Redwood National Forest are protected. While the redwoods are helpless in the face of man, their bark is surprisingly resistant to fire. On the side of the trail you will see thriving trees, their trunks completely hollowed out by fire. You can easily walk right inside the trunks.

This trail seems to be off the beaten path. Barrow says he saw no one else along the five-mile walk. "I experienced the wonderful feeling of being alone — as if I had the whole forest to myself. I marveled at the awesome immensity of the trees stretching skyward, disappearing into the misty air. I stood for a moment, listening; I was stunned by the deafening stillness around me."

JACKS PEAK REGIONAL PARK
Monterey Peninsula

Directions: From Monterey, take Highway 68 south to Olmstead Road. Turn south and follow Olmstead Road 1.5 miles until you reach Jacks Peak Road. Turn left and proceed to Jacks Peak Regional Park entrance. Turn right and follow Pine Road to Jacks Peak parking area.

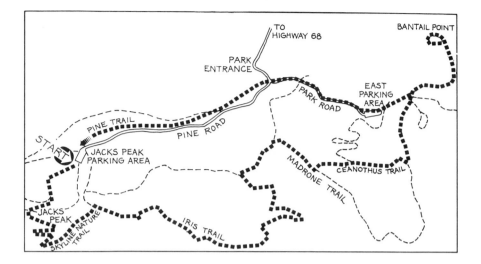

Best Season: In spring you'll find a profusion of wildflowers, but the walk is breathtaking any time of year. Watch out for poison oak off the trails, and during winter or spring you may come across a downed tree.

Length: Distance on the trail is 7.75 miles; allow three to four hours.

Degree of Difficulty: This gently rolling walk is a moderate one.

Following the Trails in Jacks Peak Park

The Monterey Peninsula, known for its abundant pine forests and breathtaking vistas of the Pacific, inspired the likes of Jack London, Henry Miller, and Robert Louis Stevenson, as well as more ordinary folk who flock here for vacations or romantic weekends. Walking along the trails of Jacks Peak Park, surrounded by groves of Monterey pine, a carpet of wildflowers underfoot, and spectacular views of the crashing surf, it's easy to understand why.

Begin your walk at the Jacks Peak parking lot and follow the signs toward the Skyline Nature Trail. Markers along the way explain the natural features; a descriptive brochure is available at the trailhead. Follow the trail through strands of fragrant Monterey pine; after about a quarter of a mile, a spectacular vista opens up. The entire Monterey Bay area fans out before you, about 2,000 feet below. The trail crosses the mountaintop for about a half mile. At this point you can see the Pacific coastline south of Point Lobos and rich, verdant Carmel Valley, which walk nominator Chris Crockett says reminds him of the Swiss Alps.

After continuing downhill another half mile, you will reach the Iris Trail junction. "From here the trail levels," Crockett explains, "winding

225

through cathedral-like forests of pine, which provide teasing glimpses of the Carmel Valley." It is here, in early spring or summer, that you'll find wildflowers in profusion. "Lucky individuals," says Crockett, "can also spot raccoons, black-tailed deer, and even a cougar!"

Walk on for about another mile and take a right on the Madrone Trail. Continue for a quarter of a mile and turn left on the Ceanothus Trail. (Ceanothus is a species of shore wildflowers found along the California coast; they fall mostly into two groups — California Lilac and Buckthorn.)

The climax of the walk comes when you take the Madrone Trail to Bantail Point and another spectacular view of Monterey Bay.

Return to the parking lot via the Park Road and Pine Trail. "From the smell of fragrant pine to the views that dazzle the eye, this walk is a true delight to the senses," concludes Crockett.

LA JOLLA

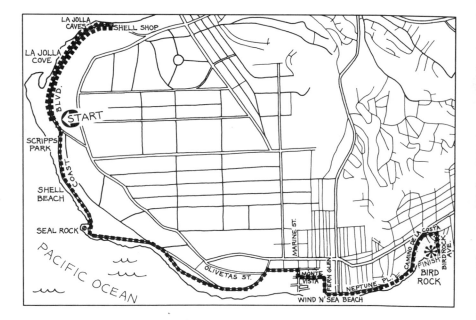

Directions: The walk begins at the Ellen Browning Scripps Park. To get there, take the La Jolla Village Drive exit from Highway 5 (the San Diego Freeway). Turn left at the third light to La Jolla Shores Drive. Turn right at the second light to Torrey Pines Road, and right again at the next light to Prospect Street. Take the second right and follow Coast Boulevard for a quarter of a mile. Park at Ellen Browning Scripps Park.

Best Season: Winter months are often rainy in La Jolla, but the walk can be enjoyed year round. Since this is an urban area, early morning expeditions are more peaceful.

Length: The walk is approximately 6 miles round trip.

Degree of Difficulty: Easy. The terrain is quite flat; you could take a young child along in a stroller. There's lots to see on this three- to four-hour fun walk.

La Jolla Cove to Bird Rock Walk

La Jolla is the "Jewel of the Pacific." This walk is an excellent way to see both its natural and human habitats. It is basically a coastal walk, but you'll pass by shops and some very special neighborhoods as well.

Conscious of their town's unique beauty, residents of La Jolla have purposely kept it from becoming a quintessential tourist town, although it certainly qualifies as a beach resort. But there is no "hotel row" and the nightlife is quiet. Furthermore, La Jolla is much more than spectacular scenery; it is home to Scripps Institution of Oceanography, a world leader in marine studies, and to the Salk Institute for Biological Studies.

To begin the walk, head north from Scripps Park to the La Jolla Caves on Coast Boulevard. The La Jolla Cave Shell Shop at 1325 Coast Boulevard has a man-made tunnel through which you can walk to the Pacific.

La Jolla Cove is part of an underwater park protecting the reefs that are found about 20 yards offshore. The cove is stuffed by nature with nautiluses, kelp, sea stars, moray eels, and lobsters. The shore side of the cove is a paradise for people of all ages. A grassy area plays host to every activity conceivable, from jazz concerts and balloon sculpting to volley ball games and cookouts. A sign at the cove reads: "Warning: Dangerous Rip Currents. Surfboards, Surf Mats, Boogie Boards Unlawful."

Follow the walk along a cliff above the Pacific where the "coastal view is gorgeous," in the words of nominator Judith Ryland. You'll see the original La Jolla Beach below, used before the population explosion of the 1940s. Past the cove is the scene of the annual La Jolla roughwater swim, out to the buoy and back.

Now the walk backtracks a little, heading south again toward Scripps Park. Continue along the cliff, looking down past Shell Beach and Seal Rock as you walk south. You will see houses on the ocean side. Turn right on Olivetas Street and follow the signs for the bike route. Turn right on Marine Street and enter the Barber Tract, an enclave of charming English Tudor-style homes with lovely little gardens.

Now turn left on Monte Vista Avenue, then right on Fern Glen, which becomes Neptune Place. You'll be walking along Windansea Beach, which has some of the best surfing in California. The surfing area is at the north end of the beach, and you might see a few world-champion surfers in training as you pass by. Windansea Beach was the setting for Tom Wolfe's *The Pump House Gang*. You'll walk by the now-famous pump house, still used to pressurize the city's sewers.

Turn right on Camino de la Costa. Wander through the exclusive residential neighborhood known, for obvious reasons, as the Gold Coast. Continue on to Bird Rock, a large, well-splattered promontory. There's a lookout here, and a bench from which you can ponder the vast Pacific before returning to Scripps Park by the same route.

Judith Ryland says, "This extraordinary walk incorporates village and cliffy seacoast with ease and with no risk to the walker. Guaranteed to make the out-of-towner see everything and move to La Jolla!"

MARIN COUNTY HEADLANDS

Directions: Take Highway 101 north from San Francisco to Marin City. Follow Donahue Road until it dead-ends. Park your car at the end of the paved road; the walk begins on the dirt fire road.

Best Season: Year round. In the summer, the late morning is best, when the fog has had a chance to burn off.

Length: 10–13 miles round trip. Allow about six hours.

Degree of Difficulty: The trip could be quite difficult for someone who is "not aerobic," in the words of nominator Suzanne Simpson. Watch out for poison oak along the trail and an occasional grass snake. Cars sometimes travel along the fire road in the first half mile, so take care to listen and watch out for them. Take food and water with you and a jacket. Leave your dog at home; they are not permitted in this area.

Walking the Headlands

Marin County is known for conspicuous consumption, hot tubs, fads, and "the good life." But Marin is much more than that. It is a place of great natural beauty, of tiny fishing villages and rolling farmland, of redwood forest and spectacular beaches, and it is a curious mixture of people. Artists live next to stockbrokers, monks next to movie stars. As you drive across the Golden Gate Bridge from San Francisco, the high cliffs of the Headlands rise before you, brown in summer, a rich green in win-

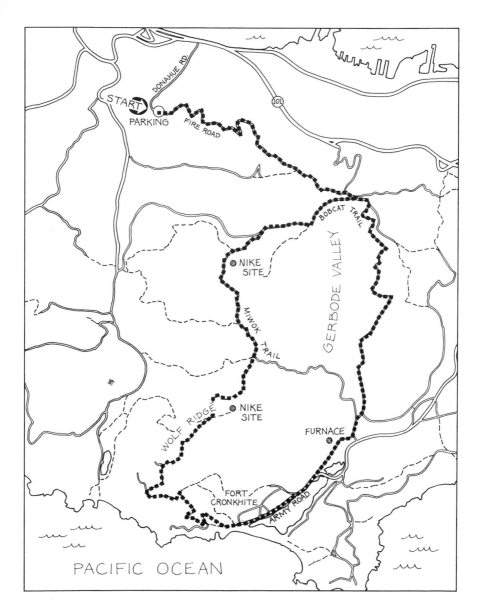

ter. More than 3 million years of geological upheaval created the dramatic ridges of the Headlands, which form the southernmost bounds of the Marine Part of California's Coastal Range. They offer an awesome, silent contrast to the sparkling man-made city across the Bay.

Suzanne Simpson, a food and wine writer for Marin's *Pacific Sun,* nominated this walk through the Headlands with great enthusiasm. She loves the exhilaration of it, the beauty. Along the walk are some magnificent panoramas of the Golden Gate Bridge, the Pacific crashing against cliffs, and the Bay, dotted with sailboats, ferries, and occasionally freighters carrying goods from China or Japan or just about anywhere. Looking the other way you can see the rolling hills of Marin and beloved Mt. Tam, "a most spectacular sight to behold!" says Simpson.

Take the dirt road from Donahue all the way up a ridge to a major fork; about a half hour, if you're walking at a good clip. From here you can see the ocean. Continue along the trail to the right, up to a Nike missile site. Walk around its north side, and then down the Miwok Trail. At the second fork, take a right and follow the trail up to the next Nike site. You will come out on an old, paved Army road. Follow it down to Fort Cronkhite Beach. From here, walk up the road to the old brick furnace (about a quarter of a mile) and get on the new trailhead. Cross over the creek and stay on the main trail (a branch goes off to the right). You'll pass through a lovely valley and will now face a giant uphill walk. Return to the area where you forked off at the first Nike site and then back down the fire road.

There is one eucalyptus stand along the trail, but otherwise this is bushy and grassy headlands country, no trees around. In the spring and early summer California wildflowers are everywhere — wild iris, Queen Ann's lace, shooting stars, and wonderful wild mustard.

PIERCE POINT TRAIL
Point Reyes National Seashore, Olema

Directions: From San Francisco, take Highway 101 north across the Golden Gate Bridge, to the San Anselmo turnoff. Head west on Sir Francis Drake Boulevard for about an hour until you reach Inverness. Take the Pierce Point Road, north of Inverness. Trailhead and parking lot are at the end of this road.

Best Season: The walk is a fine one any time of year, although days in July and August can be cold, when the fog and wind whip in off the Pacific. The walk is especially beautiful in the spring, when the Pacific Coast wild iris (*Iris douglasiana*) and other shore wildflowers (some very rare) are found in abundance. The iris species form heavy, sturdy clumps, and the stalks of these lovely lavender-hued flowers can be two feet tall. The flowering season is February through May. In winter the days are often relatively mild along the Point Reyes Peninsula.

Length: From the Pierce Point parking lot, the hiking trail is 5 miles to Tomales Bluff, 10 miles round trip. Allow at least four hours.

Degree of Difficulty: Moderately easy. There are a few sharp inclines. The cliffs are steep and crumbly; it is essential to keep away from them for safety. The National Park Service suggests that you bring your own supply of water when hiking on the Peninsula; the stream water is not fit to drink.

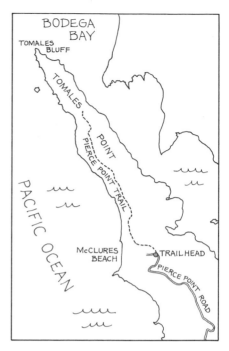

The Pierce Point Trail, Point Reyes National Seashore

Point Reyes National Seashore is 100 square miles of incomparable beauty. Formed by the constant, sometimes violent, movement of the earth's crust, its varied landscapes include rolling hills, rocky headlands, forested ridges, bays, and estuaries — all jutting out into the Pacific.

Life at Point Reyes is living on the fault line, literally. The infamous San Andreas Fault follows along the Point Reyes Peninsula, rich in geological as well as human history. The Peninsula is carried aloft by the eastern ridge of the Pacific plate, one of six forming most of the earth's crust. During the great San Francisco earthquake in 1906, Tomales Point, along the Pierce Point Trail, slid 16.4 feet northwestward. The Peninsula continues to move in that direction at a steady three inches each year.

While exploring the New World in 1579 for Queen Elizabeth I, Sir Francis Drake most likely brought his ship, the *Golden Hind,* into the estuary on Point Reyes that now bears his name. It was a Spanish adventurer, Don Sebastián Vizcaíno, who named the Peninsula itself. On January 6, 1603, the twelfth day of Christmas, he called it *La Punta de Los Reyes* — the Feast of the Three Kings.

At the Pierce Point trailhead you'll see pastureland where tule elk roam. They were returned to the area after having vanished for more than 100 years. There is a variety of other wildlife on and around the Peninsula, too, including rare white deer, more than 300 different species of birds, seals, sea lions, and, from December to April, the beautiful gray whales.

McClures Beach, below the Pierce Point trailhead, can be reached by a very steep half-mile trail. The beach is a wonderful place to observe the numerous small inhabitants of the tidepools, but the surf can be treacherous. Don't go near the water. (Note to hardy explorers: McClures Beach is a side trip you might consider after the Pierce Point Trail walk.)

The Pierce Point Trail follows along a ridge overlooking the crashing Pacific breakers and the calm beaches of Tomales Bay. Nori Nisbet, who lives in nearby Inverness and who nominated the Pierce Point Trail, says that it reminds him "of the best of Scottish hikes." The feeling of vastness, the aura of tranquility, and the movement of the earth combine to create a sense of human connectedness with nature that Nisbet experienced here and in his native land.

The Point Reyes Lighthouse is a well-known landmark on the Peninsula and worth a visit. It is also the place to call for a fog report on the day you plan to walk the trail: (415) 669-1534. After finishing your walk on the Pierce Point Trail, you can drive back past Tomales Bay State Park and then head west on Sir Francis Drake Highway to the lighthouse. It is open year round (closed on Tuesdays and Wednesdays) weather permitting. From an observation platform 300 steps above the lighthouse, it is possible to watch the gray whales on their southward and northward migrations between December and April.

SAN FRANCISCO
Golden Gate Promenade

Directions: The Golden Gate Promenade begins at Fort Mason, at the northwest corner of Van Ness Avenue and Bay Street. If you are in downtown San Francisco and heading to Fort Mason on foot, it is a fairly easy walk by a number of routes. Sutter to Polk, Polk north to Bay, left on Bay for a short block to Van Ness is an interesting one.

Best Season: This walk is beautiful any time of the year, with the exception of very windy days. Even in a gentle rain, you'll see walkers and joggers along the route. In the very early morning or late at night it's best not to walk alone.

Length: The distance from Fort Mason to Fort Point (and the Golden Gate Bridge) is 3.5 miles. Allow about three to four hours for the 7-mile round trip.

Degree of Difficulty: Easy. The terrain is quite level. Step aside for joggers when you are on the stretch from the "little" Green to Fort Point.

Walking to the Bridge: The Golden Gate Promenade

This walk begins at Fort Mason, one of the places where the city of San Francisco meets the calming waters of the Bay. Now the headquarters of the Golden Gate National Recreation Area (part of the U.S. Interior Department), Fort Mason has had an illustrious past. It was home to the commanding general of the U.S. Army in the West from 1865 to 1943, and its history reaches even further back than that. In front of McDowell Hall is a plaque celebrating Colonel Richard Mason, who chased squatters out of the military compound in the 1850s.

Spend some time leisurely looking around Fort Mason. (On Pope Street you'll see a building that has survived since the Civil War era — number 235 — a long building with open porches; and there are plenty of plaques to read for historical color.) When you are ready, find the cement stairs toward the back of the compound. Walk down them and head for the Golden Gate Bridge.

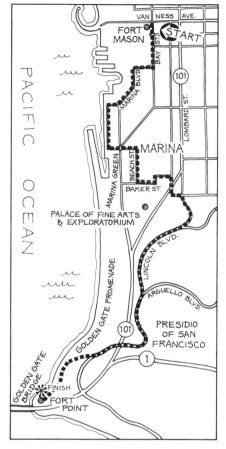

You will pass by the piers of Fort Mason's docks; during World War II more than 1.5 million soldiers and millions of tons of cargo passed through here. Today the piers are home to various civic organizations and a wonderful vegetarian restaurant — Greens at Fort Mason — run by the San Francisco Zen Buddhist community. It is open Tuesday through Thursday for lunch and dinner; lunch is available on Friday and Saturday, and on weekend nights a fixed menu is served. Demand is high. Reserve at least two weeks in advance: (415) 771-6222.

After leaving the pier area, you'll see the Marina Green — the "big" Green, as the local people call it. Here, along the water's edge, San Franciscans jog on the dirt path and exercise on the Parcourse, a series of exercise stations that follow along the Promenade. In the middle of the "big" Green, there is an almost endless scene of kite flyers, serious Frisbee throwers, frolicking children, and — like other spots in San Francisco — people doing just about everything imaginable. Along this part of the walk you'll pass by docked sailboats. If it's a sunny weekend morning you will undoubtedly see San Franciscans carrying elegant hampers into the gates, ready for a day's sailing. Stroll past those toiling to do 500 sit-ups at a Parcourse station and head down to the "little" Green.

The "little" Green is the sunbathing area. In midday in mid-winter it is here that you'll find the only naturally tanned bodies in the city. "Little" Green hosts a corps of bronzed regulars who spend much of the day just waiting for the sun to emerge from the fog, even for 10 minutes.

As you walk along the Marina, notice the dome-shaped building up ahead on the other side of the street. This is the Palace of Fine Arts. Part of the Panama-Pacific International Exposition of 1915, the building now houses a theater and a "hands-on" science museum called the Exploratorium. There's nothing quite like it; if you have time, cross the street and spend an hour or two here exploring the world.

From the Marina, take the path to Fort Point that follows along the Presidio, the lush U.S. Army compound. You'll see army jeeps, trucks, and, farther down, a little schoolhouse and some lovely residences. It is along this stretch that you can breathe deeply and feel the ocean which beckons ahead of you. The Golden Gate itself looms majestically ahead.

Fort Point, clearly visible and clearly under the Golden Gate Bridge, is a red-brick building constructed between 1853 and 1861. It has 120 cannon mounts. It is open to visitors from 10 to 5 daily, except Christmas, and admission is free.

Walk around Fort Point until you are really under the Golden Gate Bridge. Feeling the power of the Pacific Ocean combined with the strength of the bridge is an overwhelming experience. Look down at the treacherous water in the division between the Bay and the ocean. You just might see a starfish clinging tenaciously — and incredibly — to a rock.

From Fort Point's entry side there is a path leading up to the pedestrian entrance to the Golden Gate Bridge. You can choose, if you wish, to cross the bridge, adding another two miles to your walk.

For the return trip, you can pick up public transportation at the bridge toll plaza, or walk back along the Promenade the way you came.

SAN FRANCISCO
Russian Hill

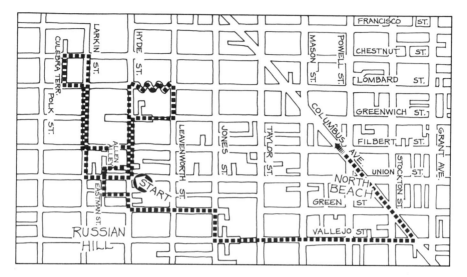

Directions: To begin this exploration of Russian Hill from downtown, take the Hyde Street cable car from Union Square to the intersection of Union and Hyde streets. You can drive, but it is not recommended; many Russian Hill neighborhoods now allow parking by permit only. If you are a dedicated walker, you will be able to walk to Russian Hill from downtown — it is a stimulating adventure. You need a map, strong legs, and a good pair of lungs.

Best Season: San Francisco has a wonderful climate. This walk may be taken at any time of the year, unless it happens to be a cold, wet, rainy winter day, but there aren't many of those. If you head out early on a summer morning, take a sweater or jacket; you'll need it until the fog lifts. September is the warmest month in San Francisco. Everyone else's summer (July and August) can be the coldest.

Length: Allow at least three hours for this leisurely stroll through Russian Hill. If you have time for breakfast or lunch, add another hour or two. Leave a full day free if you want to explore the joys of North Beach after the Russian Hill walk.

Degree of Difficulty: Moderate; be prepared for the steepest hills in San Francisco.

Russian Hill, a San Francisco Favorite

"And great is thy tenderness, O cool grey city of love!" wrote Russian Hill poet George Sterling (1869–1926); Russian Hill — a verdant, charming, relatively secluded, and mostly residential enclave in the heart of the "city of love" — could well have been his inspiration. No one really knows why the 312-foot-high hill is called "Russian," but in the 19th century it was home to some of San Francisco's finest writers and artists, including Sterling, Frank Norris, Ambrose Bierce, and George Dewey.

Two separate crests come together to create Russian Hill. The lee side of the hill is extremely steep, with intricate walkways and stairways and fabulous views of the Bay and Golden Gate. Dave Smith, the Russian Hill resident who nominated this walk, says birds of prey have returned to Russian Hill after a long period of absence. He recently saw what he thinks were young falcons swooping about.

Begin your walk at the commercial crossroads of Hyde and Union. Here you'll find the first Swensen's, a Russian Hill tradition for ice cream. Across Hyde is the Searchlight Market, and across Union from this neighborhood market is La Ferme Beaujolaise, a gentrified meat market/gourmet shop with picnic baskets and bottles of wine in the window. Head up the hill on the Searchlight Market side of Hyde. The next street is Filbert. The Filbert block between Hyde and Leavenworth has the steepest grade in San Francisco.

The next street is Greenwich where George Sterling (and O. J. Simpson) lived. Walk to the bottom of this charming cul-de-sac and note the gray stucco house on the north side of the street. This is the one used for the opening of the television show "MacMillan and Wife."

Wander down the fresh, leafy path to Leavenworth and turn left. Walk another, very short block to Lombard Street, the "Crookedest Street in the World." At the top of Lombard, you're on top of the world again. Turn left (we're backtracking a block here) and return to Hyde and Greenwich. Turn right and enter a little jewel-like haven called the Alice Marble Park. Marble was a Wimbledon and U.S. Open Tennis champion; the tennis courts bear her name. Walk on the pathway next to the tennis courts and turn right into a small arborlike area. A monument to George Sterling is at its end. Here you can read his poem about the "cool grey city of love" on the plaque.

Follow the path from the monument to a bench and sit down. From this dark apple-green perch you'll have one of the best views of the Golden Gate Bridge in all of San Francisco. You can also see the actual Golden Gate from this vantage point — the one that was here eons before the bridge was built in the 1930s — the land forming the natural gate between the Bay and the Pacific Ocean.

Take the rest of the stairs down to Larkin Street and turn right to walk up to Chestnut. Turn left onto Chestnut and then left on Culebra. This little street looks like a blind alley, but follow it anyway. Eureka! Some hidden stairs take you out of the alley and onto Lombard Street.

Now, turn right on Larkin, left on Filbert, right on Hyde, and then right again into another Russian Hill alley — Allen. Allen Alley comes out on Eastman. Cross Union Street and continue down the alley to Russell. Turn left and note #15 and #17 Russell. They are wonderful gingerbread Victorians, painted in the traditional Victorian manner. When you reach Hyde, turn right and then walk left from Hyde onto Green. (Depending on the time of day, you may want to stop at Edible Delights, at the corner of Hyde and Green, for an espresso and a sweet.) The 1000 block of Green Street is one of the most famous stretches of housing on Russian Hill. Cross Leavenworth and note the white "Spanish-Deco" 20-story building at 1101 Green. It was built in 1930. At #1088 Green is a residence that was originally a firehouse. Built in 1907, it still says "Engine Number 31" in front. Across the street from the old firehouse is one of the two remaining octagon houses in San Francisco; it was built in 1857.

Turn right on Jones Street and walk to Vallejo where you'll see a sign: "Not a Thru Street." Walk up two ramps and the first part of the Vallejo steps to one of Russian Hill's two summits. Now you'll see a bricked cul-de-sac to the north called Russian Hill Place. The townhouses are Italianate; note #7. Its plaque reads "Avec Souci," giving the onlooker cause to wonder what cares might lie within.

Continue along Vallejo Street. The houses at #1134 and #1136 withstood the 1906 conflagration. As you cross Florence Street, still on Vallejo, note the Pueblo Revival architecture, which was the rage of the 20s.

Go down the second set of Vallejo Street steps to Taylor Street. This takes you into North Beach, where you leave the quiet and can hear the cable cars again. Wander at will in this wonderful neighborhood, finding your way to Columbus Avenue and stopping for an espresso at the Bohemian Cigar Store at the corner of Union and Columbus. North Beach, rich in history, offers the walker a special opportunity to see things that can be seen only on foot. Poet Gary Snyder wrote an essay about North Beach, where he lived for over two years. In it he said, "When we of the Fifties and after walked into it, walk was the key word. Maybe no place else in urban America where a district has such a feel of on-foot: narrow streets, high blank walls and stairstep steeps of alleys and white-wood houses cheap to rent; laundry flapping in the foggy wind from flat-topped roofs." If you have time, don't miss a chance to browse through the literary heart of North Beach — City Lights Bookstore at 261 Columbus. Here poets like Snyder, Allen Ginsberg, and Lawrence Ferlinghetti, who founded the store in 1953, as well as numerous other writers, met to read together, talk together, and create together. The bookstore remains a San Francisco literary meeting place to this day. From here you can walk back downtown or take public transportation to anywhere else you might like to go.

SANTA MONICA
Palisades Park

Directions: From downtown Los Angeles, take the San Diego Freeway (10) west. Exit on Fourth Street (the final exit before the Pacific) and turn right. Turn left on Colorado Avenue and head toward the Santa Monica Pier, the south end of Palisades Park. You can park your car along Ocean Avenue. The walk begins on Ocean just off Colorado.

Best Season: Year round, but veteran Los Angeles walker Mary Jane Horton urges taking the walk in the early morning. At noon and after 5 the park is crowded with locals and tourists alike. "But these are walking tourists from all over the world," Horton says, "not busloads on tour."

Length: The distance from the Santa Monica Pier north to Inspiration Point is 1.5 miles. Plan on three hours for the 3-mile round trip, including a stop for a chocolate-covered frozen banana on the Pier and plenty of time to gaze at the Pacific.

Degree of Difficulty: The walk is paved and quite easy; expect a gently rolling terrain. The earth slips and slides along a bluff overlooking the Pacific. Observe signs and do not walk beyond the fenced boundary to the west of the path.

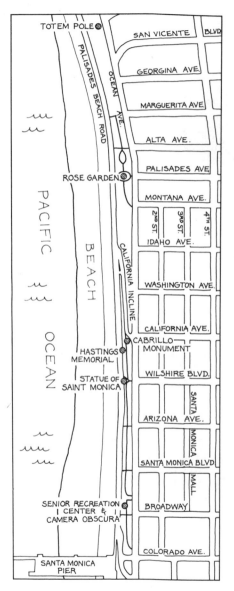

Palisades Park

Dedicated in 1892, Palisades Park, a narrow strip of land along a bluff overlooking the Pacific, has long been a favorite refuge for city dwellers. It is separated from the beach by the Pacific Coast Highway, which stretches along the foot of the cliffs (the scene of a now-classic Laurel and Hardy short). Within the park's grassy, tree-lined, 26-plus acres you'll find people walking, running, talking, reading, picnicking, playing shuffleboard, throwing Frisbees, pushing strollers, and doing just about anything you might expect in an urban park with a mild climate like southern California's.

From the Santa Monica Pier, heading north along the main path through the park, you will come to the Senior Citizen's Recreation Center. Here an unexpected treat awaits you. In a darkened chamber an example of camera obscura reflects scenes of the park and the coast through the use of revolving lenses, prisms, and mirrors.

The park is a lush natural environment of Mexican fan palms, Canary Island date palms, Australian tea trees, several varieties of *eucalyptus,* and the greenest of grass; it is also dotted with man-made monuments and memorials. A statue of Saint Monica stands at the foot of Wilshire Boulevard to remind visitors of the origin of the city's name. According to legend, Spanish soldiers camped by the springs here in 1769. Father Juan Crespi was with them. He called the springs "Santa Monica" because they reminded him of tears shed by the saint for her wayward son (who later became a saint himself — Saint Augustine).

Farther along the path is the Hastings Memorial Garden. Here a plaque honors George Hastings, a well-loved Santa Monica naturalist and teacher. At the top of the California incline you'll come to the Cabrillo Monument commemorating the discovery of Santa Monica by Juan Rodríguez Cabrillo in 1542.

Stop at the Fuschia Garden a bit farther on and the Rose Garden at the foot of Alta Street. Take note of the "Montana Hole" at the foot of Montana Avenue. It is the result of cliff erosion in the 1880s. A series of steps and a pedestrian overpass stretch above the Pacific Coast Highway and lead to the beach. You'll find pedestrian overpasses at the ends of Idaho and Broadway, too.

Opposite Adelaide Drive at the north end of the park is the 30-foot Alaskan Totem Pole. This was a gift to the city made in 1925 by J. Walter Todd, who loved Santa Monica and who thought of the totem pole as a symbol of his roots in the town.

Palisades Park ends at Inspiration Point, the northernmost section of the park. Here you'll have a grand view of the Malibu coastline; the furthest point north you can see from here is Point Doom, jutting out into the sea.

The human landscape can be fascinating, too. Mary Jane Horton saw some particularly interesting visitors strolling here during the 1984 Summer Olympics. She also saw a group of white-robed, barefooted people who seemed, for a while, to be living within the park's green boundaries. Also, it is said that the rich and famous, many of whom live along the coast highway below, jog here in the afternoons; don't be surprised if you recognize someone reading a film script in the shade of a palm tree.

If you have time for a side trip, stroll by the shops and restaurants along Montana Avenue. Add a couple of miles to the distance and at least two more hours to the trip.

When you return to the Santa Monica Pier (completed in the 1920s), be sure to stop and see the restored carousel. Here you can forget your healthful diet for a moment as you consume that quintessential beach food, the chocolate-covered frozen banana.

HISTORIC SONOMA

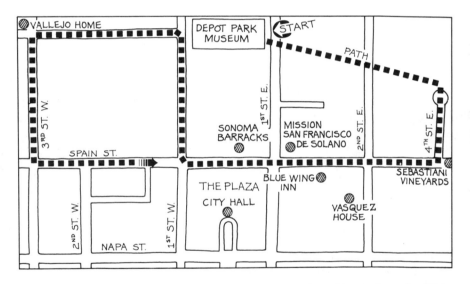

Directions: From San Francisco, follow Highway 101 north to the Vallejo/Napa (Highway 37) exit, and then take Highway 121 to Highway 12, which leads directly to the Plaza in Sonoma. Drive your car around the plaza to the public parking lot off of First Street East, behind the Sonoma Barracks building.

Best Season: The weather is good all year, but expect some rainy days from November to March.

240

Length: The walk is about 2 miles. How long it takes is up to you.

Degree of Difficulty: Easy.

Sonoma Plaza Historic Walk

From the parking lot, take the shortcut up to the Depot Park Museum, located on First Street West, north of the Plaza. The museum, which is open from 1:00 to 4:30 Wednesday through Sunday, is operated by the Sonoma Valley Historical Society. Information about the walk can be obtained here. If you prefer a guided tour, arrange to have a walking-tour guide accompany you for part of the walk. The museum itself, which features various exhibits depicting life in the Old West, is a replica of the original Sonoma Depot, built in 1880. "Allow at least 30 minutes for a tour of the museum and railroad cars," says Irma Wallem, a long-time resident of Sonoma who serves as a docent at the museum and who submitted this historic walking tour. "Everyone who comes to Sonoma loves this walk," she adds enthusiastically, "you feel as though you are in another time."

From the Depot Park Museum, follow the walk and bike path to Sebastiani Vineyards on Fourth Street East at the end of Spain. Here at Sonoma's largest winery you can go on an informative guided tour, sample wine in the tasting room, and visit the Sebastiani's Indian Artifacts Museum.

Head West, now, on Spain Street to the Mission San Francisco de Solano, the 21st (and last) mission on the Camino Real Highway. Open daily to visitors, the mission was founded in 1823 to convert Indians to Christianity and to keep an eye on the Russian fur traders who lived at Fort Ross and Bodega. As you leave the mission, take a look across the street at the Blue Wing Inn, a former stagecoach inn and a good example of Monterey colonial architecture.

Cross First Street East to the restored Sonoma Barracks, originally built in the 1800s to house the troops of General Mariano Vallejo, commander of the "northern frontier." Today the Barracks, open every day from 10:00 to 5:00, house exhibits that show life as it was lived by the Indians, Mexicans, and early Americans in and around Sonoma.

Take the walking path again to Lachryma Montis, General Vallejo's home, built in 1851. Vallejo called it Lachryma Montis ("mountain tear") because of the mineral springs on the property.

Return now to the Plaza along Third Street West to Spain again. Notice the City Hall as you walk along Spain. All four sides are identical. This building often appears on TV's "Falcon Crest."

Continue on Spain Street to 129 East Spain and enter the El Paseo Courtyard to Vasquez House. Here you can see an exhibit of early California in the house built for Colonel Joseph Hooker, who later became a general in the Civil War. Guided tours to a number of private homes, many made of adobe brick, others with interesting features of early architecture, are also available from Vasquez House.

If you are hungry, buy an ice-cream cone on the corner of Spain and First Street East; or walk down First Street to the famous Sonoma French Bakery for a loaf of sweet or sourdough French bread. You will pass the Sebastiani Theatre with its 72-foot tower and balustrade across the front. It opened in 1933; Ronald Reagan was among the stars who attended the opening.

Take one more walk around the Plaza; browse through the quaint shops and boutiques before returning to your car behind the Barracks.

A SECRET WALK
The Startling Sonoma Coast

Directions: Head north from San Francisco on Highway 101. Take the South Washington Boulevard exit in Petaluma and turn left at the light. Continue for about 29 miles to Route 1 and turn right. Watch for a sign that says "Golfing," and turn left into Bodega Harbour. Go left at the top of the hill, following the Coastal Access sign to "Pinnacle Gulch Trail." Turn left on Mockingbird to the public parking area. Total driving time from San Francisco: about an hour and 15 minutes.

Best Season: Spring or fall.

Best Time of Day: Daylight/low tide.

Length: Half hour to as long as you like.

Degree of Difficulty: Moderately difficult.

Places to Stay: Bodega Bay Lodge, The Tides Inn, or rental homes. For information on renting homes in Bodega Bay for a few days or a week, call George Haig Realty, (707) 857-2711.

Places to Eat: The Tides, Lucas Wharf, The Whaler's Inn, The Sandpiper, and a new restaurant in Pelican Plaza. There is also Bud's Ice Cream Parlor and a cookie and pastry shop called Lucy Hanna's (don't miss the sour cream coffee cake!).

Bodega Bay's Pinnacle Gulch Trail
Few people know of Pinnacle Gulch Trail, a narrow footpath that meanders around craggy cliffs on down to one of the most spectacular

242

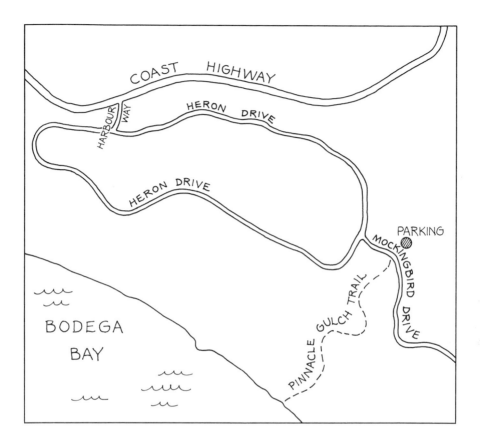

beaches in America. It's a discovery — a startling one!

The first part of the trail is steep and rocky, so watch your footing. If you are walking in the spring, you will see a profusion of wildflowers lining the path and cascading over the hills. The path, already narrow, becomes narrower still where huge cow parsnips (4–8 feet) nearly block the way. These plants with their woolly-type leaves and large white flower clusters are members of the carrot family. Butterflies dart around brightly colored orange and yellow California poppies, purple lupines, buttercups, sea daisies, geranium, wild iris, Pride of Madeira and myriad of other flowers.

Don't be surprised if you turn a corner and come upon a mule-ear deer. They're quite tame and will let you get within 10 or 20 feet before scampering off up the hillside.

Be sure to listen, too. You'll hear the sounds of hundreds of different kinds of birds. Bodega Bay is famous for them, and Alfred Hitchcock chose this tiny fishing village and nearby Bodega as the site for his film

The Birds. You'll hear seals, too, barking away on their island called, obviously enough, Seal Rock.

After about 15 minutes you'll see the ocean. Look down; the gulch fills with rocks and giant pieces of bleached driftwood. Here the path drops suddenly and ends. You're at the beach. Pelican Rock juts out of the water to your right; and, if you look beyond, out into the ocean, you'll see Seal Rock. With good binoculars you can see the seals playing in the water or sunbathing on the rock.

There's a lot to take in from this one spot. Bodega Head (the San Andreas Fault runs right through the tip) pushes out into the ocean on your right; and Point Reyes swings around on your left, marking the entrance to Tomales Bay, home of California's successful oyster farming business.

From here on your walk can be as long or as short as you like. Stretched out on either side are literally miles of beach. Remember to calculate the return walk on the Pinnacle Gulch Trail, before you start out on your beach walk.

The Sonoma Coast has a moonlike, other-worldly atmosphere, with craggy rocks jutting up around secluded coves and tidal pools. For this particular beach walk, it is important to be aware of the tides. At high tide it's impossible to get past some of the rocks.

If you walk to the right from Pinnacle Gulch, you will come to a narrow natural tunnel in the rocks. At low tide this provides entrance to another beach, where you can walk about three and a half miles toward Bodega Head without obstacles. Seagulls, falcons, and sparrowhawks soar overhead, while sandpipers play tag with the waves, running back and forth as fast as their sticklike legs will take them, as the water rushes in and out.

If you walk left from Pinnacle Gulch, the going is a little more difficult, but no less spectacular. You'll need to climb over rocks and walk around tidepools; but there, in the shallow water at ebb tide, you'll find a whole community of small creatures: starfish, barnacles, mussels, sand crabs, and flowerlike anemones, to name just a few. Life in the tidepools is precarious at best, so be careful not to disrupt it. Even turning a rock over and exposing these tiny creatures to sunlight can kill them. Remember, too, as you walk along the beach, that the Sonoma Coast is not for swimming. There is a strong undertow and sudden "sleeper" waves that can be very dangerous, not to mention the great white shark whose breeding grounds are just a few miles away.

When you're ready, return to Pinnacle Gulch and the trail back to the parking area.

Perhaps you were surprised by this walk. Surprised to discover that there is still a place in California where you can walk for miles and miles along a secluded, pristine coast. It's a secret — share it wisely.

Part 4

ALASKA AND HAWAII

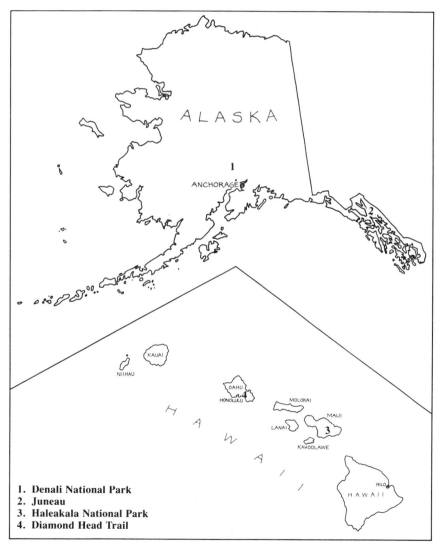

1. **Denali National Park**
2. **Juneau**
3. **Haleakala National Park**
4. **Diamond Head Trail**

Alaska

DENALI NATIONAL PARK

Directions: To reach Denali National Park in south central Alaska, take Alaska Highway 3 south from Fairbanks (120 miles) or north from Anchorage (240 miles). Denali is also accessible from Anchorage and Fairbanks via the Alaska Railroad, an eight- and four-hour trip, respectively. The train takes you to the depot 1.5 miles beyond the Visitor Information Center at Riley Creek. The rail station is next to the Denali National Park Hotel. Make reservations three to four months in advance. The number is (907) 683-2215 from mid-May through September and (907) 276-7234 from October 1 to mid-May. To get to the interior of the park, where this walk is, you need to take the shuttle bus that leaves the Visitor Information Center at Riley Creek according to a published schedule. Disembark from the shuttle at a starting point suggested by a Backcountry Ranger at Riley Creek Information Center.

Best Season: The best time to explore Denali National Park is from mid-June to August. Bring warm clothing; even in mid-summer, temperatures range from the 40s to the 60s. Remember that June in this part of Alaska brings daylight 24 hours a day. Even in mid-August, sunrise comes early — before 5:00 a.m.

Length: Hikes of varying lengths are available. Roy Bergstrom, who first told us about Denali, says, for example, that you should allow from nine to ten hours for a walk up and down Cathedral Mountain. This includes the four-hour, round-trip shuttle bus ride. During the peak visitor season, buses may be full and you will experience delays.

Degree of Difficulty: Hikes in Denali vary in difficulty. Using Cathedral Mountain again as an example, Roy Bergstrom says it is moderately difficult, with a 1,500-foot rise in elevation to the summit. It is a steep climb, but on fairly easy alpine tundra slopes; there are no rocks, and Bergstrom says it is "almost like walking on a very steep golf course." Take a pair of tennis shoes in your day-pack; you won't find any bridges here, so when you need to cross water you can take off your hiking boots, put on the tennis shoes and forge ahead. On the other side, put the soggy tennis shoes back into your pack and the dry hiking boots back on your feet. You should be prepared for wet weather; raingear is a must.

A Walk near "the High One"

Denali means "the high one," in the language of the original south-central Alaskan people, and the park takes this name because within its borders is the highest mountain in North America — the majestically beautiful Mount McKinley. In addition to this giant peak, Denali encompasses more than 9,000 square miles of wilderness and only one road and one area of development. Hiking in Denali National Park and Preserve gives the walker a chance to explore one of the truly last frontiers of the West and to experience up close the incredible beauty and isolation of untouched wilderness.

It is essential to check into the Visitor Information Center before you begin your walk in Denali. In fact, before you plan a trip to the park, contact park officials for information. Call (907) 683-2294 or write: Superintendent, Denali National Park and Preserve, Box 9, Denali National Park, AK 99755. The ecosystem of this area is so fragile that trails do not exist, park rangers direct walkers and hikers to different areas so there will never be too many people in one place at one time. Everywhere in Denali there is spectacular scenery and potential for unique wildlife viewing. A staff member who has hiked the backcountry in Denali for the past three summers explains some of the wonder of the place: "To hike here, you have to think for yourself. There is no trail to lead the way. That is both exciting and frightening, and it is what makes hiking here such a potentially powerful experience. You explore, you decide, and you take the consequences. You can ask ten people what their favorite hikes are and get ten or more different answers. Denali's uniqueness is not in any individual 'greatest hike,' but in its unusual mix of easy access, and as yet comparatively pristine character."

Denali National Park was established primarily to protect wildlife. There are about 37 species of animals and more than 155 species of birds, including the willow ptarmigan, Alaska's State Bird. Keep an eye out for caribou, bull moose and Dall sheep, as well as marmots, the Arctic ground squirrel, and if you're lucky and savvy enough, wolf tracks. And this is grizzly country. Be sure you heed all information and warnings about traveling in bear habitat.

As you walk along the ridges, a panorama of landscapes passes before you — rivers, lakes, thickets, the wildflowers of the tundra. Best of all, if the weather is clear, you'll see "the high one," snow-covered Mount McKinley rising from about 2,000 feet above sea level to its 20,000-foot-plus summit. This place is very special.

JUNEAU
Perseverance Trail

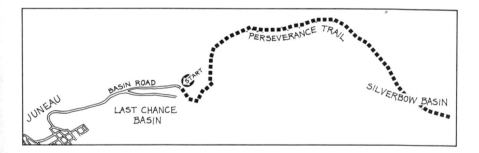

Directions: From downtown Juneau, walk to the end of Basin Road. The trailhead is clearly marked.

Best Season: Summer and autumn are the best times to take this walk. Summer nights never get quite dark, so you can start out late. In the afternoons, you'll see many residents jogging or walking their dogs on the trail.

Length: Round trip on this maintained trail (Alaska Department of Natural Resources, Division of Parks) is 7 miles. Allow two hours — or much more — in order to appreciate the exquisite beauty of Juneau.

Degree of Difficulty: About 100 inches of rain fall on Juneau each year, but this is a hazard only in summer on this moderately easy walk. Avalanche danger precludes winter use of this route.

The Perseverance Trail

Juneau, in the southeast corner of "mainland" Alaska, is located on the Gastineau Channel, quite near British Columbia. The trail is named for the abandoned Perseverance Mine, one of the largest hardrock mines in the United States, found at the end of the trail. The city of Juneau takes its name from old Joe Juneau, who, along with Dick Harris, struck one of the largest lodes of gold quartz in the world back in 1880.

Nominator Bill Johnson, a 10-year Alaska resident (and New York transplant), calls the Perseverance Trail: "A rarity. One walks through a modern downtown into a reclaimed wilderness. You walk right into the mountains!"

The beauty of the trail reflects, of course, the beauty of Juneau itself. A town of 30,000, it is built on a small piece of land on a salt-water inland bay. The town is nestled between two mountains, Mt. Juneau (3,576 feet) and Mt. Roberts (3,819 feet). Bill Johnson tells us that "waterfalls run right off the mountains into people's backyards."

The trail begins at a short spur to the left at the end of Basin Road behind the city. It leads past Last Chance Basin to Silverbow Basin, the site of the Perseverance Mine. Goldmines and tunnels honeycomb under the trail and into the mountain. Bill Johnson says only the initiated can find their way in to explore the netherlands of the old mines.

At the top, the view of the mountains and old railyards, abandoned prospectors' houses and antiquated mining machinery, is enhanced by an occasional view of black bears, porcupines, marmots, and grouse. Wildflowers appear along the trail in the summer, just two weeks after the snow melts. They stay through September or until the snows return.

Wooden bridges cross Gold Creek at several points along this trail; if the path seems a little tame for you, there are glaciers that peek out of cracks in the mountains. Bill Johnson grabs his crampons and ice axe, after working hard all day, and thinks about heading for Canada.

Hawaii (Maui)

HALEAKALA NATIONAL PARK
Sliding Sands and Halemauu Trails

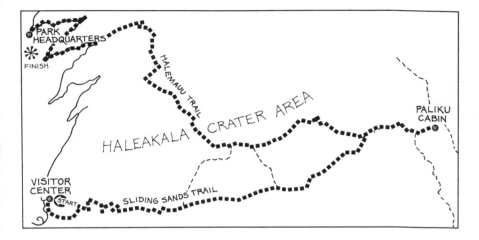

Directions: There is no local transportation to Haleakala. Most visitors drive rental cars. From Lahaina, 59 miles away, travel southeast on Route 30, turn right on Route 38, right on Route 36, right on Route 37, left on Route 377, and left on Route 378. Park at the House of the Sun Visitors Center. The Sliding Sands trailhead, where this walk begins, is accessible from the parking lot. The Halemauu Trail, which is your exit route, ends at Halemauu Trail parking lot, six miles from the Visitors Center, so you need to arrange transportation back to your car at the Visitors Center.

Best Season: The walk is possible any time of year, but when you go depends on when you are able to make your reservations to stay at Paliku cabin. Paliku cabin, on Sliding Sands Trail, is one of three cabins maintained by the Park Service in this unique environment (sometimes called the "moon on earth"). The cabins are available through a lottery system. You must write to Haleakala National Park, Box 369, Makawao, HI 96768, to request the night or nights you wish to stay at Paliku cabin. Include an alternate night. You will be notified by mail only if you are selected by lottery. Selections are made at the first of the month. Reservations must be made at least three months in advance and are limited to three nights per month, with no more than two consecutive nights at any one cabin. The charge is $5 per night for each adult ($15 minimum), with a refundable $15 key and cleaning deposit.

Two primitive campgrounds are also available in Haleakala, one of them at Paliku. But staying at Paliku campground requires serious backpacking, including carrying a waterproof tent.

Length: The hike takes two days, with an overnight stay at Paliku cabin in Haleakala crater. The distance to the cabin along Sliding Sands Trail is 9.8 miles and takes a full day. The return trip on the second day is along the 10.2-mile Halemauu Trail.

Degree of Difficulty: This walk is difficult. Many people take it, but weather conditions and high elevations (the trail begins at more than 9,700 feet) combine with loose cinders on the first quarter of the descent to make the walk a challenging one. Both trails have easy grades (except for the hike up out of the crater, which is steep) and are well maintained; but your level of comfort will depend on your level of fitness, the load you are carrying, and the weather. Remember, too, that Paliku cabin is not to be confused with the Diamond Head Hilton. The dormitory-style cabin has 12 bunks and a small kitchen with running water; toilet facilities are found in an outhouse. It is old, Spartan, "but sturdy, well-built, and clean" says Park Ranger Pete Sanchez.

Hypothermia is the greatest danger to the hiker at Haleakala. It is common to set out in warm and sunny weather, only to experience mist, rain, cold, and high winds in short order, which can sap your body's heat. Dress in layers: shorts or light pants, a light shirt, sweater, jacket, and a rainshell. Rain often comes down horizontally; there are no trees for shelter. It can be in the 30s at the summit in winter, in the 50s in summer. Snow is not usual, but freezing conditions can occur at any time of the year. (Haleakala National Park will provide you with a brochure, "Four Lines of Defense against Hypothermia.") Carry your own water and food. For this particular trip, you will need to carry two lunches, one breakfast, and a dinner to prepare in Paliku cabin.

The Journey to Haleakala Crater

Haleakala National Park is 45 square miles, 19 of which are taken up by the huge Haleakala crater. The volcano has not erupted since the mid-1700s, yet Haleakala is considered dormant, not extinct. One legend of this volcanic island tells the story of Hina, mother of the demigod Maui, who had trouble drying her bark cloth because the day was too short. Maui snared the rays of the sun and held them fast with ropes. "Give me my life," pleaded the sun. "I will give you your life," replied Maui, "if you promise to go more slowly across the sky." To this day, the sun is careful to go slowly across the heavens, and the great mountain is known as Haleakala, the house of the sun.

This difficult walk may sound a bit formidable, but there is nothing else on earth quite like Haleakala. The crater is cone-studded and streaked with color. Its contrasting beauty is the result of an underwater plume that gave birth to the island after eons of eruptions caused sheets of lava to build up until the volcano emerged from the sea. Haleakala's greatest height reached 30,000 feet from its base on the ocean floor. Wind and rain erosion, geologic submergences and emergences, and the sputtering of Haleakala itself formed the crater as it is today.

The volcanic, moonlike, landscape of Haleakala crater is bereft of vegetation, but the northeast corner, where Paliku is located, is rich and verdant. Paliku cabin is at the foot of a vertical wall of rock with unclimbable cliffs. Paliku is rainy (200 inches per year); even the mists there can leave you soaked. Tall grass, some native trees, and ferns make up this oasis at the base of the cinder-covered slopes of Haleakala.

The rare silversword plant, found only on the islands of Hawaii and Maui, grows in the crater. When it blooms, within 4 to 20 years of age, it produces a thick stalk with hundreds of small flowers. The Hawaiian goose, the nene, can also be seen in the crater; and at Paliku, you might see honey creepers. These small, robin-sized birds are an endangered species.

The Halemauu Trail was built in the 1930s by the Civilian Conservation Corps. It is your exit from Paliku. You'll pass by Pele's Paintpot (named for the volcano goddess), a part of the trail with exotic volcanic formations. Leave Paliku early for the 10-mile walk away from the crater to the Halemauu parking lot.

For more information about Haleakala, call (808) 572-9306, or write to Haleakala National Park, Box 369, Makawao, HI 96768.

Hawaii (Oahu)

HONOLULU
Diamond Head Trail

Directions: The Diamond Head trailhead is easily accessible from downtown Honolulu, four miles away. A bus takes you to Diamond Head from the Ala Moana Shopping Center in Honolulu. By car, Diamond Head can be reached by Diamond Road, which circles the crater. Take King Street east in Honolulu and then Kalakaua Avenue east through Waikiki. Turn left at the sign marked "Civ-Alert USPFO" opposite 18th Street. Follow the road to Diamond Head State Monument. Leave your car at the base of the crater. The trailhead is clearly marked. It is also possible to walk to Diamond Head from Waikiki Beach. Take Kalakaua Avenue to Monsarrat Avenue, which becomes Diamond Head Road.

Best Season: Diamond Head Trail is open all year, seven days a week, from 6 a.m. to 6 p.m., but it is not advisable to walk it during an intense rainstorm. The temperature is usually between 75 and 78 degrees, although during summer it may reach 90. You can expect the area to be lush and green from November until May and dry during the warmer months. There is no ventilation in the crater, so when it's hot it's best to take this walk in the early morning or late afternoon.

Length: The trail is a 1.5-mile loop. Allow about two hours.

Degree of Difficulty: Easy. Walkers are advised to carry a flashlight for use during passage through two short, man-made tunnels. Although there are restrooms and drinking fountains at the base of the trail, make sure to carry your own water.

The Diamond Head Trail

Pele, Hawaiian goddess of volcanoes, is said to have tried to make her home on each of the Hawaiian Islands. The "fire-eyed goddess," as Pele is sometimes called, dwelled on the island of Oahu some 400,000 years ago. When she moved on, she left the extinct crater given the name "Diamond Head" by British sailors in the 1800s. They found calcite crystals on the slopes of the crater and mistook their glitter for diamonds.

Diamond Head was used as a military installation during World War II and, for years before, as a military lookout. Its elevation is only 760 feet, but you can see the horizon for 180 degrees and all of Honolulu. Hidden in the crater are the lookout towers, gun placements, and tunnels.

The Diamond Head Trail is lined with botanical plants indigenous to Hawaii: the small, wild yellow flower, the ilima; the Hawaiian cotton and Hawaiian pea plant; red frangipani; and the pungent keawe bush, which looks like a fern with thorny branches. The common weed haole koa is everywhere. As you walk along, you will probably encounter two species of doves, as well as the bright red male cardinal, and a few mongooses.

After you leave the first tunnel you will see a concrete building. To the left of the bunker behind the building is a viewpoint overlooking the crater. Take the steep stairs to the room from which you can observe Waikiki and Honolulu; then enter the room with a spiral staircase that leads to the apex of Diamond Head. From this vantage point you can see some of the famous Hawaiian surfing spots, as well as the Koolau Mountains and the other Oahu craters.

When you leave the crater, consider a stop at the nearby Honolulu Zoo or Honolulu Rose Garden. If it's time for lunch, restaurant choices along Monsarrat Avenue in Waikiki are dizzying: Korean, Hawaiian, Filipino, Italian, American, Vietnamese, and Thai.

Notes on Contributors

GARY YANKER

Gary Yanker has been dubbed "Mr. Walk," America's and Europe's foremost authority on walking, and the guru of the walking movement by *American Health Magazine, The Miami Herald,* NBC's "Today Show," *Footwear Magazine* and *The Frankfurter Allgemeine,* among others. After practicing corporate and intellectual property law for eight years, Yanker gave up full time practice to devote his energies to making walking America's number one exercise activity. He is walking editor of *American Health* and founding editor of *Walking World* magazine. His articles and excerpts of his books have appeared in *Saturday Review, Family Circle, McCall's, Print, American Health, Cosmopolitan, Vital,* and *Reader's Digest.*

Yanker is the author of seven books, including two others on walking: *The Complete Book of Exercisewalking* (Contemporary Books) and *Gary Yanker's Walking Workouts* (Warner Books).

Gary Yanker conceived of a walking guide for the best walks while traveling and walking in Europe. He noticed that European countries each have definitive walking guides and that these combined walking with motoring. Gary's own 100-day-a-year traveling schedule throughout the United States made it possible for him to personally identify and walk more than half of the great walks included in this book. Gary will continue his quest for great walks, adding his new finds to future editions. Look for Gary when he comes to your city or write him with your candidates for Greatest Walks. He will most likely want to join you in walking them.

CAROL D. TARLOW

Carol Tarlow heads up her own writing and editing business in Sausalito, California, where she is involved with a variety of publishing projects. She is a member of the editorial board of Mercury House, a new Bay Area publishing company, writes articles for business publications, works with authors and publishers to develop book manuscripts, and is the book editor of *Walking World* magazine. Prior to her move west, she was a senior editor with Reader's Digest Condensed Books.

Of all the many projects she has worked on, *America's Greatest Walks* has been one of the most rewarding and certainly one of the most fun. "I knew this was a beautiful and diverse country," she says, "but I was surprised by the wonderful, out-of-the-way places people nominated. I kept wanting to jump out of my 'editor's' chair and discover each one for myself."

DAVID F. CLOW
Eastern States Regional Editor

David F. Clow is a Philadelphia-based writer with a strong interest in planning and development issues as they affect pedestrians. He is the screenwriter of the award-winning documentary series "Understanding Cities," which examines the history and development of Rome, Paris, London, and other great walking cities, with an eye toward building better pedestrian developments in the United States.

Clow has written for various magazines and business journals, including *Philadelphia Magazine* and *Pennsylvania Outlook*. He also writes articles for *USA Today* on a variety of subjects, including sports and special news features. He is currently working on a screenplay, as well as a first novel.

MARILYN GREEN
Central States Regional Editor

Marilyn Green is a free-lance writer living in Cincinnati, Ohio. Her travel, food, and feature articles appear in such national magazines and newspapers as *Travel and Leisure* and *Islands*. She is a contributing editor for *Recommend* and *Travel Smart* and is currently working on three travel books, two on U.S. destinations and one on Scotland. In addition, she has coauthored several video and theater scripts and is a consultant for film and video grants.

Green owes her love of walking to her father, a Thoreauist. When she was very young, he taught her the pleasures of traveling on foot. She has since walked extensively in nearly every state in the United States and in much of Western Europe, as well as in Canada and the Caribbean.

Presently on the faculty of the University of Cincinnati, she is a cultural historian with degrees in art, music, and the humanities.

PAULA PANICH
Western States Regional Editor

Paula Panich fell in love with Egypt when she was a junior high school English and history teacher in San Mateo County, California. It was the beginning of a passion for travel and writing that took her to Irish castles, Egyptian temples, an English Victorian Hotel (for a "murder weekend"), and a wedding on a tiny island in the middle of Lake Bled, Yugoslavia.

After teaching for seven years, she worked for *San Francisco Theatre Magazine,* was the media director of Arizona Governor Bruce Babbitt's successful 1978 campaign, and served as a public relations account supervisor for Bozell & Jacobs in Phoenix.

To support her writing habit, she has been operating her own public relations firm in Phoenix for the past six years. As a free-lance writer, she has written pieces on travel and health for the *Arizona Republic, Scottsdale Daily Progress, Arizona Business Gazette, Today's Business, Yoga Journal,* and *Backstage* and is a monthly contributing editor to *Phoenix Home & Garden.* She was also the editor of *Film Arizona,* a monthly newsletter on the film industry in Arizona, published by Arizona's Department of Commerce. She is a coauthor of the Phoenix chapter in the forthcoming book, *25 Cities for Women Who Travel.*

Panich began walking in earnest for fitness and serenity during her pregnancy. She is now a dedicated walker and the mother of a beautiful two-year-old daughter, Ilana. Married to a commercial film director, Bill Linsman, Panich and her family live in Phoenix.

CATHERINE GORDON TICER
Art Editor/Coordinator

Catherine Ticer was born in Alexandria, Virginia, where she developed a firm commitment to physical fitness through high school competitive sports such as rowing and tennis. After graduating from the University of Virginia in 1984 with a degree in English, she moved to New York where she currently works for a publisher of educational textbooks.

In February 1985, Catherine left New York briefly for a month-long sojourn through the wilds of Kenya and Southern Africa where she discovered yet another love for travel and photography. Soon after her return, she became involved in the *Walks* project organizing the photography and artwork for walks from every state across the country which has thereby allowed her to feed her new interests simultaneously.

A cross-country trip has been on Catherine's agenda since college and there is now a good chance that much of it will be done on foot.

BEST WALK NOMINATION FORM
(use additional paper if necessary)

Type of walk: _____

Region: _____

How to get there from the highway: _____

_____

_____

Why selected: _____

_____

Degree of difficulty: (Easy, moderate, moderately difficult, difficult, very difficult) Why?

_____

Best time of year to go: _____

Description of Walk

Physical environment: _____

Points of interest along the route: _____

_____

Walking time and distance: _____

Any warnings or hazards? _____

Opinions: (Special comments from experts, local walkers, or yourself)

_____

_____

_____

(please turn the page)

Additional comments and/or information: _____

_____

_____

The information I have provided is true to the best of my knowledge. I understand and agree that this information becomes the property of Walking World *Magazine, to be used at their discretion.*

_____
(Signature)

Please print: Name: _____

Address: _____

_____

Telephone: _____

Please send nominations and any comments to:
Walking World
Box K
Gracie Station
New York, NY 10028

By the year 2000, 2 out of 3 Americans could be illiterate.

It's true.

Today, 75 million adults...about one American in three, can't read adequately. And by the year 2000, U.S. News & World Report envisions an America with a literacy rate of only 30%.

Before that America comes to be, you can stop it...by joining the fight against illiteracy today.

Call the Coalition for Literacy at toll-free **1-800-228-8813** and volunteer.

Volunteer Against Illiteracy. The only degree you need is a degree of caring.

Ad Council Coalition for Literacy

THIS AD PRODUCED BY MARTIN LITHOGRAPHERS
A MARTIN COMMUNICATIONS COMPANY